Lee Williams

D1577215

HYMNS
FOR
CHURCH & SCHOOL

MELODY EDITION

GRESHAM BOOKS
HENLEY-ON-THAMES, OXFORDSHIRE

Published by GRESHAM BOOKS,
P.O. Box 61, Henley-on-Thames, Oxfordshire.

Hymns for Church & School
ISBN 0 9502121 5 6 – Melody
ISBN 0 905418 05 0 – Full Music

Hymns for Church & School with Praise and Thanksgiving
ISBN 0 946095 20 5 – Melody
Hymns for Church & School with Praise and Thanksgiving
ISBN 0 946095 21 3 – Full Music

This edition first printed 1985

Music Processed by M.S.S. Studios, Wimborne, Dorset
and Typeset by Ferndown Typesetters, Christchurch, Dorset

FOREWORD

by

THE ARCHBISHOP OF YORK

THE Headmasters' Conference is to be congratulated on its wisdom in appointing in 1960 a committee of four to prepare the Fourth Edition of *The Public School Hymn Book* under the new name of HYMNS FOR CHURCH AND SCHOOL. May it receive a warm welcome and a wide circulation.

Too many congregations are content with a lamentably small selection of hymns which they use almost *ad nauseam*. This is to live in poverty when in fact we are surrounded by wealth. It is much to be hoped that if, to begin with, this book is still used mainly in schools, those who there learn the delight of good new hymns will pass on their discoveries to their home churches. It is likely that in time this book will come to be used increasingly outside as well as inside the schools. I hope it will.

I foresee HYMNS FOR CHURCH AND SCHOOL as being an instrument in the forwarding of union among the churches. There are, thank God, many areas of life and work in which we co-operate. Apart from the intercourse of theological debate, we share one another's books. When I take up a book by C. H. Dodd or Niebuhr, or Tillich or Temple, I do not ask whether he is an Anglican or a Baptist or a Methodist. Scholarship transcends denominationalism. So in the realms of social and ethical endeavour—there is a problem to be faced and we work at it together. It is so, also, in the matter of hymnody. Newman jostles Wesley; Gellert keeps company with Addison—and it is well that they should.

There is much to commend this book. Not least among the features of this radical revision of an already valuable work are the following:

The omission of silly sentiment and feeble theology. To hear a crowd of lusty confirmation candidates singing about themselves as 'frail and trembling sheep' is hardly to be impressed with reality in religion! It is a pity that some good hymns are spoilt by one or two bad lines. I note for example that 'Art thou weary? Art thou languid?' is omitted in this book, presumably because the questions invite, at least from the young, the reply 'Not at all, thank you'. It would not be difficult to cite hymns whose theology is as ragged and tattered as the covers of the books which sometimes disgrace our churches. Such hymns are noticeably absent from this book.

Its editorial notes, as unobtrusive as they are enlightening. These, we may be sure, will lead not only to an intelligent use of the book, but to the stimulation of interest in hymnology on the part of many who use it. 'I will sing with the understanding also'—St Paul's ideal will be considerably furthered when in public worship such a book as this is used in company with the Revised Psalter (approved by the Convocations of Canterbury and York in 1963 with a view to legislation for its permissive use).

The admixture of hymns of all periods of history. Dr Erik Routley in his admirable historical survey illustrates this profusely, and at the same time draws attention to the exceptionally high proportion of twentieth-century tunes that the book contains.

The lowering of the key in which many of the tunes are given. This will make for congregational singing and is greatly to be welcomed.

Let me add one other word, more by way of an expression of hope than of complaint. It is significant that even in this

Foreword

book the section of hymns on the Holy Spirit is so slender. But was there ever an age in which we needed Him more? Without His breath of life, all our efforts, our conferences, our schemes of union will be of no avail. There is need for co-operative effort and thinking on the part of theologians and poets with a view to the production of some strong hymns on this highly important part of Christian theology.

Donald Ebor:.

BISHOPTHORPE
YORK
EASTER 1964

ACKNOWLEDGEMENTS

THE Editors desire to express their obligation to many authors, composers, and owners or holders of copyright for permission to use hymns and tunes. Every effort has been made to trace all copyright-owners; but if, through inadvertence, any surviving rights have been overlooked, the necessary correction will gladly be made in subsequent editions.

The following Hymns and Melodies are copyright. Details of Acknowledgement will be found in the Full Music Edition of this book:—

HYMNS

Nos. 8, 11, 12, 13, 14, 16, 31, 40, 42, 44, 45, 51, 62, 63, 64, 66, 68, 70, 81, 84, 86, 92, 105, 106, 111, 113, 125, 139, 144, 145, 149, 151, 156, 157, 158, 164, 176, 177, 178, 181, 183, 185, 189, 190, 191, 193, 195, 196, 197, 211, 212, 219, 220, 226, 230, 231, 251, 252, 260, 266, 270, 272, 276, 281, 283, 285, 286, 287, 293, 295, 301, 309, 310, 311, 312, 313, 315, 316, 317, 325, 329, 331, 339, 340, 345, 346.

MELODIES

Nos. 7, 9(ii), 11, 12(i), 12(ii), 13(i), 14(i), 14(ii), 16(i), 28(ii), 31, 34(i), 38(ii), 39(ii), 40, 41, 42(i), 49, 55, 57, 58(i), 58(ii), 63, 66, 70, 71, 73(ii), 75, 81, 83(i), 83(ii), 85, 87, 89(i), 93(ii), 99(i), 101, 110(ii), 119, 121(ii), 122(i), 126, 130(i), 130(ii), 132, 137(i), 138(i), 140, 143, 144(i), 144(ii), 145, 147(ii), 149, 151, 152(i), 152(ii), 153(i), 154(i), 157, 162, 164, 177(i), 178, 182, 185, 186, 187(i), 187(ii), 188, 189, 190, 193, 194(ii), 195, 202(i), 202(ii), 206(i), 211(i), 216, 217(ii), 218(i), 218(ii), 219, 220, 225(i), 225(ii), 226, 229(i), 230(ii), 231, 232, 236, 237, 245, 246(ii), 251, 256(ii), 257, 260(i), 260(ii), 261, 265(i), 265(ii), 268(ii), 269, 272, 273, 280, 281, 283, 289, 290(i), 292, 293, 298, 299, 302, 305(i), 305(ii), 306(ii), 307, 308(i), 310(i), 311(i), 311(ii), 312, 315(i), 315(ii), 317(i), 318, 321, 324, 329, 330, 338(i), 342, 344, 345(ii), 346.

† is added to an Author's name when there has been a small alteration of his original text.

‡ implies a more considerable alteration.

* is set against a verse or verses which may be omitted when it is desired to shorten a hymn.

Amen is printed only when a musical setting requires it.

THE HYMNS

The Hymns

God the Father

1 ABBEY C.M.

Melody from *Scottish Psalter* (1615)
(Rhythm slightly varied)

THE heav'n of heav'ns cannot contain
The universal Lord:
Yet he in humble hearts will deign
To dwell and be adored.

2 Where'er ascends the sacrifice
Of fervent praise and prayer,
Or in the earth or in the skies,
The heav'n of God is there.

3 His presence there is spread abroad
Through realms, through worlds, unknown;
Who seeks the mercies of his God
Is ever near his throne.

W. Drennan (1754-1820)

God the Father:

FIRST VERSION

ST MARY   C.M.

Melody from E. PRYS's *Llyfr y Psalmau* (1621)
Harmony based on setting in PLAYFORD's *Psalms* (1677)

SECOND VERSION
(with later form of rhythm)

ST MARY   C.M.

Harmonized by S. S. WESLEY (1810-76)

His Nature

O GOD, my strength and fortitude,
   Of force I must love thee.
Thou art my castle and defence
   In my necessity.

2 I when beset with pain and grief
   Did pray to God for grace;
And he forthwith did hear my plaint,
   Out of his holy place.

3 The Lord descended from above,
   And bowed the heavens high;
And underneath his feet he cast
   The darkness of the sky.

4 On cherubs and on cherubim
   Full royally he rode;
And on the wings of all the winds
   Came flying all abroad.

5 Unspotted are the ways of God,
   His word is purely tried;
He is a sure defence to such
   As in his faith abide.

6 Most blessèd be the living Lord,
   Most worthy of all praise,
Who is my rock and saving health—
   Praisèd be he always.

Thomas Sternhold† (d. 1549)

This early metrical psalm is discussed in §5 of the Introductory Essay.

God the Father:

FIRST VERSION

ST ANNE   C.M.

Modern form of tune
(See 2nd version below)

SECOND VERSION
(with original rhythm)

ST ANNE   C.M.

Melody and bass from
A Supplement to the New Version (1708)
Probably by Dr WILLIAM CROFT (1678-1727)

His Nature

Man frail and God eternal

O GOD, our help in ages past,
    Our hope for years to come,
Our shelter from the stormy blast,
    And our eternal home;

2 Under the shadow of thy throne
    Thy saints have dwelt secure;
Sufficient is thine arm alone,
    And our defence is sure.

3 Before the hills in order stood,
    Or earth received her frame,
From everlasting thou art God,
    To endless years the same.

4 A thousand ages in thy sight
    Are like an evening gone,
Short as the watch that ends the night
    Before the rising sun.

5 Time, like an ever-rolling stream,
    Bears all its sons away;
They fly forgotten, as a dream
    Dies at the opening day.

6 O God, our help in ages past,
    Our hope for years to come,
Be thou our guard while life shall last,
    And our eternal home.

Isaac Watts† (1674-1748)
Based on Psalm 90. 1-5

God the Father:

4 LEONI 6 6.8 4. D. Hebrew Melody, as adapted *c.*1770

His Nature

THE God of Abraham praise,
Who reigns enthroned above,
Ancient of everlasting days,
    And God of love:
To him uplift your voice,
At whose supreme command
From earth we rise, and seek the joys
    At his right hand.

2   He by himself hath sworn,
I on his oath depend;
I shall, on eagle's wings upborne,
    To heav'n ascend;
I shall behold his face,
I shall his power adore,
And sing the wonders of his grace
    For evermore.

3   There dwells the Lord our King,
The Lord our Righteousness,
Triumphant o'er the world and sin,
    The Prince of Peace;
On Zion's sacred height
His Kingdom he maintains,
And glorious with his saints in light
    For ever reigns.

4   Before the great Three-One
They all exulting stand:
And tell the wonders he hath done
    Through all their land:
The listening spheres attend,
And swell the growing fame,
And sing, in songs which never end,
    The wondrous Name.

5   The whole triumphant host
Give thanks to God on high;
'Hail! Father, Son, and Holy Ghost,'
    They ever cry:
Hail, Abraham's God—and mine!
(I join the heav'nly lays,)
All might and majesty are thine,
    And endless praise.

Thomas Olivers‡ (1725-99)

This hymn is a paraphrase, in Christian terms, of part of the 'Yigdal', a medieval statement of the principles of the Hebrew Faith. The tune is named after the synagogue singer Meyer Leoni, who gave this traditional 'Yigdal' melody to Thomas Olivers.

God the Father:

5 REDHEAD No. 46 87.87.   R. REDHEAD (1820-1901)

His Nature

BRIGHT the vision that delighted
　　Once the sight of Judah's seer;
Sweet the countless tongues united
　　To entrance the prophet's ear.

2 Round the Lord in glory seated
　　Cherubim and seraphim
Filled his temple and repeated
　　Each to each the alternate hymn:

3 'Lord, thy glory fills the heaven;
　　Earth is with its fullness stored;
Unto thee be glory given,
　　Holy, Holy, Holy, Lord.'

4 Heaven is still with glory ringing,
　　Earth takes up the angels' cry,
'Holy, Holy, Holy,' singing,
　　'Lord of hosts, the Lord most high.'

5 With his seraph train before him,
　　With his holy Church below,
Thus unite we to adore him,
　　Bid we thus our anthem flow:

6 'Lord, thy glory fills the heaven;
　　Earth is with its fullness stored;
Unto thee be glory given,
　　Holy, Holy, Holy, Lord.'

R. Mant† (1776-1848)

This hymn is based on the account of Isaiah's vision in Isaiah 6. 1-3.

God the Father:

6 ST DENIO 11 11.11 11.

Welsh Hymn Melody (1839)
(Founded on a folk-tune)

IMMORTAL, invisible, God only wise,
In light inaccessible hid from our eyes,
Most blessèd, most glorious, the Ancient of Days,
Almighty, victorious, thy great name we praise.

2 Unresting, unhasting, and silent as light,
Nor wanting, nor wasting, thou rulest in might—
Thy justice like mountains high-soaring above
Thy clouds which are fountains of goodness and love.

3 To all life thou givest, to both great and small;
In all life thou livest, the true life of all;
We blossom and flourish as leaves on the tree,
And wither and perish; but naught changeth thee.

4 Great Father of Glory, pure Father of Light,
Thine angels adore thee, all veiling their sight;
All laud we would render: O help us to see
'Tis only the splendour of light hideth thee.

W. Chalmers Smith (1824-1908)
Based on 1 *Timothy* 1. 17

His Nature

GONFALON ROYAL L.M.   P. C. BUCK (1871-1947)
With movement

A - - men.

God's Omnipresence

Lord of all being, throned afar,
Thy glory flames from sun and star;
Centre and soul of every sphere,
Yet to each loving heart how near!

2 Sun of our life, thy quickening ray
Sheds on our path the glow of day;
Star of our hope, thy softened light
Cheers the long watches of the night.

3 Our midnight is thy smile withdrawn,
Our noontide is thy gracious dawn,
Our rainbow arch thy mercy's sign;
All, save the clouds of sin, are thine.

4 Lord of all life, below, above,
Whose light is truth, whose warmth is love,
Before thy ever-blazing throne
We ask no lustre of our own.

5 Grant us thy truth to make us free,
And kindling hearts that burn for thee,
Till all thy living altars claim
One holy light, one heavenly flame.   Amen.

Oliver Wendell Holmes (1809-94)

God the Father:

CREATION'S HYMN
(DIE EHRE GOTTES AUS DER NATUR)
Majestically and with exaltation

L. VAN BEETHOVEN (1770-1827)
(from *Sechs Lieder*, op. 48)

The heav'ns de-clare the Cre-a-tor's glo-ry; Their sound forth tells his won-drous Name. The earth doth praise him, the o-ceans pro-claim him, Re-ceive, O Man, their God-like word! Who holds the num-ber-less stars in the hea-vens? Who lead-eth forth the fla-ming sun?

His Work in Creation

It shines re - splen-dent, his won - der re - veal - ing; With joy a he - ro's course to run, With joy a he - ro's course to run.

From the German of C. F. Gellert (1715-69)

God the Father:

FIRST TUNE

LONDON (or ADDISON'S) D.L.M.

Melody, and most of the harmony,
by JOHN SHEELES (1688-1761)
(Composed for this hymn)

His Work in Creation

THE spacious firmament on high,
With all the blue, ethereal sky,
And spangled heav'ns, a shining frame,
Their great Original proclaim.
Th'unwearied sun, from day to day,
Does his Creator's power display,
And publishes to every land
The work of an Almighty Hand.

2 Soon as the evening shades prevail,
The moon takes up the wondrous tale,
And nightly to the listening earth
Repeats the story of her birth;
Whilst all the stars that round her burn,
And all the planets in their turn,
Confirm the tidings as they roll,
And spread the truth from pole to pole.

3 What though, in solemn silence, all
Move round the dark terrestrial ball?
What though nor reäl voice nor sound
Amid their radiant orbs be found?
In reason's ear they all rejoice,
And utter forth a glorious voice,
For ever singing, as they shine,
'The Hand that made us is Divine'.

J. Addison (1672-1719)
Based on Psalm 19. 1-4

When the tune LONDON *is sung, the last line of each verse is repeated.*

God the Father:

SECOND TUNE

FIRMAMENT D.L.M.

WALFORD DAVIES (1869-1941)

cresc.

ff

A - men.

His Work in Creation

THE spacious firmament on high,
With all the blue, ethereal sky,
And spangled heav'ns, a shining frame,
Their great Original proclaim.
Th'unwearied sun, from day to day,
Does his Creator's power display,
And publishes to every land
The work of an Almighty Hand.

2 Soon as the evening shades prevail,
The moon takes up the wondrous tale,
And nightly to the listening earth
Repeats the story of her birth;
Whilst all the stars that round her burn,
And all the planets in their turn,
Confirm the tidings as they roll,
And spread the truth from pole to pole.

3 What though, in solemn silence, all
Move round the dark terrestrial ball?
What though nor reäl voice nor sound
Amid their radiant orbs be found?
In reason's ear they all rejoice,
And utter forth a glorious voice,
For ever singing, as they shine,
'The Hand that made us is Divine'.

Amen.

J. Addison (1672-1719)
Based on Psalm 19. 1-4

God the Father:

10 HANOVER 10 10.11 11.

Melody (and most of the bass) from
A Supplement to the New Version (1708)
Probably by Dr WILLIAM CROFT (1678-1727)

His Work in Creation

O WORSHIP the King, all-glorious above;
O gratefully sing his power and his love:
Our Shield and Defender, the Ancient of Days,
Pavilioned in splendour, and girded with praise.

2 O tell of his might, O sing of his grace,
   Whose robe is the light, whose canopy space;
   His chariots of wrath the deep thunder-clouds form,
   And dark is his path on the wings of the storm.

3 The earth with its store of wonders untold,
   Almighty, thy power hath founded of old;
   Hath stablished it fast by a changeless decree,
   And round it hath cast, like a mantle, the sea.

4 Thy bountiful care what tongue can recite?
   It breathes in the air, it shines in the light;
   It streams from the hills, it descends to the plain,
   And sweetly distils in the dew and the rain.

5 Frail children of dust, and feeble as frail,
   In thee do we trust, nor find thee to fail;
   Thy mercies how tender, how firm to the end,
   Our Maker, Defender, Redeemer, and Friend.

6 O measureless Might, ineffable Love,
   While angels delight to hymn thee above,
   Thy humbler creation, though feeble their lays,
   With true adoration shall sing to thy praise.

Robert Grant‡ (1779-1838)
Based on Psalm 104

God the Father:

11 LASST UNS ERFREUEN   88.44.88 and Alleluias
Melody from *Geistliche Kirchengesang*, Cologne, 1623
Arranged by R. VAUGHAN WILLIAMS (1872-1958)

O — praise him, O —

praise him, Al - le - lu - ia, Al - le - lu - ia, Al - le - lu — ia!

His Work in Creation

Laudato sia Dio mio Signore

ALL creatures of our God and King,
Lift up your voice and with us sing
   Alleluia, Alleluia!
Thou burning sun with golden beam,
Thou silver moon with softer gleam,

     O praise him, O praise him,
     Alleluia, Alleluia, Alleluia!

2 Thou rushing wind that art so strong,
  Ye clouds that sail in heaven along,
     O praise him, Alleluia!
  Thou rising morn, in praise rejoice,
  Ye lights of evening, find a voice:

3 Thou flowing water, pure and clear,
  Make music for thy Lord to hear,
     Alleluia, Alleluia!
  Thou fire so masterful and bright,
  That givest man both warmth and light:

4 Dear mother earth, who day by day
  Unfoldest blessings on our way,
     O praise him, Alleluia!
  The flowers and fruits that in thee grow,
  Let them his glory also show:

5 And all ye men of tender heart,
  Forgiving others, take your part,
     O sing ye, Alleluia!
  Ye who long pain and sorrow bear,
  Praise God and on him cast your care:

6 And thou most kind and gentle Death,
  Waiting to hush our latest breath,
     O praise him, Alleluia!
  Thou leadest home the child of God,
  And Christ our Lord the way hath trod:

7 Let all things their Creator bless,
  And worship him in humbleness,
     O praise him, Alleluia!
  Praise, praise the Father, praise the Son,
  And praise the Spirit, Three in One:

    W. H. Draper (1855-1933), *based on the*
    'Cantico di frate sole' of St Francis of Assisi (1182-1226)

God the Father:

12

FIRST TUNE

ST AUDREY 87.87.87.   BASIL HARWOOD (1859-1949)

1 Lord of Beauty, thine the splendour

Shown in earth and sky and sea,

Burning sun and moonlight tender,

Hill and river, flow'r and tree:

Lest we fail our praise to render,

Touch our eyes that we may see.

His Work in Creation

LORD of Beauty, thine the splendour
    Shown in earth and sky and sea,
Burning sun and moonlight tender,
    Hill and river, flow'r and tree:
Lest we fail our praise to render,
    Touch our eyes that we may see.

2 Lord of Wisdom, whom obeying
    Mighty waters ebb and flow,
While unhasting, undelaying,
    Planets on their courses go;
In thy laws thyself displaying,
    Teach our minds thy truth to know.

3 Lord of Life, alone sustaining
    All below and all above,
Lord of Love, by whose ordaining
    Sun and stars sublimely move:
In our earthly spirits reigning,
    Lift our hearts that we may love.

4 Lord of Beauty, bid us own thee,
    Lord of Truth, our footsteps guide,
Till as Love our hearts enthrone thee,
    And, with vision purified,
Lord of All, when all have known thee,
    Thou in all art glorified.

C. A. Alington (1872-1955)

A small figure indicates the number of notes to a syllable.

God the Father:

12 *(continued)* SECOND TUNE

OBIIT 87.87.87

WALTER PARRATT (1841-1924)

His Work in Creation

LORD of Beauty, thine the splendour
  Shown in earth and sky and sea,
Burning sun and moonlight tender,
  Hill and river, flow'r and tree:
Lest we fail our praise to render,
  Touch our eyes that we may see.

2 Lord of Wisdom, whom obeying
    Mighty waters ebb and flow,
  While unhasting, undelaying,
    Planets on their courses go;
  In thy laws thyself displaying,
    Teach our minds thy truth to know.

3 Lord of Life, alone sustaining
    All below and all above,
  Lord of Love, by whose ordaining
    Sun and stars sublimely move:
  In our earthly spirits reigning,
    Lift our hearts that we may love.

4 Lord of Beauty, bid us own thee,
    Lord of Truth, our footsteps guide,
  Till as Love our hearts enthrone thee,
    And, with vision purified,
  Lord of All, when all have known thee,
    Thou in all art glorified.

                    C. A. Alington (1872-1955)

God the Father:

First Tune

RERUM CREATOR   11 10.11 10.
Unison. Moving easily.

JOHN WILSON (1905-   )

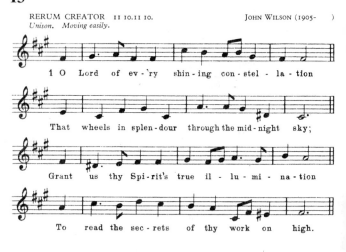

1 O Lord of ev-'ry shin-ing con-stel-la-tion
That wheels in splen-dour through the mid-night sky;
Grant us thy Spi-rit's true il-lu-mi-na-tion
To read the sec-rets of thy work on high.

Second Tune

DONNE SECOURS   11 10.11 10.

Melody of Psalm 12 in *Genevan Psalter* (1551)
Probably by L. BOURGEOIS (died *c.* 1561)

His Work in Creation

O LORD of every shining constellation
    That wheels in splendour through the midnight sky;
Grant us thy Spirit's true illumination
    To read the secrets of thy work on high.

2 And thou who mad'st the atom's hidden forces,
    Whose laws its mighty energies fulfil;
Teach us, to whom thou giv'st such rich resources,
    In all we use, to serve thy holy will.

3 O Life, awaking life in cell and tissue,
    From flow'r to bird, from beast to brain of man;
O help us trace, from birth to final issue,
    The sure unfolding of thine ageless plan.

4 Thou who hast stamped thine image on thy creatures,
    And though they marred that image, lov'st them still;
Uplift our eyes to Christ, that in his features
    We may discern the beauty of thy will.

5 Great Lord of nature, shaping and renewing,
    Who mad'st us more than nature's sons to be;
Help us to tread, with grace our souls enduing,
    The road to life and immortality.

Albert F. Bayly (1901-   )

God the Father:

FIRST TUNE

MOSELEY 77.77.77
Andante con moto

JOHN JOUBERT (1927-   )

Lord of all, to thee we raise This our grate-ful hymn of praise.

SECOND TUNE

LUCERNA LAUDONIAE 77.77.77

DAVID EVANS (1874-1948)

Lord of all, to thee we raise This our grate-ful hymn of praise.

His Work in Creation

FOR the beauty of the earth,
  For the beauty of the skies,
For the love which from our birth
  Over and around us lies:

    Lord of all, to thee we raise
    This our grateful hymn of praise.

2 For the beauty of each hour
  Of the day and of the night,
Hill and vale, and tree and flow'r,
  Sun and moon and stars of light:

3 For the joy of ear and eye,
  For the heart and brain's delight,
For the mystic harmony
  Linking sense to sound and sight:

4 For the joy of human love,
  Brother, sister, parent, child,
Friends on earth, and friends above,
  Pleasures pure and undefiled:

5 For each perfect gift of thine
  To our race so freely given,
Graces human and divine,
  Flow'rs of earth and buds of heaven:

6 For thy Church which evermore
  Lifteth holy hands above,
Off'ring up on every shore
  Her pure sacrifice of love:

F. S. Pierpoint‡ (1835-1917)

God the Father:

15 NUN DANKET 67.67.66.66.   Later form of a melody from
J. CRÜGER's *Praxis Pietatis Melica* (c. 1647)
Harmony chiefly from MENDELSSOHN's *Lobgesang* (1840)

His Love and Providence

✓

Nun danket alle Gott

NOW thank we all our God,
With heart and hands and voices,
　Who wondrous things hath done,
In whom his world rejoices;
　Who from our mother's arms
　　Hath blessed us on our way
With countless gifts of love,
　And still is ours to-day.

2　O may this bounteous God
Through all our life be near us,
　With ever joyful hearts
And blessèd peace to cheer us;
　And keep us in his grace,
　　And guide us when perplexed,
And free us from all ills
　In this world and the next.

3　All praise and thanks to God
The Father now be given,
　The Son, and him who reigns
With them in highest heaven,
　The one eternal God,
　　Whom earth and heaven adore,
For thus it was, is now,
　And shall be evermore.

Martin Rinkart (1586-1649)
Based on Ecclesiasticus 50.22-24
Tr. C. Winkworth (1827-78)

God the Father:

FIRST TUNE

MICHAEL 87.87.337.

HERBERT HOWELLS (1892-)

SECOND TUNE

MEINE HOFFNUNG 87.87.337.

Later form of a melody from
J. NEANDER's *Alpha und Omega* (1680)

His Love and Providence

ALL my hope on God is founded;
   He doth still my trust renew,
Me through change and chance he guideth,
   Only good and only true.
      God unknown,
      He alone
Calls my heart to be his own.

2 Pride of man and earthly glory,
   Sword and crown betray his trust;
What with care and toil he buildeth,
   Tower and temple, fall to dust.
      But God's power,
      Hour by hour,
Is my temple and my tower.

3 God's great goodness aye endureth,
   Deep his wisdom, passing thought:
Splendour, light, and life attend him,
   Beauty springeth out of naught.
      Evermore
      From his store
New-born worlds rise and adore.

4*Daily doth th' Almighty Giver
   Bounteous gifts on us bestow;
His desire our soul delighteth,
   Pleasure leads us where we go.
      Love doth stand
      At his hand;
Joy doth wait on his command.

5 Still from man to God eternal
   Sacrifice of praise be done,
High above all praises praising
   For the gift of Christ his Son.
      Christ doth call
      One and all:
Ye who follow shall not fall.

Robert Bridges (1844-1930)
Based on the German of J. Neander (1650-80)

God the Father:

17 WILTSHIRE C.M.

G. T. SMART (1776-1867)

Psalm 34, *vv.* 1, 3-4, 7-9

THROUGH all the changing scenes of life,
　In trouble and in joy,
The praises of my God shall still
　My heart and tongue employ.

2 O magnify the Lord with me,
　　With me exalt his name;
　When in distress to him I called,
　　He to my rescue came.

3 The hosts of God encamp around
　　The dwellings of the just;
　Deliverance he affords to all
　　Who on his succour trust.

4 O make but trial of his love;
　　Experience will decide
　How blest they are, and only they,
　　Who in his truth confide.

5 Fear him, ye saints, and you will then
　　Have nothing else to fear;
　Make you his service your delight,
　　Your wants shall be his care.

6 To Father, Son, and Holy Ghost,
　　The God whom we adore,
　Be glory, as it was, is now,
　　And shall be evermore.

N. Tate (1652-1715) and N. Brady (1659-1726),
in 'A New Version of the Psalms'

His Love and Providence

18 MONKLAND 77.77.

Arranged by J. WILKES (1861) from a tune composed or adapted by JOHN ANTES (1740-1811)

For his mer-cies aye en-dure, Ev-er faith-ful, ev-er sure.

From Psalm 136

LET us, with a gladsome mind,
Praise the Lord, for he is kind:
For his mercies aye endure,
Ever faithful, ever sure.

2 Let us blaze his name abroad,
For of gods he is the God:

3 He, with all-commanding might,
Filled the new-made world with light:

4 He the golden-tressèd sun
Caused all day his course to run:

5 Th' hornèd moon to shine by night,
'Mid her spangled sisters bright:

6 All things living he doth feed,
His full hand supplies their need:

7 Let us, with a gladsome mind,
Praise the Lord, for he is kind:

John Milton‡ (1608-74)

God the Father:

R. HARRISON (1748-1810)
(Original harmony, except in last 2 bars)

His Love and Providence

GIVE to our God immortal praise,
Mercy and truth are all his ways:
    Wonders of grace to God belong,
    Repeat his mercies in your song.

2 Give to the Lord of Lords renown:
  The King of Kings with glory crown:
    His mercies ever shall endure,
    When lords and kings are known no more.

3 He built the earth, he spread the sky,
  And fixed the starry lights on high:
    Wonders of grace to God belong,
    Repeat his mercies in your song.

4 He fills the sun with morning light,
  He bids the moon direct the night:
    His mercies ever shall endure,
    When suns and moons shall shine no more.

5 He sent his Son with power to save
  From guilt and darkness and the grave:
    Wonders of grace to God belong,
    Repeat his mercies in your song.

6 Through this vain world he guides our feet,
  And leads us to his heavenly seat;
    His mercies ever shall endure,
    When this vain world shall be no more.

Isaac Watts (1674-1748)
Based on Psalm 136

20 SOLEMNIS HAEC FESTIVITAS L.M.   Melody from *Paris Gradual* (1685)

SING to the Lord a joyful song,
  Lift up your hearts, your voices raise;
To us his gracious gifts belong,
  To him our songs of love and praise.

2 For life and love, for rest and food,
    For daily help and nightly care,
  Sing to the Lord, for he is good,
    And praise his name, for it is fair.

3 For strength to those who on him wait,
    His truth to prove, his will to do,
  Praise ye our God, for he is great;
    Trust in his name, for it is true.

4 For joys untold, that from above
    Cheer those who love his sweet employ,
  Sing to our God, for he is Love,
    Exalt his name, for it is Joy.

5 Sing to the Lord of heav'n and earth,
    Whom angels serve and saints adore,
  The Father, Son, and Holy Ghost,
    To whom be praise for evermore.

J. S. B. Monsell (1811-75)

His Love and Providence

Melody, and most of the harmony,
from J. RANDALL's *Psalm and Hymn Tunes* (1794)
Probably by C. COLLIGNON (1725-85)

21 UNIVERSITY C.M.

Psalm 23

THE God of love my Shepherd is,
    And he that doth me feed:
While he is mine, and I am his,
    What can I want or need?

2 He leads me to the tender grass,
    Where I both feed and rest;
Then to the streams that gently pass:
    In both I have the best.

3 Or if I stray, he doth convert
    And bring my mind in frame:
And all this not for my desert,
    But for his holy name.

4 Yea, in death's shady black abode
    Well may I walk, not fear;
For thou art with me, and thy rod
    To guide, thy staff to bear.

5 Surely thy sweet and wondrous love
    Shall measure all my days;
And as it never shall remove,
    So neither shall my praise.

George Herbert (1593-1633)

God the Father:

FIRST TUNE

CRIMOND   C.M.

Melody by JESSIE S. IRVINE (1836-87)
Harmonized by T. C. L. PRITCHARD (1885-1960)

SECOND TUNE

WILTSHIRE   C.M.

G. T. SMART (1776-1867)

His Love and Providence

Psalm 23

THE Lord's my Shepherd, I'll not want.
    He makes me down to lie
In pastures green; he leadeth me
    The quiet waters by.

2 My soul he doth restore again,
    And me to walk doth make
Within the paths of righteousness,
    E'en for his own name's sake.

3 Yea, though I walk in death's dark vale,
    Yet will I fear none ill;
For thou art with me, and thy rod
    And staff me comfort still.

4 My table thou hast furnishèd
    In presence of my foes;
My head thou dost with oil anoint,
    And my cup overflows.

5 Goodness and mercy all my life
    Shall surely follow me;
And in God's house for evermore
    My dwelling-place shall be.

Scottish Psalter (1650)

God the Father:

23 SURREY 88.88.88.

Melody by HENRY CAREY (c.1687-1743)
(slightly decorated)

His Love and Providence

THE Lord my pasture shall prepare,
And feed me with a shepherd's care;
His presence shall my wants supply,
And guard me with a watchful eye;
My noonday walks he shall attend,
And all my midnight hours defend.

2*When in the sultry glebe I faint,
Or on the thirsty mountain pant,
To fertile vales and dewy meads
My weary wandering steps he leads,
Where peaceful rivers, soft and slow,
Amid the verdant landscape flow.

3 Though in the paths of death I tread,
With gloomy horrors overspread,
My steadfast heart shall fear no ill,
For thou, O Lord, art with me still:
Thy friendly crook shall give me aid,
And guide me through the dreadful shade.

4 Though in a bare and rugged way
Through devious lonely wilds I stray,
Thy bounty shall my pains beguile;
The barren wilderness shall smile,
With sudden greens and herbage crowned,
And streams shall murmur all around.

Joseph Addison (1672-1719)

God the Father:

FIRST TUNE

DOMINUS REGIT ME 87.87.   J. B. DYKES (1823–76)

SECOND TUNE

ST COLUMBA 87.87.   Traditional Irish melody

His Love and Providence

Psalm 23

THE King of love my Shepherd is,
  Whose goodness faileth never;
I nothing lack if I am his
  And he is mine for ever.

2 Where streams of living water flow
  My ransomed soul he leadeth,
And where the verdant pastures grow
  With food celestial feedeth.

3 Perverse and foolish oft I strayed,
  But yet in love he sought me,
And on his shoulder gently laid,
  And home rejoicing brought me.

4 In death's dark vale I fear no ill
  With thee, dear Lord, beside me;
Thy rod and staff my comfort still,
  Thy Cross before to guide me.

5 Thou spread'st a table in my sight;
  Thy unction grace bestoweth;
And O what transport of delight
  From thy pure chalice floweth!

6 And so through all the length of days
  Thy goodness faileth never:
Good Shepherd, may I sing thy praise
  Within thy house for ever.

H. W. Baker (1821-77)

God the Father:

FIRST TUNE

STRACATHRO C.M.

Melody by C. HUTCHESON (1792-1860)
Harmonized by GEOFFREY SHAW (1879-1943)

SECOND TUNE

BURFORD C.M.

Melody from J. CHETHAM's *Psalmody* (1718)

His Love and Providence

O GOD of Bethel, by whose hand
  Thy people still are fed;
Who through this earthly pilgrimage
  Hast all our fathers led:

2 Our vows, our prayers, we now present
  Before thy throne of grace:
God of our fathers, be the God
  Of their succeeding race.

3 Through each perplexing path of life
  Our wandering footsteps guide;
Give us each day our daily bread,
  And raiment fit provide.

4 O spread thy covering wings around,
  Till all our wanderings cease,
And at our Father's loved abode
  Our souls arrive in peace.

Philip Doddridge (1702-51) and John Logan† (1748-88)

This hymn is based on Genesis 28. 19-21. 'Bethel', in the Hebrew, is literally 'house of God'.

God the Father:

FIRST VERSION

LONDON NEW C.M.

Melody from *Scottish Psalter* (1635)
as adapted in PLAYFORD'S *Psalms* (1671)

SECOND VERSION
(with later form of rhythm)

LONDON NEW C.M.

His Love and Providence

GOD moves in a mysterious way
  His wonders to perform;
He plants his footsteps in the sea,
  And rides upon the storm.

2 Deep in unfathomable mines
    Of never-failing skill
  He treasures up his bright designs,
    And works his sovereign will.

3 Ye fearful saints, fresh courage take;
    The clouds ye so much dread
  Are big with mercy, and will break
    In blessings on your head.

4 Judge not the Lord by feeble sense,
    But trust him for his grace:
  Behind a frowning providence
    He hides a smiling face.

5 His purposes will ripen fast,
    Unfolding every hour;
  The bud may have a bitter taste,
    But sweet will be the flower.

6 Blind unbelief is sure to err,
    And scan his work in vain;
  God is his own interpreter,
    And he will make it plain.

William Cowper (1731-1800)

God the Father:

First Tune

BELGRAVE C.M.

WILLIAM HORSLEY (1774-1858)

Second Tune

CONTEMPLATION C.M.

F. A. GORE OUSELEY (1825-89)

His Love and Providence

WHEN all thy mercies, O my God,
  My rising soul surveys,
Transported with the view, I'm lost
  In wonder, love, and praise.

2 Unnumbered comforts to my soul
    Thy tender care bestowed,
  Before my infant heart conceived
    From whom those comforts flowed.

3 When in the slippery paths of youth
    With heedless steps I ran,
  Thine arm unseen conveyed me safe
    And led me up to man.

4 Through every period of my life
    Thy goodness I'll pursue;
  And after death, in distant worlds,
    The glorious theme renew.

5 When nature fails, and day and night
    Divide thy works no more,
  My ever-grateful heart, O Lord,
    Thy mercy shall adore.

6 Through all eternity to thee
    A joyful song I'll raise;
  For O! eternity's too short
    To utter all thy praise.

Joseph Addison (1672-1719)

28

FIRST TUNE

CROSS OF JESUS 87.87   J. STAINER (1840-1901)

SECOND TUNE

RUSTINGTON 87.87.D   C. HUBERT H. PARRY (1848-1918)

His Love and Providence

THERE'S a wideness in God's mercy,
  Like the wideness of the sea;
There's a kindness in his justice,
  Which is more than liberty.

2 There is welcome for the sinner,
  And more graces for the good;
There is mercy with the Saviour;
  There is healing in his blood.

3 For the love of God is broader
  Than the measures of man's mind;
And the heart of the Eternal
  Is most wonderfully kind.

4 But we make his love too narrow
  By false limits of our own;
And we magnify his strictness
  With a zeal he will not own.

5 'Tis not all we owe to Jesus;
  It is something more than all:
Greater good because of evil,
  Larger mercy through the fall.

6 If our love were but more simple,
  We should take him at his word;
And our lives would fill with sunshine
  In the glory of the Lord.

F. W. Faber† (1814-63)

29 ES IST KEIN TAG 88.84. Melody by J. D. MEYER (*Geistliche Seelen-Freud*, 1692)
(arr. R. VAUGHAN WILLIAMS, 1906)

O LORD of heav'n, and earth, and sea,
To thee all praise and glory be;
How shall we show our love to thee,
   Giver of all?

2 For peaceful homes, and healthful days,
For all the blessings earth displays,
We owe thee thankfulness and praise,
   Giver of all!

3 Thou didst not spare thine only Son,
But gav'st him for a world undone,
And freely with that Blessèd One
   Thou givest all.

4 Thou giv'st the Spirit's blessèd dower,
Spirit of life, and love, and power,
And dost his sev'nfold graces shower
   Upon us all.

5 For souls redeemed, for sins forgiven,
For means of grace and hopes of heaven,
Father, what can to thee be given,
   Who givest all?

6*We lose what on ourselves we spend,
We have as treasure without end
Whatever, Lord, to thee we lend,
   Who givest all;

7 To thee, from whom we all derive
Our life, our gifts, our power to give:
O may we ever with thee live,
   Giver of all!

C. Wordsworth (1807-85)

His Love and Providence

30 STRACATHRO C.M.

Melody by C. HUTCHESON (1792-1860)
Harmonized by GEOFFREY SHAW (1879-1943)

ALL as God wills, who wisely heeds
  To give or to withhold,
And knoweth more of all my needs
  Than all my prayers have told!

2 Enough that blessings undeserved
    Have marked my erring track;
  That wheresoe'er my feet have swerved
    His chastening turned me back;

3 That more and more a Providence
    Of love is understood,
  Making the springs of time and sense
    Sweet with eternal good;

4 That death seems but a covered way
    Which opens into light,
  Wherein no blinded child can stray
    Beyond the Father's sight.

5 And so the shadows fall apart,
    And so the west winds play;
  And all the windows of my heart
    I open to the day.

J. G. Whittier (1807-92)

God the Father:

31 TWIGWORTH 87.87 D.   HERBERT HOWELLS (1892-   )

1 God is Love: let heav'n a - dore him; God is
Love: let earth re - joice; Let cre - a - tion sing be -
fore him, And ex - alt him with one voice.
He who laid the earth's foun - da - tion, He who
spread the heav'ns a - bove, He who breathes through all cre -
a - tion, He is Love, E - ter - nal Love.

His Love and Providence

GOD is Love: let heav'n adore him;
  God is Love: let earth rejoice;
Let creation sing before him,
  And exalt him with one voice.
He who laid the earth's foundation,
  He who spread the heav'ns above,
He who breathes through all creation,
  He is Love, Eternal Love.

2 God is Love: and he enfoldeth
    All the world in one embrace;
  With unfailing grasp he holdeth
    Every child of every race.
  And when human hearts are breaking
    Under sorrow's iron rod,
  That same sorrow, that same aching,
    Wrings with pain the heart of God.

3 God is Love: and though with blindness
    Sin afflicts the souls of men,
  God's eternal loving-kindness
    Holds and guides them even then.
  Sin and death and hell shall never
    O'er us final triumph gain;
  God is Love, so Love for ever
    O'er the universe must reign.

Timothy Rees† (1874-1939)

God the Father:

32 CHRISTUS DER IST
MEIN LEBEN 76.76.

Melody by M. VULPIUS (c. 1560-1615),
arranged by J. S. BACH (1685-1750)

*v.*1 Far___

Peace

MY soul, there is a country
Fär beyond the stars,
Where stands a wingèd sentry
All skilful in the wars.

2 There, above noise and danger,
Sweet peace sits, crowned with smiles,
And One born in a manger
Commands the beauteous files.

3 He is thy gracious Friènd,
And—O my soul, awake!—
Did in pure love descènd,
To die here for thy sake.

4 If thou canst get but thither,
There grows the flower of peace,
The rose that cannot wither,
Thy fortress and thy ease.

5 Leave then thy foolish ranges,
For none can thee secure
But One, who never changes,
Thy God, thy life, thy cure.

Henry Vaughan (1622-95)

v.5 ranges] rangings, or wanderings
A small figure indicates the number of notes to a syllable.

His Kingdom

Later form of a tune by
DR WILLIAM BOYCE (c. 1710-1779)
as given in S. S. WESLEY's *European Psalmist* (1872)

33 HALTON HOLGATE 87.87.

The future Peace and Glory of the Church

HEAR what God the Lord hath spoken:—
O my people, faint and few,
Comfortless, afflicted, broken,
Fair abodes I build for you.

2 Thorns of heart-felt tribulation
Shall no more perplex your ways;
You shall name your walls Salvation,
And your gates shall all be Praise.

3 There, like streams that feed the garden,
Pleasures, without end, shall flow:
For the Lord, your faith rewarding,
All his bounty shall bestow.

4 Still in undisturbed possession
Peace and righteousness shall reign:
Never shall you feel oppression,
Hear the voice of war again.

5 Ye no more your sun descending,
Waning moons no more shall see,
But, your griefs for ever ending,
Find eternal noon in me.

6 God shall rise, and shining o'er you
Change to day the gloom of night;
He, the Lord, shall be your glory,
God your everlasting light.

William Cowper (1731-1800)
Based on Isaiah 60. 15-20

God the Father:

FIRST TUNE

ABBOT'S LEIGH 87.87.D. C. V. TAYLOR (1907-   )

SECOND TUNE

AUSTRIA 87.87.D. J. HAYDN (1732-1809)

His Kingdom

Zion, or The City of God

GLORIOUS things of thee are spoken,
    Zion, city of our God!
He whose word cannot be broken
    Formed thee for his own abode:
On the Rock of Ages founded,
    What can shake thy sure repose?
With salvation's walls surrounded,
    Thou may'st smile at all thy foes.

2 See, the streams of living waters,
    Springing from eternal love,
Well supply thy sons and daughters,
    And all fear of want remove:
Who can faint while such a river
    Ever flows their thirst to assuage?
Grace, which like the Lord the Giver,
    Never fails from age to age.

3*Round each habitation hov'ring,
    See the cloud and fire appear
For a glory and a cov'ring,
    Showing that the Lord is near.
Thus they march, the pillar leading,
    Light by night and shade by day;
Daily on the manna feeding
    Which he gives them when they pray.

4 Saviour, if of Zion's city
    I, through grace, a member am,
Let the world deride or pity,
    I will glory in thy name:
Fading is the worldling's pleasure,
    All his boasted pomp and show;
Solid joys and lasting treasure
    None but Zion's children know.

John Newton (1725-1807)
Based on Isaiah 33.20-21 and Psalm 87

God the Father:

35 RUSSIA 11.10.11.9(10).   Melody by A. F. Lvov (1799-1870)

GOD, the Omnipotent! King, who ordainest
   Great winds thy clarions, the lightnings thy sword;
Show forth thy pity on high where thou reignest:
   Give to us peace in our time, O Lord.

2 God, the All-righteous One! man hath defied thee;
   Yet to eternity standeth thy word;
Falsehood and wrong shall not tarry beside thee:
   Give to us peace in our time, O Lord.

3 God, the All-merciful! earth hath forsaken
   Thy ways of blessedness, slighted thy word;
Bid not thy wrath in its terrors awaken:
   Give to us peace in our time, O Lord.

4 So shall thy children, in thankful devotion,
   Laud him who saves them from peril abhorred,
Singing in chorus, from ocean to ocean,
   'Peace to the nations, and praise to the Lord!'

Verses 1, 3, 4, by H. F. Chorley† (1808-72)
Verse 2, by J. Ellerton† (1826-93)

His Kingdom

Melody from *A Collection of Hymns and Sacred Poems* (Dublin, 1749)

The Day of God

'THY Kingdom come!' on bended knee
　　The passing ages pray;
And faithful souls have yearned to see
　　On earth that Kingdom's day.

2 But the slow watches of the night
　　Not less to God belong;
And for the everlasting right
　　The silent stars are strong.

3 And lo, already on the hills
　　The flags of dawn appear;
Gird up your loins, ye prophet souls,
　　Proclaim the day is near:

4 The day in whose clear-shining light
　　All wrong shall stand revealed;
When justice shall be throned in might,
　　And every hurt be healed;

5 When knowledge, hand in hand with peace,
　　Shall walk the earth abroad:
The day of perfect righteousness,
　　The promised day of God.

F. L. Hosmer (1840-1929)

God the Father:

37 RICHMOND C.M.

Melody by T. HAWEIS (1734-1820),
as adapted by S. WEBBE the younger (c. 1770-1843)

His Kingdom

The Church the City of God

CITY of God, how broad and far
    Outspread thy walls sublime!
The true thy chartered freemen are
    Of every age and clime.

2 One holy Church, one army strong,
      One steadfast, high intent;
  One working band, one harvest-song,
      One King omnipotent.

3 How purely hath thy speech come down
      From man's primeval youth!
  How grandly hath thine empire grown,
      Of freedom, love, and truth!

4 How gleam thy watch-fires through the night
      With never-fainting ray!
  How rise thy towers, serene and bright,
      To meet the dawning day!

5 In vain the surge's angry shock,
      In vain the drifting sands:
  Unharmed upon the eternal Rock
      The eternal City stands.

Samuel Johnson (1822-82)

God the Father:

First Tune

OLD 120th 66.66.66.

Melody from *Psalms* (1570)
Harmony from Ravenscroft's *Psalmes* (1621)

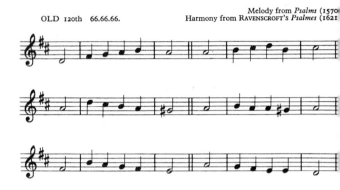

Second Tune

FRILFORD 66.66.66.

W. H. Ferguson (1874-1950)

His Kingdom

To the Kingdom of God within

O THOU not made with hands,
  Not throned above the skies,
Nor walled with shining walls,
  Nor framed with stones of price,
More bright than gold or gem,
God's own Jerusalem!

2 Where'er the gentle heart
  Finds courage from above;
Where'er the heart forsook
  Warms with the breath of love;
Where faith bids fear depart,
City of God, thou art.

3 Thou art where'er the proud
  In humbleness melts down;
Where self itself yields up;
  Where martyrs win their crown;
Where faithful souls possess
Themselves in perfect peace.

4 Where in life's common ways
  With cheerful feet we go;
Where in his steps we tread,
  Who trod the way of woe;
Where he is in the heart,
City of God, thou art.

5 Not throned above the skies,
  Nor golden-walled afar,
But where Christ's two or three
  In his name gathered are,
Lo, in the midst of them,
God's own Jerusalem!

F. T. Palgrave† (1824-97)

God the Father:

39

ST CECILIA 66.66.

L. G. Hayne (1836-83)

Second Version
(with original form of rhythm)

ST CECILIA 66.66.

L. G. Hayne (1836-83)

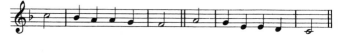

His Kingdom

ACKERGILL 66.66.   LEONARD BLAKE (1907-   )

THY Kingdom come, O God,
  Thy rule, O Christ, begin;
Break with thine iron rod
  The tyrannies of sin.

2 Where is thy reign of peace,
    And purity, and love?
  When shall all hatred cease,
    As in the realms above?

3 When comes the promised time
    That war shall be no more—
  Oppression, lust, and crime
    Shall flee thy face before?

4 We pray thee, Lord, arise,
    And come in thy great might;
  Revive our longing eyes,
    Which languish for thy sight.

5 Men scorn thy sacred name,
    And wolves devour thy fold;
  By many deeds of shame
    We learn that love grows cold.

6 Where peoples near or far
    In darkness linger yet,
  Arise, O Morning Star,
    Arise, and never set!

L. Hensley† (1827-1905)

God the Father:

40 THAXTED 13 13.13 13.13 13.

GUSTAV HOLST (1874-1934)
(adapted from his Suite *The Planets*)

(The Two Fatherlands)

I VOW to thee, my country—all earthly things above—
Entire and whole and perfect, the service of my love:
The love that asks no question, the love that stands the test,
That lays upon the altar the dearest and the best;
The love that never falters, the love that pays the price,
The love that makes undaunted the final sacrifice.

2 And there's another country, I've heard of long ago,
Most dear to them that love her, most great to them that know;
We may not count her armies, we may not see her King;
Her fortress is a faithful heart, her pride is suffering;
And soul by soul and silently her shining bounds increase,
And her ways are ways of gentleness and all her paths are Peace.

Cecil Spring Rice (1859-1918)

The author, at the end of his service as Ambassador in Washington in 1918, and at a dark hour of the First World War, sent these verses to an American friend, adding that 'the greatest object of all—at the most terrific cost and the most tremendous sacrifice—will, I hope, at last be permanently established, Peace'.

His Kingdom

41 SANCTA CIVITAS 86.86.86.   HERBERT HOWELLS (1892-   )

With warmth, but moving easily

1 O Holy City, seen of John, Where
2 O shame to us who rest content While
3 Give us, O God, the strength to build The

Christ, the Lamb, doth reign, Within whose four-square walls shall come No
lust and greed for gain In street and shop and ten-e-ment Wring
Ci-ty that hath stood Too long a dream, whose laws are love, Whose

night, nor need, nor pain,___ And where the tears are
gold from hu-man pain,___ And bit-ter lips in
ways are bro-ther-hood,___ And where the sun that

wiped from eyes That shall not weep___ a-gain!
blind des-pair Cry, 'Christ hath died in vain!'
shi-neth is God's grace for hu-man good.

4 Al-rea-dy in the mind of God That Ci-ty ri-seth

fair: Lo, how its splen-dour chal-len-ges The

souls that great-ly dare — Yea, bids us seize the

whole of life And build its glo-ry there.

W. Russell Bowie (1882-   )
(suggested by St John's vision in Revelation 21)

God the Father:

42

HILLSBOROUGH S.M.   JOHN GARDNER (1917-   )

SECOND TUNE

ST THOMAS S.M.   Melody by AARON WILLIAMS (1731-76)

His Kingdom

O DAY of God, draw nigh
In beauty and in power,
Come with thy timeless judgment now
To match our present hour.

2 Bring to our troubled minds,
Uncertain and afraid,
The quiet of a steadfast faith,
Calm of a call obeyed.

3 Bring justice to our land,
That all may dwell secure,
And finely build for days to come
Foundations that endure.

4 Bring to our world of strife
Thy sovereign word of peace,
That war may haunt the earth no more
And desolation cease.

5 O Day of God, draw nigh
As at creation's birth;
Let there be light again, and set
Thy judgments in the earth.

R. B. Y. Scott (1899-   )

The Lord Jesus Christ:

43 VENI EMMANUEL 88.88.88.   Melody from *The Hymnal Noted* (Pt. II, 1856)
Copied by J. M. NEALE (1818-66) 'from a French Missal'

Re - joice!   Re - joice!

Em-ma - nu-el Shall come to thee, O Is - ra-el.

His Advent

Veni, veni, Emmanuel

O COME, O come, Emmanuel,
And ransom captive Israel,
That mourns in lonely exile here,
Until the Son of God appear:
  Rejoice! Rejoice! Emmanuel
  Shall come to thee, O Israel.

2 O come, thou Rod of Jesse, free
  Thine own from Satan's tyranny;
  From depths of hell thy people save,
  And give them vict'ry o'er the grave:

3 O come, thou Day-spring, come and cheer
  Our spirits by thine advent here;
  Disperse the gloomy clouds of night,
  And death's dark shadows put to flight:

4 O come, thou Key of David, come,
  And open wide our heav'nly home;
  Make safe the way that leads on high,
  And close the path to misery:

5 O come, O come, thou Lord of Might,
  Who to thy tribes, on Sinai's height,
  In ancient times didst give the law
  In cloud, and majesty, and awe:

18th century Latin
Tr. J. M. Neale (1818-66) *and others*

These verses are based on the ancient Advent Antiphons, each of which salutes the coming Messiah
under one of the titles ascribed to him in Holy Scripture.

The Lord Jesus Christ:

44 WACHET AUF 898.898.664.88.

Melody by P. Nicolai (1556-1608)
Adapted and harmonized by J. S. Bach (1685-1750)

His Advent

Wachet auf

Wake, O wake! with tidings thrilling
The watchmen all the air are filling,
        Arise, Jerusalem, arise!
Midnight strikes! no more delaying,
'The hour has come!' we hear them saying.
        Where are ye all, ye virgins wise?
            The Bridegroom comes in sight,
            Raise high your torches bright!
                Alleluia!
            The wedding song
            Swells loud and strong:
        Go forth and join the festal throng.

2 Zion hears the watchmen shouting,
Her heart leaps up with joy undoubting,
        She stands and waits with eager eyes;
See her Friend from heaven descending,
Adorned with truth and grace unending!
        Her light burns clear, her star doth rise.
            Now come, thou precious Crown,
            Lord Jesu, God's own Son!
                Alleluia!
            Let us prepare
            To follow there,
        Where in thy supper we may share.

3 Every soul in thee rejoices;
From men and from angelic voices
        Be glory giv'n to thee alone!
Now the gates of pearl receive us,
Thy presence never more shall leave us,
        We stand with Angels round thy throne.
            Earth cannot give below
            The bliss thou dost bestow.
                Alleluia!
            Grant us to raise,
            To length of days,
        The triumph-chorus of thy praise.

P. Nicolai (1556-1608)
Tr. F. C. Burkitt† (1864-1935)

This hymn, in which the coming of Christ is likened to the arrival of the Bridegroom at a wedding-feast, draws its imagery from the Parable of the Wise and Foolish Virgins in Matthew 25.1-13, and also from Revelation 19.6-9.

45 MERTON 87.87.   W. H. MONK (1823-89)

Vox clara ecce intonat

HARK, a clarion call is sounding
  Through the shadows of the night:
'Cast away the dreams of darkness,
  Christ descends with heavenly light'.

2 Wakened by the solemn warning
  Let the earth-bound soul arise:
Bethlem's star, all ill dispelling,
  Lights anew the morning skies.

3 Lo! the Lamb, so long expected,
  Comes with pardon down from heaven:
Let us pray, with hearts repentant,
  By his grace to be forgiven.

4 So, when next he comes with glory,
  And his judgment-day draws near,
Faithful he may find his servants,
  Watching till their Lord appear.

5 Honour, glory, might and blessing
  To the Father and the Son,
With the co-eternal Spirit,
  While unending ages run.

10th century or earlier
Tr. E. Caswall (1814-78) and others

His Advent

Jordanis oras praevia

On Jordan's bank the Baptist's cry
Announces that the Lord is nigh;
Awake and hearken, for he brings
Glad tidings from the King of Kings.

2 Then cleansed be every Christian breast,
And furnished for so great a guest!
Yea, let us each our hearts prepare
For Christ to come and enter there.

3 For thou art our salvation, Lord,
Our refuge, and our great reward;
Without thy grace we waste away
Like flowers that wither and decay.

4 To heal the sick stretch out thine hand,
And bid the fallen sinner stand;
Shine forth, and let thy light restore
Earth's own true loveliness once more.

5 All praise, eternal Son, to thee
Whose advent sets thy people free,
Whom, with the Father, we adore,
And Holy Ghost, for evermore.

C. Coffin (1676-1749)
Tr. J. Chandler (1806-76) and others

The Lord Jesus Christ:

FIRST VERSION

BRISTOL C.M.

Melody, and most of the harmony,
from T. RAVENSCROFT's *Psalmes* (1621)

SECOND VERSION
(*with later form of rhythm*)

BRISTOL C.M.

Christ's Message

HARK the glad sound! the Saviour comes,
The Saviour promised long;
Let every heart prepare a throne,
And every voice a song.

2 He comes the prisoners to release
In Satan's bondage held;
The gates of brass before him burst,
The iron fetters yield.

3 He comes the broken heart to bind,
The wounded soul to cure,
And with the treasures of his grace
To enrich the humble poor.

4 Our glad hosannas, Prince of Peace,
Thy welcome shall proclaim;
And heav'n's eternal arches ring
With thy belovèd name.

Philip Doddridge† (1702-51)
Based on Luke 4.18-19

48

DUNDEE C.M.

Later form of a melody in *Scottish Psalter* (1615)
Harmony from RAVENSCROFT'S *Psalmes* (1621)

SECOND TUNE

ST FULBERT C.M.

H. J. GAUNTLETT (1805-76)

Isaiah 9, *vv.* 2, 3, 6, 7

THE race that long in darkness pined
Have seen a glorious light:
The people dwell in day, who dwelt
In death's surrounding night.

2 To hail thy rise, thou better Sun,
The gathering nations come,
Joyous as when the reapers bear
The harvest treasures home.

3 To us a Child of hope is born,
To us a Son is given;
Him shall the tribes of earth obey,
Him all the hosts of heaven.

4 His name shall be the Prince of Peace,
For evermore adored,
The Wonderful, the Counsellor,
The great and mighty Lord.

5 His power increasing still shall spread,
His reign no end shall know;
Justice shall guard his throne above,
And peace abound below.

John Morison (1749-98),
as in Scottish Paraphrases (1781)

The Lord Jesus Christ:

49 LOWER MARLWOOD 84.84.884.
In free time, but boldly and with spirit.

BASIL HARWOOD (1859-1949)

1 Lift up your heads, ye might-y gates, *Al - le - lu - ia!*

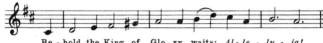

Be - hold, the King of Glo-ry waits; *Al - le - lu - ia!*

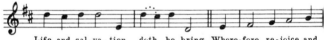

Life and sal-va-tion doth he bring, Where-fore re-joice and

vv. 1-3

glad - ly sing: *Al - le - lu - ia!*

v. 4

Al - le - lu - ia! Al - le - lu - ia! A - men.

His Advent

Macht hoch die Thür

LIFT up your heads, ye mighty gates,   *Alleluia!*
Behold, the King of Glory waits;   *Alleluia!*
Life and salvation doth he bring,
Wherefore rejoice and gladly sing: *Alleluia!*

2 O blest the land, the city blest,   *Alleluia!*
  Where Christ the Ruler is confessed;   *Alleluia!*
  Happy the hearts, and happy the homes,
  To whom this King in triumph comes: *Alleluia!*

3 Fling wide the portals of your heart,   *Alleluia!*
  To make a temple set apart;   *Alleluia!*
  So shall your Sovereign enter in,
  And new and nobler life begin: *Alleluia!*

4 Redeemer, come! with us abide,   *Alleluia!*
  Our hearts to thee we open wide;   *Alleluia!*
  May thy blest Spirit guide us on
  Until our glorious crown is won!
          Alleluia!   Alleluia!   Amen.

Georg Weissel (1590-1635)
Tr. adapted from C. Winkworth (1827-78)

50 CROSS OF JESUS 87.87.

J. STAINER (1840-1901)

COME, thou long-expected Jesus,
  Born to set thy people free;
From our fears and sins release us;
  Let us find our rest in thee.

2 Israel's strength and consolation,
  Hope of all the earth thou art;
Dear Desire of every nation,
  Joy of every longing heart.

3 Born thy people to deliver,
  Born a Child and yet a King,
Born to reign in us for ever,
  Now thy gracious kingdom bring:

4 By thy own eternal Spirit
  Rule in all our hearts alone;
By thy all-sufficient merit
  Raise us to thy glorious throne.

Charles Wesley† (1707-88)

His Incarnation

51 ST COLUMBA C.M.

Irish Traditional Melody

(For an Evening Service)

THE Maker of the sun and moon,
   The Maker of our earth,
Lo! late in time, a fairer boon,
   Himself is brought to birth!

2 How blest was all creation then,
   When God so gave increase;
And Christ, to heal the hearts of men,
   Brought righteousness and peace!

3 No star in all the heights of heaven
   But burned to see him go;
Yet unto earth alone was given
   His human form to know.

4 His human form, by man denied,
   Took death for human sin:
His endless love, through faith descried,
   Still lives the world to win.

5 O perfect Love, outpassing sight,
   O Light beyond our ken,
Come down through all the world to-night,
   And heal the hearts of men!

Laurence Housman (1865-1959)

The Lord Jesus Christ:

FIRST VERSION

WIE SCHÖN LEUCHTET   887.887.48.48.

Melody by P. NICOLAI (1556-1608)
Adapted and harmonized by J. S. BACH
(1685-1750)

SECOND VERSION

WIE SCHÖN LEUCHTET   887.887.48.48.

Harmonized by MENDELSSOHN
in his oratorio *Christus* (1847)

His Incarnation

Wie schön leuchtet der Morgenstern

How brightly shines the Morning Star!
The nations see and hail afar
   The Light in Judah shining.
Thou David's son of Jacob's race,
The Bridegroom, and the King of grace,
   For thee our hearts are pining!
        Lowly, holy,
Great and glorious, thou victorious
         Prince of graces,
Filling all the heavenly places!

2 Though circled by the hosts on high,
  He deigns to cast a pitying eye
    Upon his helpless creature;
  The whole Creation's Head and Lord,
  By highest seraphim adored,
    Assumes our very nature.
         Jeśu, grant us,
  Through thy merit, to inherit
         Thy salvation;
  Hear, O hear our supplication.

3 Rejoice, ye heav'ns; thou earth, reply;
  With praise, ye sinners, fill the sky,
    For this his Incarnation.
  Incarnate God, put forth thy power,
  Ride on, ride on, great Conqueror,
    Till all know thy salvation.
         Amen, Amen!
  Alleluia, Alleluia!
         Praise be given
  Evermore by earth and heaven.

     P. Nicolai (1556-1608)
       Tr. H. Harbaugh† (1860) *and W. Mercer†* (1859)

The Lord Jesus Christ:

Melody from T. Est's *Psalmes* (1592)
Harmony adapted from Est (1592) and Ravenscroft
(1621)

53 WINCHESTER OLD C.M.

If preferred, this tune may be sung in its original rhythm, with a minim for the first and last note of each line.

St Luke 2. 8-14

WHILE shepherds watched their flocks by night,
All seated on the ground,
The angel of the Lord came down,
And glory shone around.

2 'Fear not,' said he (for mighty dread
Had seized their troubled mind),
'Glad tidings of great joy I bring
To you and all mankind.

3 'To you in David's town this day
Is born of David's line
A Saviour, who is Christ the Lord;
And this shall be the sign:

4 'The heavenly Babe you there shall find
To human view displayed,
All meanly wrapped in swathing bands,
And in a manger laid.'

5 Thus spake the seraph; and forthwith
Appeared a shining throng
Of angels praising God, who thus
Addressed their joyful song:

6 'All glory be to God on high,
And to the earth be peace;
Good will henceforth from heaven to men
Begin and never cease.'

Nahum Tate† (1652-1715)

His Incarnation

54 ERMUNTRE DICH 87.87.88.77.

Melody by J. SCHOP (1641), as set by
J. S. BACH in the *Christmas Oratorio* (1734)

Break forth, O pure ce - les-tial light, And u - sher in the morn-ing; O draw us up to hea-ven's height, To hear the an-gel's warn - ing. A Child, now weak in in - fan - cy, Our con - fi - dence and joy shall be, The pow'r of Sa - tan break - ing, Our peace e - ter - nal mak - ing.

*J. Rist (1607-77), as used in Bach's 'Christmas Oratorio' (1734)
Tr. J. Troutbeck‡ (1832-99)*

The Lord Jesus Christ:

A solis ortus cardine

FROM East to West, from shore to shore,
   Let earth awake and sing
The holy Child whom Mary bore,
   The Christ, the Lord, the King!

2 For lo! the world's Creator wears
   The fashion of a slave:
Our human flesh the Godhead bears,
   His creature, man, to save.

3*For this how wondrously he wrought!
   A maiden, in her place,
Became in ways beyond all thought
   The vessel of his grace.

4 He shrank not from the oxen's stall,
   Nor scorned the manger-bed;
And he, whose bounty feedeth all,
   At Mary's breast was fed.

5 To shepherds poor the Lord most high,
   Great Shepherd, was revealed;
While angel-choirs sang joyously
   Above the midnight field.

6 All glory be to God above,
   And on the earth be peace
To all who long to taste his love,
   Till time itself shall cease.

Coelius Sedulius (c. 450)
Tr. J. Ellerton† (1826-93)

His Incarnation

German Carol Melody
Harmonized by M. PRAETORIUS (1571-1621)

56 ES IST EIN' ROS' 76.76.676.

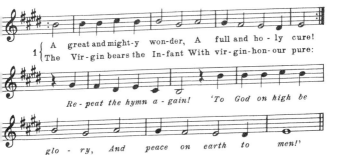

A great and might-y won-der, A full and ho-ly cure!
The Vir-gin bears the In-fant With vir-gin-hon-our pure:
Re-peat the hymn a-gain! 'To God on high be
glo-ry, And peace on earth to men!'

Μέγα καὶ παράδοξον θαῦμα

A GREAT and mighty wonder,
  A full and holy cure!
The Virgin bears the Infant
  With virgin-honour pure:
    Repeat the hymn again!
    'To God on high be glory,
    And peace on earth to men!'

2 The Word becomes incarnate
    And yet remains on high!
  And Cherubim sing anthems
    To shepherds from the sky:

3* While thus they sing your Monarch,
    Those bright angelic bands,
  Rejoice, ye vales and mountains,
    Ye oceans, clap your hands:

4 Since all he comes to ransom,
    By all be he adored,
  The Infant born in Bethl'em,
    The Saviour and the Lord:

5 And idol forms shall perish,
    And error shall decay,
  And Christ shall wield his sceptre,
    Our Lord and God for aye:

St Germanus (c. 634-c. 734)
Tr. J. M. Neale† (1818-66)

The Lord Jesus Christ:

57 MENDELSSOHN 77 77.77 77.77. From a chorus in MENDELSSOHN's *Festgesang* (1840) originally adapted by W. H. CUMMINGS (1855)

Hark! the her-ald-an-gels sing Glo-ry— to the new-born King.

His Incarnation

HARK! the herald-angels sing
Glory to the new-born King,
Peace on earth, and mercy mild,
God and sinners reconciled.
Joyful, all ye nations, rise,
Join the triumph of the skies;
With the angelic host proclaim,
'Christ is born in Bethlehem.'
     Hark! the herald-angels sing
     Glory to the new-born King.

2 Christ, by highest heaven adored,
  Christ, the everlasting Lord,
  Late in time behold him come,
  Offspring of a Virgin's womb.
  Veiled in flesh the Godhead see!
  Hail, the incarnate Deity!
  Pleased as Man with man to dwell,
  Jesus, our Emmanuel:

3 Hail, the heaven-born Prince of Peace!
  Hail, the Sun of Righteousness!
  Light and life to all he brings,
  Risen with healing in his wings.
  Mild he lays his glory by,
  Born that man no more may die,
  Born to raise the sons of earth,
  Born to give them second birth:

Charles Wesley (1707-88) *and others*

The Lord Jesus Christ:

58

English Traditional Melody
FOREST GREEN   D.C.M. (Irregular)   Harmonized by R. VAUGHAN WILLIAMS
(1872-1958)

SECOND TUNE

CHRISTMAS CAROL   D.C.M. (Irregular)   WALFORD DAVIES (1869-1941)

His Incarnation

O LITTLE town of Bethlehem,
  How still we see thee lie!
Above thy deep and dreamless sleep
  The silent stars go by.
Yet in thy dark streets shineth
  The everlasting light;
The hopes and fears of all the years
  Are met in thee to-night.

2 For Christ is born of Mary;
    And gathered all above,
  While mortals sleep, the angels keep
    Their watch of wondering love.
  O morning stars, together
    Proclaim the holy birth,
  And praises sing to God the King,
    And peace to men on earth!

3 How silently, how silently,
    The wondrous gift is given!
  So God imparts to human hearts
    The blessings of his heaven.
  No ear may hear his coming;
    But in this world of sin,
  Where meek souls will receive him still,
    The dear Christ enters in.

4* Where children pure and happy
    Pray to the blessèd Child,
  Where misery cries out to thee,
    Son of the mother mild;
  Where charity stands watching
    And faith holds wide the door,
  The dark night wakes, the glory breaks,
    And Christmas comes once more.

5 O holy Child of Bethlehem,
    Descend to us, we pray;
  Cast out our sin, and enter in;
    Be born in us to-day!
  We hear the Christmas angels
    The great glad tidings tell;
  O come to us, abide with us,
    Our Lord Emmanuel!

                    Phillips Brooks (1835-93)

The Lord Jesus Christ:

59   BONN   8.33.6.D.

Melody and bass by J. G. EBELING (1637-76)

His Incarnation

Fröhlich soll mein Herze springen

ALL my heart this night rejoices,
      As I hear,
      Far and near,
Sweetest angel voices:
'Christ is born!' their choirs are singing,
      Till the air
      Everywhere
Now with joy is ringing.

2 Hark, a voice from yonder manger,
      Soft and sweet,
      Doth entreat,
'Flee from woe and danger;
Brethren, come; from all doth grieve you
      You are freed,
      All you need
I will surely give you'.

3 Come then, let us hasten yonder;
      Here let all,
      Great and small,
Kneel in awe and wonder;
Love him who with love is yearning;
      Hail the star
      That from far
Bright with hope is burning!

4 Thee, O Lord, with heed I'll cherish,
      Live to thee,
      And with thee
Dying, shall not perish;
But shall dwell with thee for ever,
      Far on high,
      In the joy
That can alter never.

P. Gerhardt (1607-76)
Tr. C. Winkworth† (1827-78)

60 ADESTE FIDELES Irregular

Melody found in MS about 174.
Perhaps by J. F. WADE (*c.*1711-1786)

1 A-des-te, fi-de-les, Lae-ti tri-um-phan-tes;
2   De-um de De-o,   Lu-men de __ Lu-mi-ne,
3   Can-tet nunc 'I-o',   Cho-rus an-ge-lo-rum;
4   Er-go qui na-tus   Di-e ho-di-er-na,

Ve-ni-te, ve-ni-te in   Beth-le-hem:
Par-tu-rit   Vir-go __   Ma-ter,
Can-tet nunc au-la cae-les-ti-um:
Je-   su, ti-bi sit   glo-ri-a:

Na-tum vi-de-te   Re-gem an-ge-lo-rum:
De-   um ve-rum,   Ge-ni-tum non fac-tum:
Glo-   ri-a   In ex-cel-sis De-o!
Pa-tris ae-ter-ni   Ver-bum ca-ro fac-tum:

Ve-ni-te, a-do-re-mus, Ve-ni-te, a-do-re-mus, Ve-

ni-te, a-do-re-mus __   Do-   mi-num.

Anon.; found in MS about 1745
Perhaps by J. F. Wade (c. 1711-1786)

His Incarnation

61 ADESTE FIDELES Irregular

Melody found in MS about 1745
Perhaps by J. F. WADE (c.1711-1786)

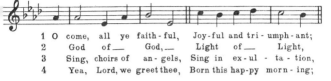

1 O come, all ye faith-ful,   Joy-ful and tri - umph-ant;
2 God   of __   God, __   Light   of __   Light,
3 Sing, choirs of   an - gels, Sing in ex-ul - ta - tion,
4 Yea, Lord, we greet thee, Born this hap-py morn - ing;

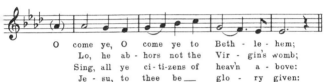

O   come ye, O   come ye to   Beth - le - hem;
Lo, he ab - hors not the   Vir - gin's womb;
Sing, all ye ci - ti-zens of   heav'n a - bove:
Je - su, to   thee be __   glo - ry given:

Come and be - hold him, Born the King of An - gels:
Ve - ry __   God, Be - got - ten, not cre - a - ted:
'Glo - ry to God __   In __ the __ high - est':
Word of the Fa - ther, Now in flesh ap - pear - ing:

O   come, let us a - dore him, O come, let us a - dore him, O

come, let us a - dore   him, __ Christ __ the Lord.

Anon.; found in MS about 1745
Perhaps by J. F. Wade (c. 1711-1786)
Tr. F. Oakeley (1802-80) and others

The Lord Jesus Christ:

62 VRUECHTEN 67.67.D.

Dutch Melody, 17th century

O men with sor - row worn, Your chains the Lord hath ri - ven; To you a Child is born, To you a Son is gi - ven, is gi - ven, is gi - ven, To you a Son _____ is gi - ven.

His Incarnation

Let joy your carols fill;
　Away with sin and sadness!
To men of gentle will
　Be peace on earth and gladness!
　　O men with sorrow worn,
　　　Your chains the Lord hath riven;
　　To you a Child is born,
　　　To you a Son is given.

2 Mid cares and toil and stress
　And worldly hearts unheeding,
In paths of humbleness
　A little Child is leading:

3 All ye that labours bear,
　Take now his yoke upon you;
Your toil he comes to share,
　Light burden lays he on you:

4 O holy humble birth!
　Sing forth the joyful story!
Good will, good will on earth,
　And in the highest, glory!

Frank Fletcher (1870-1954)

The Lord Jesus Christ:

63 SUSSEX CAROL 88.88.88.

English Traditional Melody
Harmonized by R. VAUGHAN WILLIAMS (1872-1958)

(Choir)

1 On Christ-mas night all Chris-tians sing To

hear the news the an-gels bring: *(All)* On Christ-mas night all

Chris-tians sing To hear the news the an-gels bring:

News of great joy,— news of— great mirth,

News of our mer-ci-ful King's birth.

His Incarnation

A Sussex Carol

Choir

On Christmas night all Christians sing
To hear the news the angels bring:

All

On Christmas night all Christians sing
To hear the news the angels bring:
News of great joy, news of great mirth,
News of our merciful King's birth.

Choir

2   Then why should men on earth be sad,
Since our Redeemer made us glad,

All

Then why should men on earth be sad,
Since our Redeemer made us glad,
When from our sin he set us free,
All for to gain our liberty.

Choir

3   When sin departs before his grace,
Then life and health come in its place;

All

When sin departs before his grace,
Then life and health come in its place;
Angels and men with joy may sing,
All for to see the new-born King.

Choir

4   All out of darkness we have light,
Which made the angels sing this night:

All

All out of darkness we have light,
Which made the angels sing this night:
'Glory to God and peace to men,
Now and for evermore—Amen.'

Traditional Carol

The Lord Jesus Christ:

64 IRIS 87.87. and Refrain

French or Flemish Melody
Harmonized by CHARLES WOOD (1866-1926)

Glo - - - - - - - ri - a in ex - cel - sis De - o,

Glo - - - - - - - ri - a in ex - cel - sis De - o!

His Incarnation

SHEPHERDS, in the field abiding,
  Tell us, when the seraph bright
Greeted you with wondrous tiding,
  What ye saw and heard that night:
    Gloria in excelsis Deo!

2 'We beheld (it is no fable)
  God incarnate, King of bliss,
Swathed and cradled in a stable,
  And the angel-strain was this:

3 'Quiristers on high were singing
  Jesus and his Virgin-birth;
Heavenly bells the while a-ringing:
  Peace, goodwill to men on earth':

4 Thanks, good herdmen; true your story;
  Have with you to Bethlehem:
Angels hymn the King of Glory;
  Carol we with you and them:

G. R. Woodward (1848-1934)
Based on an ancient Antiphon

The Lord Jesus Christ:

65 GOD REST YOU MERRY 86.86.86. and Refrain   English Traditional Melody

O＿ ti - dings of com - fort and joy, com-fort and joy, O＿ ti - dings of. com - fort and joy!

His Incarnation

GOD rest you merry, gentlemen,
　Let nothing you dismay,
For Jesus Christ our Saviour
　Was born upon this day,
To save us all from Satan's power
　When we were gone astray:
O tidings of comfort and joy, comfort and joy!
　O tidings of comfort and joy!

2 From God our Heav'nly Father
　　A blessèd angel came,
　And unto certain shepherds
　　Brought tidings of the same,
　How that in Bethlehem was born
　　The Son of God by name:

3 The shepherds at those tidings
　　Rejoicèd much in mind,
　And left their flocks a-feeding
　　In tempest, storm and wind,
　And went to Bethlehem straightway
　　This blessèd Babe to find:

4 But when to Bethlehem they came,
　　Whereat this Infant lay,
　They found him in a manger,
　　Where oxen feed on hay;
　His mother Mary kneeling
　　Unto the Lord did pray:

5 Now to the Lord sing praises,
　　All you within this place,
　And with true love and brotherhood
　　Each other now embrace;
　This holy tide of Christmas
　　All others doth deface:

Traditional Carol

The Lord Jesus Christ:

66 SOMERSET CAROL 86.86.86. and Refrain

English Traditional Melody
Arranged by WILLIAM LLEWELLYN
(1925-   )

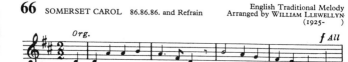

1 Come

all you wor-thy gen-tle-men That may be stand-ing by;

Christ our bless-ed Sa - viour Was born on Christ-mas Day. The

bless-ed Vir-gin Ma - ry Un - to the Lord did say: 'O we

wish you the com-fort and ti - dings of joy!'

2 Christ our bless-ed Sa - viour Now

in the man-ger lay—He's ly-ing in the man-ger While the

His Incarnation

ox - en feed on hay. The bless-ed Vir-gin Ma - ry Un -

to the Lord did say: 'O we wish you the com-fort and

ti - dings of joy!' 3 God

bless the ru-ler of this house, And long on may he

reign, Ma-ny hap-py Christ-mas-es He live to see a -

gain! God bless our ge - ner - a - tion, Who

live both far and near, And we wish them a hap - py, a

hap - py New Year!

Traditional Carol

The Lord Jesus Christ:

67 THE FIRST NOWELL   Irregular

English Traditional Melody
Arranged with Descant by LEONARD BLAKE
(1907-   )

No - well,__ No - well, No - well, No - well!

Born is the King__ of Is - ra - el!

His Incarnation

THE first Nowell the angel did say
Was to certain poor shepherds in fields as they lay;
In fields where they lay keeping their sheep,
On a cold winter's night that was so deep:
    Nowell, Nowell, Nowell, Nowell!
    Born is the King of Israel!

2 They lookèd up and saw a star,
   Shining in the east, beyond them far;
   And to the earth it gave great light,
   And so it continued both day and night:

3 And by the light of that same star,
   Three Wise Men came from country far;
   To seek for a King was their intent,
   And to follow the star wherever it went:

4* This star drew nigh to the north-west,
    O'er Bethlehem it took its rest,
    And there it did both stop and stay,
    Right over the place where Jesus lay:

5 Then entered in those Wise Men three,
   Full reverently upon their knee,
   And offered there, in his Presence,
   Their gold and myrrh and frankincense:

6 Then let us all with one accord
   Sing praises to our Heav'nly Lord,
   That hath made heav'n and earth of naught,
   And with his blood mankind hath bought:

Traditional Carol

The Lord Jesus Christ:

68 PUER NOBIS. 76.77.

Melody from *Piae Cantiones* (1582)
Arranged by GEOFFREY SHAW (1879-1943)

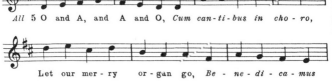

All   1   Un - to   us   is born a Son,   King of Quires su -
Trebles   2 Christ, from heav'n des-cend-ing low,   Comes on earth   a
Tenors & Basses 3   This   did He - rod sore af - fray, And griev-ous-ly   be -
Trebles   4   Of   his love and mer-cy mild   This the Christ-mas

1 per - nal: See   on   earth his   life be - gun,   Of
2 stran - ger: Ox   and   ass their   Own - er know   Be -
3 wil - der;   So   he   gave the   word to slay,   And
4 sto - ry: And   O   that   Ma - ry's   gen - tle Child Might

1 lords the Lord e - ter - nal,   Of   lords the Lord e - ter - nal.
2 cra - dled in the   man - ger,   Be - cra - dled in the man - ger.
3 slew the lit - tle   chil - der,   And slew the lit - tle chil - der.
4 lead us   up to   glo - ry! Might lead us up to   glo - ry!

All 5 O   and   A,   and   A   and   O,   *Cum can - ti - bus   in   cho - ro,*

Let   our   mer - ry   or - gan   go,   *Be - ne - di - ca - mus*

Do - mi - no,   Be - ne - di - ca - mus   Do - mi - no.

15th century Latin
Tr. G. R. Woodward (1848-1934)

His Incarnation

Adapted from a melody in
C. F. Witt's *Harmonia Sacra* (Gotha, 1715)

O sola magnarum urbium

Bᴇᴛʜʟᴇʜᴇᴍ, of noblest cities
None can once with thee compare;
Thou alone the Lord from heaven
Didst for us incarnate bear.

2 Fairer than the sun at morning
Was the star that told his birth;
To the lands their God announcing,
Hid beneath a form of earth.

3 By its lambent beauty guided
See the eastern kings appear;
See them bend, their gifts to offer,
Gifts of incense, gold and myrrh.

4 Sacred gifts of mystic meaning:
Incense doth the God disclose,
Gold a royal child proclaimeth,
Myrrh a future tomb foreshows.

5 Holy Jesu, in thy brightness
To the Gentile world displayed,
With the Father and the Spirit
Endless praise to thee be paid.

Prudentius (348-c.410)
Tr. E. Caswall (1814-78)

The Lord Jesus Christ:

70 TRES MAGI DE GENTIBUS 777.7.   C. S. LANG (1891-

1 East-ern Mon-archs,

Sa-ges three, Come with gifts in great plen-ty;

Wor-ship Christ on_ bend-ed knee. *Cum Vir-gi-ne_ Ma-*

ri - a.____   *ri - a.____*

His Incarnation

Tres magi de gentibus

Eastern Monarchs, Sages three,
Come with gifts in great plenty;
Worship Christ on bended knee,
   Cum Virgine Maria.

2 Gold, in honour of the King,
  Incense to the Priest they bring,
  Myrrh, for time of burying,
     Cum Virgine Maria.

Trebles only
3 On that dreadful day, the last,
  He forgive our sinful past!
  To his mercy cling we fast!
(*All*)   *Cum Virgine Maria.*

4 His the praise and glory be,
  Laud and honour, victorie,
  Power supreme, and so sing we,
     Cum Virgine Maria.

mf 5 On the feast-day of his birth,
  Set on thrones above the earth,
  Angels chant in holy mirth,
     Cum Virgine Maria.

ff 6 Thus to bless the One in Three,
  Let the present company
  Raise the voice of melody,
     Cum Virgine Maria.

15*th century Latin*
Tr. G. R. Woodward (1848-1934)

The Lord Jesus Christ:

71 KING'S WESTON 65.65.D. R. Vaughan Williams (1872-1958)

* *If Descant is used with v.5, sustain this note for 9 beats.*

His Incarnation

FROM the eastern mountains
   Pressing on they come,
Wise Men in their wisdom,
   To his humble home;
Stirred by deep devotion,
   Hasting from afar,
Ever journeying onward,
   Guided by a Star.

2 There their Lord and Saviour
   In a stable lay,
Wondrous Light that led them
   Onward on their way,
Ever now to lighten
   Nations from afar,
As they journey homeward
   By that guiding Star.

3 Thou who in a manger
   Once hast lowly lain,
Who dost now in glory
   O'er all kingdoms reign,
Gather in the peoples
   Who in lands afar
Have not seen the brightness
   Of thy guiding Star.

4*Gather in the outcasts,
   All who've gone astray,
Throw thy radiance o'er them,
   Guide them on their way;
Those who never knew thee,
   Or have wandered far,
Guide them by the brightness
   Of thy guiding Star.

5 Light of Life that shinedst
   Ere the worlds began,
Draw thou near, and lighten
   Every heart of man;
Gather all the nations
   Homeward from afar,
Young and old together,
   By thy guiding Star.

G. Thring‡ (1823-1903)

See overleaf for an Alternative Setting of Verse 5

The Lord Jesus Christ:

72 DIX 77.77.77.

C. KOCHER (1786-1872)
Adapted by W. H. MONK (1823-89)

His Incarnation

As with gladness men of old
Did the guiding star behold,
As with joy they hailed its light,
Leading onward, beaming bright,
So, most gracious Lord, may we
Evermore be led to thee.

2 As with joyful steps they sped
To that lowly manger-bed,
There to bend the knee before
Him whom heav'n and earth adore,
So may we with willing feet
Ever seek thy mercy-seat.

3 As they offered gifts most rare
At that manger rude and bare,
So may we with holy joy,
Pure, and free from sin's alloy,
All our costliest treasures bring,
Christ, to thee our heavenly King.

4 Holy Jesus, every day
Keep us in the narrow way;
And, when earthly things are past,
Bring our ransomed souls at last
Where they need no star to guide,
Where no clouds thy glory hide.

5 In the heav'nly country bright
Need they no created light;
Thou its light, its joy, its crown,
Thou its sun which goes not down:
There for ever may we sing
Alleluias to our King.

W. Chatterton Dix (1837-98)

The Lord Jesus Christ:

FIRST TUNE

73

BEDE 11 10.11 10.

Adapted from HANDEL's *Athaliah* (1733)
by J. GOSS (1800-80)

SECOND TUNE

WALLOG 11 10.11 10.

WALFORD DAVIES (1869-1941)

His Incarnation

BRIGHTEST and best of the sons of the morning,
  Dawn on our darkness and lend us thine aid;
Star of the east, the horizon adorning,
  Guide where our infant Redeemer is laid.

2 Cold on his cradle the dew-drops are shining,
    Low lies his head with the beasts of the stall:
  Angels adore him in slumber reclining,
    Maker and Monarch and Saviour of all.

3 Say, shall we yield him, in costly devotion,
    Odours of Edom and offerings divine?
  Gems of the mountain and pearls of the ocean,
    Myrrh from the forest or gold from the mine?

4 Vainly we offer each ample oblation,
    Vainly with gifts would his favour secure;
  Richer by far is the heart's adoration,
    Dearer to God are the prayers of the poor.

5 Brightest and best of the sons of the morning,
    Dawn on our darkness and lend us thine aid;
  Star of the east, the horizon adorning,
    Guide where our infant Redeemer is laid.

                                    R. Heber (1783-1826)

The Lord Jesus Christ:

74 LEWES 87.87.87.

JOHN RANDALL (1715-99)
(Harmony slightly altered)

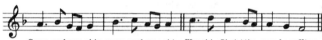

Come and wor-ship, come and wor-ship, Wor-ship Christ the new-born King.

His Incarnation

ANGELS, from the realms of glory,
  Wing your flight o'er all the earth;
Ye who sang creation's story
  Now proclaim Messiah's birth:
    Come and worship, come and worship,
    Worship Christ, the new-born King.

2 Shepherds in the field abiding,
    Watching o'er your flocks by night,
  God with man is now residing;
    Yonder shines the Infant Light:

3 Sages, leave your contemplations;
    Brighter visions beam afar;
  Seek the great Desire of Nations;
    Ye have seen his natal star:

4 Saints before the altar bending,
    Watching long in hope and fear,
  Suddenly the Lord, descending,
    In his temple shall appear:

5 Sinners, moved with true repentance,
    Else condemned to endless pains,
  Justice now revokes the sentence:
    Mercy calls you—break your chains:

J. Montgomery† (1771-1854)

The Lord Jesus Christ:

75 CRANHAM Irregular   GUSTAV HOLST (1874-1934)

1   In the bleak mid - win - ter   Frost - y wind made moan,
2 Our God, heav'n can - not hold him,   Nor — earth sus - tain;
3   An - gels and arch - an - gels   May have ga-thered there,
4   What — can I give him,   Poor — as I   am?

1 Earth stood hard as   i - ron,   Wa - ter like a stone;
2 Heav'n and earth shall flee a - way   When he comes to reign:
3 Che - ru - bim and se - ra-phim   Thronged the — air — But
4 If   I were a   shep - herd   I would bring a lamb;

1 Snow had fall - en, snow on snow,   Snow   on — snow,
2 In the bleak mid - win - ter A   sta-ble-place suf - ficed The
3 on - ly his mo - ther,   In her mai-den bliss,
4 If I were a   wise — man   I would do my part; Yet

1 In   the bleak mid - win - ter,   Long — a — go.
2 Lord — God Al - migh - ty,   Je - sus — Christ.
3 Wor-shipped the Be - lov - ed   With — a — kiss.
4 what I can I give him —   Give — my — heart.

His Incarnation

In the bleak mid-winter
    Frosty wind made moan,
Earth stood hard as iron,
    Water like a stone;
Snow had fallen, snow on snow,
    Snow on snow,
In the bleak mid-winter,
    Long ago.

2 Our God, heav'n cannot hold him,
    Nor earth sustain;
Heav'n and earth shall flee away
    When he comes to reign:
In the bleak mid-winter
    A stable-place sufficed
The Lord God Almighty,
    Jesus Christ.

3 Angels and archangels
    May have gathered there,
Cherubim and seraphim
    Thronged the air—
But only his mother,
    In her maiden bliss,
Worshipped the Belovèd
    With a kiss.

4 What can I give him,
    Poor as I am?
If I were a shepherd
    I would bring a lamb;
If I were a wise man
    I would do my part;
Yet what I can I give him—
    Give my heart.

Christina Rossetti (1830-94)

The Lord Jesus Christ:

76 IRBY 87.87.77.

H. J. GAUNTLETT (1805-76)

His Incarnation

ONCE in royal David's city
Stood a lowly cattle shed,
Where a mother laid her baby
In a manger for his bed:
Mary was that Mother mild,
Jesus Christ her little Child.

2 He came down to earth from heaven
Who is God and Lord of all,
And his shelter was a stable,
And his cradle was a stall;
With the poor and mean and lowly
Lived on earth our Saviour holy.

3*And through all his wondrous childhood
He would honour and obey,
Love and watch the lowly Maiden,
In whose gentle arms he lay:
Christian children all must be
Mild, obedient, good as he.

4*For he is our childhood's pattern,
Day by day like us he grew,
He was little, weak, and helpless,
Tears and smiles like us he knew;
And he feeleth for our sadness,
And he shareth in our gladness.

5 And our eyes at last shall see him,
Through his own redeeming love,
For that Child so dear and gentle
Is our Lord in heaven above;
And he leads his children on
To the place where he is gone.

6 Not in that poor lowly stable,
With the oxen standing by,
We shall see him; but in heaven,
Set at God's right hand on high;
When like stars his children crowned
All in white shall wait around.

Mrs C. F. Alexander (1818-95)

The Lord Jesus Christ:

77 NOEL D.C.M.

English Traditional Melody, adapted and
extended by ARTHUR SULLIVAN (1842-1900)

His Incarnation

IT came upon the midnight clear,
  That glorious song of old,
From angels bending near the earth
  To touch their harps of gold:
'Peace on the earth, good-will to men,
  From heav'n's all-gracious King!'
The world in solemn stillness lay
  To hear the angels sing.

2 Still through the cloven skies they come,
  With peaceful wings unfurled;
And still their heavenly music floats
  O'er all the weary world;
Above its sad and lowly plains
  They bend on hovering wing;
And ever o'er its Babel sounds
  The blessèd angels sing.

3 But with the woes of sin and strife
  The world has suffered long;
Beneath the angel-strain have rolled
  Two thousand years of wrong;
And man, at war with man, hears not
  The love-song which they bring:
O hush the noise, ye men of strife,
  And hear the angels sing!

4 For lo! the days are hastening on,
  By prophet-bards foretold,
When, with the ever-circling years,
  Comes round the age of gold;
When peace shall over all the earth
  Its ancient splendours fling,
And all mankind give back the song
  Which now the angels sing.

E. H. Sears† (1810-76)

The Lord Jesus Christ:

78 DIVINUM MYSTERIUM 87.87.87.7.

Late form of a Plainsong Melody
as given in *Piae Cantiones* (1582)

Freely and with breadth

1 Of the Fa-ther's love be-got - ten Ere the worlds be-

gan_ to be, He is Al-pha and O - me - ga,

He the source, the end-ing he, Of the things that are, that

have _____ been, And that fu-ture years shall see,

Ev - er-more and ev - er - more. _

His Incarnation

Corde natus ex Parentis

Of the Father's love begotten
Ere the worlds began to be,
He is Alpha and Omega,
He the source, the ending he,
Of the things that are, that háve been,
And that future years shall see,
Evermore and evermore.

2*O that ever-blessèd birthday,
When the Virgin, full of grace,
Of the Holy Ghost incarnate,
Bare the Saviour of our race;
And the Child, the world's Redeémer,
First revealed his sacred face,
Evermore and evermore.

3 O ye heights of heav'n, adore him;
Angel hosts, his praises sing;
All dominions, bow before him,
And extol our God and King;
Let no tongue on earth be silent,
Every voice in concert ring,
Evermore and evermore.

4 This is he whom seers in old time
Chanted of with one accord;
Whom the voices of the prophets
Promised in their faithful word;
Now he shines, the long-expécted;
Let creation praise its Lord,
Evermore and evermore.

5 Christ, to thee, with God the Father,
And, O Holy Ghost, to thee,
Hymn and chant and high thanksgiving,
And unwearied praises be,
Honour, glory, and domínion,
And eternal victory,
Evermore and evermore.

Prudentius (348-*c*.410)
Tr. J. M. Neale (1818-66) *and H. W. Baker* (1821-77)

The Lord Jesus Christ:

EISENACH L.M.

Melody by J. H. SCHEIN (1586-1630)
Harmony from settings by J. S. BACH (1685-1750)

O amor quam ecstaticus

O LOVE, how deep, how broad, how high!
How passing thought and fantasy
That God, the Son of God, should take
Our mortal form for mortals' sake.

2*He sent no angel to our race
Of higher or of lower place,
But wore the robe of human frame,
And he himself to this world came.

3 For us baptized, for us he bore
His holy fast, and hungered sore;
For us temptations sharp he knew;
For us the tempter overthrew.

4 For us to wicked men betrayed,
Scourged, mocked, in crown of thorns arrayed,
He bore the shameful Cross and death;
For us at length gave up his breath.

5 For us he rose from death again,
For us he went on high to reign,
For us he sent his Spirit here,
To guide, to strengthen, and to cheer.

6 To him whose boundless love has won
Salvation for us through his Son,
To God the Father, glory be
Both now and through eternity.

15th century Latin
Tr. Benjamin Webb‡ (1820-85)

His Life and Ministry

80 THIS ENDRIS NYGHT   C.M.   English Carol Melody, 15th century
Harmonized by R. VAUGHAN WILLIAMS (1872-1958)

Satus Deo, volens tegi

THE Son of God his glory hides
    To dwell with parents poor;
And he who made the heav'ns abides
    In dwelling-place obscure.

2 Those mighty hands that stay the sky
    No earthly toil refuse;
And he who set the stars on high
    An humble trade pursues.

3 He in whose sight the angels stand,
    At whose behest they fly,
Now yields himself to man's command,
    And lays his glory by.

4 For this thy lowliness revealed,
    Jesu, we thee adore,
And praise to God the Father yield
    And Spirit evermore.

J.-B. de Santeuil (1630-97)
Tr. J. Chandler (1806-76) and others

The Lord Jesus Christ:

81 HEMPRIGGS 66.66.88.

LEONARD BLAKE (1907-   )

1 Son of the Lord— Most High, Who gave the
worlds their birth, He came to live— and
die— The Son of Man— on earth:
In Beth-lem's sta-ble born— was he,
And humb-ly bred— in Ga - li - lee.

His Life and Ministry

SON of the Lord Most High,
  Who gave the worlds their birth,
He came to live and die
    The Son of Man on earth:
      In Bethlem's stable born was he,
      And humbly bred in Galilee.

2 Born in so low estate,
    Schooled in a workman's trade,
Not with the high and great
    His home the Highest made:
      But labouring by his brethren's side,
      Life's common lot he glorified.

3 Then, when his hour was come,
    He heard his Father's call:
And leaving friends and home,
    He gave himself for all:
      Glad news to bring, the lost to find;
      To heal the sick, the lame, the blind.

4 Toiling by night and day,
    Himself oft burdened sore,
Where hearts in bondage lay,
    Himself their burden bore:
      Till, scorned by them he died to save,
      Himself in death, as life, he gave.

5 O lowly Majesty,
    Lofty in lowliness!
Blest Saviour, who am I
    To share thy blessedness?
      Yet thou hast called me, even me,
      Servant Divine, to follow thee.

G. W. Briggs (1875-1959)

The Lord Jesus Christ:

82 ST MATTHEW D.C.M.

Later form of a tune in
A Supplement to the New Version (1708)
Probably by DR WILLIAM CROFT (1678-1727)

His Life and Ministry

THINE arm, O Lord, in days of old
  Was strong to heal and save;
It triumphed o'er disease and death,
  O'er darkness and the grave.
To thee they went, the blind, the dumb,
  The palsied and the lame,
The leper with his tainted life,
  The sick with fevered frame.

2 And lo, thy touch brought life and health,
  Gave speech and strength and sight;
And youth renewed and frenzy calmed
  Owned thee the Lord of Light.
And now, O Lord, be near to bless,
  Almighty as of yore,
In crowded street, by restless couch,
  As by Gennesareth's shore.

3 Be thou our great Deliv'rer still,
  Thou Lord of life and death;
Restore and quicken, soothe and bless,
  With thine almighty breath.
To hands that work and eyes that see
  Give wisdom's heav'nly lore,
That whole and sick, and weak and strong,
  May praise thee evermore.

E. H. Plumptre (1821-91)

83

EUROCLYDON 64.64.D.

C. S. LANG (1891-)

(*Small notes in vv. 2 & 3*)

FIERCE was the wild billow,
  Dark was the night;
Oars laboured heavily,
  Foam glimmered white;
Trembled the mariners,
  Peril was nigh;
Then said the God of God,
  'Peace! It is I!'

2 Ridge of the mountain-wave,
    Lower thy crest!
  Wail of Euroclydon,
    Be thou at rest!
  Sorrow can never be,
    Darkness must fly,
  Where saith the Light of Light,
    'Peace! It is I!'

3 Jesu, Deliverer,
    Come thou to me;
  Soothe thou my voyaging
    Over life's sea!
  Thou, when the storm of death
    Roars, sweeping by,
  Whisper, O Truth of Truth,
    'Peace! It is I!'

J. M. Neale (1818-66)
Based on St Mark 4. 35-41

His Life and Ministry

GENNESARETH 64.64.D.   LEONARD BLAKE (1907-   )

1 Fierce was the wild bil - low, Dark was the night;
2 Ridge of __ the moun - tain-wave, Low - er thy crest!
3 Je - su, __ De - li - ve - rer, Come thou to me;

Oars la - boured hea - vi - ly, Foam glim - mered white;
Wail of Eu - ro - cly - don, Be thou at rest!
Soothe thou my voy - a - ging O - ver __ life's sea!

Tremb - led the ma - ri - ners, Pe - ril was nigh;
Sor - row can ne - ver be, Dark - ness must fly,
Thou, when the storm of death Roars, sweep - ing by,

Then said the God of God,   }
Where saith the Light of Light, } 'Peace! __ It is I!'
Whis - per, O Truth of Truth,   }

'Euroclydon' was the name given to the north-easterly gale (Acts 27. 14).

84 QUEM PASTORES LAUDAVERE 888.7. Melody adapted from a German MS of 1410

JESUS, good above all other,
Gentle child of gentle mother,
In a stable born our brother,
   Give us grace to persevere.

2 Jesus, cradled in a manger,
For us facing every danger,
Living as a homeless stranger,
   Make we thee our King most dear.

3 Jesus, for thy people dying,
Risen Master, death defying,
Lord in heav'n, thy grace supplying,
   Keep us to thy presence near.

4 Jesus, who our sorrows bearest,
All our thoughts and hopes thou sharest;
Thou to man the truth declarest;
   Help us all thy truth to hear.

5 Lord, in all our doings guide us;
Pride and hate shall ne'er divide us;
We'll go on with thee beside us,
   And with joy we'll persevere!

Percy Dearmer (1867-1936),
partly based on J. M. Neale (1818-66)

His Life and Ministry

85 ST ENODOC C.M.   C. S. LANG (1891-   )

For Lent

LORD, who throughout these forty days
  For us didst fast and pray,
Teach us with thee to mourn our sins,
  And close by thee to stay.

2 As thou with Satan didst contend,
    And didst the victory win,
  O give us strength in thee to fight,
    In thee to conquer sin.

3 As thirst and hunger thou didst bear,
    So teach us, gracious Lord,
  To die to self, and daily live
    By thy most holy word.

4 And through these days of penitence,
    And through thy Passiontide,
  Yea, evermore, in life and death,
    Jesu, with us abide.

                              Claudia F. Hernaman† (1838-98)

The Lord Jesus Christ:

86 PANGE LINGUA 87.87.87. Plainsong Melody (Sarum form), Mode iii

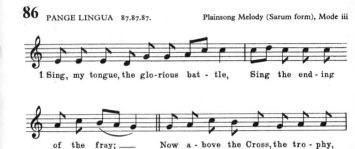

1 Sing, my tongue, the glo-rious bat-tle, Sing the end-ing

of the fray; ⎯ Now a-bove the Cross, the tro-phy,

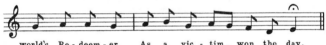

Sound the loud tri-um-phant lay: ⎯ Tell how Christ, the

world's Re-deem-er, As a vic-tim⎯ won the day.

A - men. ⎯

His Suffering and Death

Pange lingua gloriosi proelium certaminis

Sing, my tongue, the glorious battle,
  Sing the ending of the fray;
Now above the Cross, the trophy,
  Sound the loud triumphant lay:
Tell how Christ, the world's Redeemer,
  As a victim won the day.

2 Tell how, when at length the fullness
    Of th' appointed time was come,
  He, the Word, was born of woman,
    Left for us his Father's home,
  Showed to men the perfect manhood,
    Shone as light amidst the gloom.

3 Thus, with thirty years accomplish'd,
    Went he forth from Nazareth,
  Destined, dedicate, and willing,
    Wrought his work, and met his death;
  Like a lamb he humbly yielded
    On the Cross his dying breath.

4 Faithful Cross, thou sign of triumph,
    Now for man the noblest tree,
  None in foliage, none in blossom,
    None in fruit thy peer may be;
  Symbol of the world's redemption,
    For the weight that hung on thee!

5 Unto God be praise and glory:
    To the Father and the Son,
  To the eternal Spirit, honour
    Now and evermore be done;
  Praise and glory in the highest,
    While the timeless ages run.   Amen.

Venantius Fortunatus (c.535-c.600)
Tr. Percy Dearmer (1867-1936)

A small figure indicates the number of notes to a syllable.

87 LOVE UNKNOWN 66.66.44.44.   JOHN IRELAND (1879-1962)

MY song is love unknown,
My Saviour's love to me,
Love to the loveless shown,
    That they might lovely be.
        O, who am I,
            That for my sake
            My Lord should take
        Frail flesh, and die?

2 He came from his blest throne,
    Salvation to bestow:
But men made strange, and none
    The longed-for Christ would know.
        But O, my Friend,
            My Friend indeed,
            Who at my need
        His life did spend!

3 Sometimes they strow his way,
    And his sweet praises sing;
Resounding all the day
    Hosannas to their King.
        Then 'Crucify!'
            Is all their breath,
            And for his death
        They thirst and cry.

4 Why, what hath my Lord done?
      What makes this rage and spite?
  He made the lame to run,
      He gave the blind their sight.
          Sweet injuries!
              Yet they at these
              Themselves displease,
          And 'gainst him rise.

5 They rise, and needs will have
      My dear Lord made away;
  A murderer they save,
      The Prince of Life they slay.
          Yet cheerful he
              To suffering goes,
              That he his foes
          From thence might free.

6 In life no house, no home,
      My Lord on earth might have;
  In death no friendly tomb,
      But what a stranger gave.
          What may I say?
              Heav'n was his home;
              But mine the tomb
          Wherein he lay.

7 Here might I stay and sing,
      No story so divine;
  Never was love, dear King,
      Never was grief like thine!
          This is my Friend,
              In whose sweet praise
              I all my days
          Could gladly spend.

                    Samuel Crossman (1624-83)

The Lord Jesus Christ:

FIRST VERSION

ST THEODULPH   76.76.D.   Later form of a melody by M. TESCHNER (1615)

v.7 ends here.

SECOND VERSION

ST THEODULPH   76.76.D.   Melody by M. TESCHNER (1615), as set
by J. S. BACH in the *St John Passion* (1723)

v.7 ends here.

His Suffering and Death

Palm Sunday

Gloria, laus, et honor

ALL glory, laud, and honour
To thee, Redeemer, King,
To whom the lips of children
Made sweet hosannas ring.

2 Thou art the King of Israel,
   Thou David's royal Son,
Who in the Lord's name comest,
   The King and Blessèd One.

3 The company of angels
   Are praising thee on high,
And mortal men and all things
   Created make reply.

4 The people of the Hebrews
   With palms before thee went;
Our praise and prayer and anthems
   Before thee we present.

5 To thee before thy passion
   They sang their hymns of praise;
To thee now high exalted
   Our melody we raise.

6 Thou didst accept their praises:
   Accept the prayers we bring,
Who in all good delightest,
   Thou good and gracious King.

7 *All glory, laud, and honour*
   To thee, Redeemer, King,
To whom the lips of children
   Made sweet hosannas ring.

                    Theodulph of Orleans (d. 821)
                    Tr. J. M. Neale‡ (1818-66)

This hymn may be sung either in the form shown, or else in verses of four lines with the italicised words as a Refrain.

89

THE KING'S MAJESTY L.M. GRAHAM GEORGE (1912-   )
With dignity

1 Ride on! ride on in ma - jes - ty! Hark, all the

tribes ho-san-na cry; Thine hum-ble beast pur-sues his road

With palms and scat-tered gar-ments strowed.

SECOND TUNE

WINCHESTER NEW L.M. Adapted from a melody in
Musicalisches Hand-Buch (Hamburg, 1690)

His Suffering and Death

Ride on! ride on in majesty!
Hark, all the tribes hosanna cry;
Thine humble beast pursues his road
With palms and scattered garments strowed.

2 Ride on! ride on in majesty!
In lowly pomp ride on to die:
O Christ, thy triumphs now begin
O'er captive death and conquered sin.

3 Ride on! ride on in majesty!
The wingèd squadrons of the sky
Look down with sad and wondering eyes
To see the approaching sacrifice.

4 Ride on! ride on in majesty!
Thy last and fiercest strife is nigh;
The Father, on his sapphire throne,
Expects his own anointed Son.

5 Ride on! ride on in majesty!
In lowly pomp ride on to die;
Bow thy meek head to mortal pain,
Then take, O God, thy power, and reign.

H. H. Milman (1791-1868)

The Lord Jesus Christ:

90

FIRST TUNE

WESTMINSTER C.M.

J. TURLE (1802-82)

SECOND TUNE

CHESHIRE C.M.

From T. Est's *Psalmes* (1592)
(Harmony slightly altered)

For an Alternative Version of this tune, see No. 277.

For Holy Week

O THOU who through this holy week
    Didst suffer for us all,
The sick to cure, the lost to seek,
    To raise up them that fall:

2 We cannot understand the woe
    Thy love was pleased to bear;
O Lamb of God, we only know
    That all our hopes are there.

3 Thy feet the path of suffering trod;
    Thy hand the victory won:
What shall we render to our God
    For all that he hath done?

4 O grant us, Lord, with thee to die,
    With thee to rise anew;
Grant us the things of earth to fly,
    The things of heaven pursue.

Verses 1-3 by J. M. Neale (1818-66)
Verse 4 by W. Denton (1853)

His Suffering and Death

Melody from W. TANS'UR'S *Compleat Melody* (1735)

Solus ad victimam procedis, Domine

Alone thou goest forth, O Lord,
    In sacrifice to die;
Is this thy sorrow naught to us
    Who pass unheeding by?

2 Our sins, not thine, thou bearest, Lord,
    Make us thy sorrow feel,
Till through our pity and our shame
    Love answers love's appeal.

3 This is earth's darkest hour, but thou
    Dost light and life restore;
Then let all praise be given thee
    Who livest evermore.

4 Grant us with thee to suffer, Lord,
    That, as we share this hour,
Thy Cross may bring us to thy joy
    And resurrection power.

Peter Abélard (1079-1142)
Tr. F. Bland Tucker† (1895-   )

The Lord Jesus Christ:

92 HERZLIEBSTER JESU 11 11 11.5

Melody from J. CRÜGER's *Gesangbuch* (1640), as set
by J. S. BACH in the *St Matthew Passion* (1729)

AH, holy Jesu, how hast thou offended,
That man to judge thee hath in hate pretended?
By foes derided, by thine own rejected,
O most afflicted.

2*Who was the guilty? Who brought this upon thee?
Alas, my treason, Jesu, hath undone thee.
'Twas I, Lord Jesu, I it was denied thee:
I crucified thee.

3 Lo, the good Shepherd for the sheep is offered:
The slave hath sinnèd, and the Son hath suffered:
For man's atonement, while he nothing heedeth,
God intercedeth.

4 For me, kind Jesu, was thy Incarnation,
Thy mortal sorrow, and thy life's oblation;
Thy death of anguish and thy bitter passion,
For my salvation.

5 Therefore, kind Jesu, since I cannot pay thee,
I do adore thee, and will ever pray thee
Think on thy pity and thy love unswerving,
Not my deserving.

Robert Bridges (1844-1930), *based on a*
Latin Meditation of the 11th century

His Suffering and Death

FIRST TUNE

VEXILLA REGIS L.M.

Plainsong Melody (Sarum form), Mode i

Vexilla Regis prodeunt,
Fulget crucis mysterium . . .

1 The roy - al ban - ners for - ward go,
2 His feet and hands out - stretch - ing there,
3 There whilst he hung, his sa - cred side
4 Ful - filled is now what Da - vid told
5 Blest Three in One, our praise we sing

1 The Cross shines forth in mys - tic glow;
2 He willed the pierc - ing nails to bear,
3 By sol - dier's spear was o - pen'd wide,
4 In true pro - phe - tic song of old;
5 To thee from whom all gra - ces spring:

1 Where he, the Life, did death en - dure,
2 For us and our re - demp - tion's sake
3 To cleanse us in the pre - cious flood
4 To all the na - tions, 'Lo,' saith he,
5 As by the Cross thou dost re - store,

1 And yet by death did life pro - cure.
2 A vic - tim of him - self to make.
3 Of wa - ter min - gled with his blood.
4 'Our God is reign - ing from the Tree'.
5 So rule and guide us ev - er - more. A - men.

Venantius Fortunatus (c.535–c.600)
Tr. J. M. Neale (1818–66) and others

This hymn is thought to have been inspired by a procession at the opening of the convent of
St Croix at Poitiers, where the author later became Bishop. Verse 4 refers to Psalm 96, v. 10,
which in some versions included the words 'Dominus regnavit a ligno'.

The plainsong melody is probably as old as the Latin hymn itself.

The Lord Jesus Christi:

GONFALON ROYAL L.M.   P. C. BUCK (1871-1947)
With movement

A - - men.

His Suffering and Death

Vexilla Regis prodeunt

THE royal banners forward go,
The Cross shines forth in mystic glow;
Where he, the Life, did death endure,
And yet by death did life procure.

2 His feet and hands outstretching there,
He willed the piercing nails to bear,
For us and our redemption's sake
A victim of himself to make.

3 There whilst he hung, his sacred side
By soldier's spear was opened wide,
To cleanse us in the precious flood
Of water mingled with his blood.

4 Fulfilled is now what David told
In true prophetic song of old;
To all the nations, 'Lo', saith he,
'Our God is reigning from the Tree'.

5 Blest Three in One, our praise we sing
To thee from whom all graces spring:
As by the Cross thou dost restore,
So rule and guide us evermore.
                                    Amen.

Venantius Fortunatus (c. 535-c. 600)
Tr. J. M. Neale (1818-66) and others

This hymn is thought to have been inspired by a procession at the opening of the convent of
t Croix at Poitiers, where the author later became Bishop. Verse 4 refers to Psalm 96, v. 10,
hich in some versions included the words 'Dominus regnavit a ligno'.

The Lord Jesus Christ:

FIRST VERSION

PASSION CHORALE   76.76.D.

Melody by H. L. HASSLER (1564-1612), as set
by J. S. BACH in the *St Matthew Passion* (1729)

SECOND VERSION

PASSION CHORALE   76.76.D.

Melody by H. L. HASSLER (1564-1612), as set
by J. S. BACH in the *St Matthew Passion* (1729)

This version may be used for a verse by the Choir alone.

His Suffering and Death

O Haupt voll Blut und Wunden

O SACRED Head! sore wounded,
  With grief and shame weighed down,
O Kingly Head! surrounded
  With thorns, thy only crown;
O Lord of Life and Glory,
  What bliss till now was thine!
I read the wondrous story,
  And joy to call thee mine.

2 Thy grief and bitter passion
    Were all for sinners' gain:
  Mine, mine was the transgression,
    But thine the deadly pain.
  Lo, here I fall, my Saviour,
    'Tis I deserve thy place;
  Look on me with thy favour,
    Vouchsafe to me thy grace.

3 What language shall I borrow
    To thank thee, dearest Friend,
  For this, thy dying sorrow,
    Thy love that hath no end?
  Lord, make me thine for ever,
    O may I faithful be!
  And, Saviour, let me never
    Outlive my love to thee.

P. Gerhardt (1607-76) *from a Latin poem*
Tr. J. W. Alexander (1804-59) *and others*

95 ST CROSS L.M.

J. B. DYKES (1823-76)

Jesus Crucified

O COME and mourn with me awhile;
　O come ye to the Saviour's side;
　O come, together let us mourn:
　　Jesus, our Lord, is crucified!

2 Seven times he spoke, seven words of love;
　　And all three hours his silence cried
　For mercy on the souls of men:
　　Jesus, our Lord, is crucified!

3 O break, O break, hard heart of mine!
　　Thy weak self-love and guilty pride
　His Pilate and his Judas were:
　　Jesus, our Lord, is crucified!

4 O love of God! O sin of man!
　　In this dread act your strength is tried;
　And victory remains with Love:
　　For he, our Lord, is crucified!

F. W. Faber‡ (1814-63)

His Suffering and Death

HORSLEY C.M.   WILLIAM HORSLEY (1774-1858)

THERE is a green hill far away,
　　Without a city wall,
Where the dear Lord was crucified,
　　Who died to save us all.

2 We may not know, we cannot tell,
　　What pains he had to bear,
But we believe it was for us
　　He hung and suffered there.

3 He died that we might be forgiven,
　　He died to make us good;
That we might go at last to heaven,
　　Saved by his precious blood.

4 There was no other good enough
　　To pay the price of sin;
He only could unlock the gate
　　Of heaven, and let us in.

5 O dearly, dearly has he loved,
　　And we must love him too,
And trust in his redeeming blood,
　　And try his works to do.

Mrs C. F. Alexander (1818-95)

The Lord Jesus Christ:

97

FIRST TUNE

Melody from E. PRYS's *Llyfr y Psalmau* (1621)
Bass by ORLANDO GIBBONS (1623)
(Rhythm slightly altered)

SONG 67   C.M.

SECOND TUNE

Melody, and most of the bass, from
Easy Hymn-Tunes for Catholic Schools (185?)
(based on an 18th-century German melody)

ST BERNARD   C.M.

His Suffering and Death

O Deus, ego amo te

MY God, I love thee—not because
I hope for heaven thereby,
Nor yet because who love thee not
Are lost eternally.

2 Thou, O my Jesus, thou didst me
Upon the Cross embrace;
For me didst bear the nails and spear,
And manifold disgrace;

3 And griefs and torments numberless,
And sweat of agony,
Yea, death itself, and all for one
Who was thine enemy.

4 Then why, O blessèd Jesu Christ,
Should I not love thee well,
Not for the sake of winning heaven,
Nor of escaping hell;

5 Not with the hope of gaining aught,
Not seeking a reward;
But as thyself hast lovèd me,
O ever-loving Lord!

6 E'en so I love thee, and will love,
And in thy praise will sing;
Solely because thou art my God,
And my eternal King.

17th century Latin, based on a Spanish sonnet
Tr. E. Caswall† (1814-78)

The Lord Jesus Christ:

98 ROCKINGHAM L.M.

Adapted by E. MILLER (1790) from an
anonymous tune of c.1780.

His Suffering and Death

Galatians 6. 14

W HEN I survey the wondrous Cross,
  On which the Prince of Glory died,
My richest gain I count but loss,
  And pour contempt on all my pride.

2 Forbid it, Lord, that I should boast
     Save in the death of Christ my God;
   All the vain things that charm me most,
     I sacrifice them to his blood.

3 See from his head, his hands, his feet,
     Sorrow and love flow mingled down;
   Did e'er such love and sorrow meet,
     Or thorns compose so rich a crown?

4* His dying crimson, like a robe,
     Spreads o'er his body on the Tree;
   Then am I dead to all the globe,
     And all the globe is dead to me.

5 Were the whole realm of nature mine,
     That were a present far too small;
   Love so amazing, so divine,
     Demands my soul, my life, my all.

Isaac Watts (1674-1748)

*Verse 1, line 2, is the author's revised version. He had originally printed 'Where the young
Prince of Glory died'.*

The Lord Jesus Christ:

99

FIRST TUNE

BOW BRICKHILL L.M.

S. H. NICHOLSON (1875-1947)

SECOND TUNE

BRESLAU L.M.

German Traditional Melody, in
form used by MENDELSSOHN (1836)

His Suffering and Death

WE sing the praise of him who died,
  Of him who died upon the Cross:
The sinner's hope let men deride;
  For this we count the world but loss.

2 Inscribed upon the Cross we see
    In shining letters 'God is love';
  He bears our sins upon the Tree;
    He brings us mercy from above.

3 The Cross! it takes our guilt away;
    It holds the fainting spirit up;
  It cheers with hope the gloomy day,
    And sweetens every bitter cup;

4 It makes the coward spirit brave,
    And nerves the feeble arm for fight;
  It takes all terror from the grave,
    And gilds the bed of death with light;

5 The balm of life, the cure of woe,
    The measure and the pledge of love,
  The sinner's refuge here below,
    The angels' theme in heaven above.

Thomas Kelly† (1769-1855)

The Lord Jesus Christ:

100 ELLACOMBE 76.76.D.

18th century German melody,
as adapted and set in the St Gall *Gesangbuch* (1863)

His Resurrection

'Αναστάσεως ἡμέρα

THE day of Resurrection,
  Earth, tell it out abroad!
The passover of gladness,
  The passover of God!
From death to life eternal,
  From earth unto the sky,
Our Christ hath brought us over
  With hymns of victory.

2 Our hearts be pure from evil,
  That we may see aright
The Lord in rays eternal
  Of Resurrection-light;
And, listening to his accents,
  May hear, so calm and plain,
His own 'All hail,' and, hearing,
  May raise the victor strain.

3 Now let the heav'ns be joyful,
  Let earth her song begin,
The round world keep high triumph,
  And all that is therein;
Let all things seen and unseen
  Their notes of gladness blend,
For Christ the Lord is risen,
  Our joy that hath no end.

St John of Damascus (died c. 750)
Tr. J. M. Neale‡ (1818-66)

A hymn sung in the Eastern Church when the striking of midnight announced that Easter Day had begun.

101 ILFRACOMBE   L.M. with Alleluias   JOHN GARDNER (1917-   )

Aurora lucis rutilat
Caelum laudibus intonat . . .

1 Light's glitt-'ring morn be-decks the sky: __
2 Through Christ our Lord, the might-y King, __
3 O Lord of all, with us a-bide __
4 All praise be thine, O ri-sen Lord, __

Al - le - lu - ia, Al - le - lu - ia, Al - le - lu - ia!

1 Heav'n thun-ders forth its vic-tor-y cry; __
2 Death's age-long pow'r hath lost its sting; __
3 In this our joy-ful Eas-ter-tide; __
4 From death to end-less life re-stored; __

Al - le - lu - ia, Al - le - lu - ia, Al - le - lu - ia!

1 This glad earth shouts her joy be-low, __
2 An an-gel robed in light hath said, __
3 From ev-'ry wea-pon death can wield __
4 All praise to God the Fa-ther be, __

Al - le - lu - ia, Al - le - lu - ia, Al - le - lu - ia!

His Resurrection

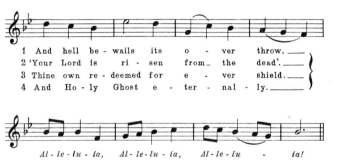

1 And hell be - wails its o - ver throw. ___
2 'Your Lord is ri - sen from_ the dead'. ___
3 Thine own re - deemed for e - ver shield. ___
4 And Ho - ly Ghost e - ter - nal - ly. _____

Al - le - lu - ia, Al - le - lu - ia, Al - le - lu - ia!

From the Latin of the 8th century or earlier
Tr. J. M. Neale (1818-66) and others

The Lord Jesus Christ:

102

WÜRTEMBERG 77.77.4.

Melody from *Hundert Arien* (Dresden, 1694)
Harmonized by W. H. Monk (1823-89)

Al - le - lu - ia!

Second Tune

ORIENTIS PARTIBUS 77.77.4.

Medieval French Melody
Arranged by R. Vaughan Williams (1872-1958)

Al - le - lu - ia!

His Resurrection

Christus ist erstanden

CHRIST the Lord is risen again!
Christ hath broken every chain!
Hark, the angels shout for joy,
Singing evermore on high:
                    Alleluia!

2 He who gave for us his life,
   Who for us endured the strife,
   Is our Paschal Lamb to-day;
   We too sing for joy, and say:
                    Alleluia!

3 He who bore all pain and loss
   Comfortless upon the Cross,
   Lives in glory now on high,
   Pleads for us, and hears our cry:
                    Alleluia!

4 He who slumbered in the grave
   Is exalted now to save;
   Now through Christendom it rings
   That the Lamb is King of Kings:
                    Alleluia!

5 Now he bids us tell abroad
   How the lost may be restored,
   How the penitent forgiven,
   How we too may enter heaven:
                    Alleluia!

6 Thou, our Paschal Lamb indeed,
   Christ, to-day thy people feed;
   Take our sins and guilt away,
   That we all may sing for aye:
                    Alleluia!

                    M. Weisse (c. 1480-1534)
                    Tr. C. Winkworth (1827-78)

103 EASTER HYMN 74.74.D.

Melody from *Lyra Davidica* (1708),
as altered in the mid-18th century

Al - le - lu - ia!

Al - le - lu - ia!

Al - le - lu - ia!

Al - le - lu - ia!

JESUS CHRIST is risen today, *Alleluia!*
Our triumphant holy day, *Alleluia!*
Who did once, upon the Cross, *Alleluia!*
Suffer to redeem our loss. *Alleluia!*

2 Hymns of praise then let us sing,
Unto Christ our heavenly King,
Who endured the Cross and grave,
Sinners to redeem and save.

3 But the pains which he endured,
Our salvation have procured;
Now beyond our sight he's King,
Where the angels ever sing.

Verse 1, 'Lyra Davidica'† (1708)
Verses 2 & 3, J. Arnold's 'Compleat Psalmodist'‡ (1749

His Resurrection

Hymn for Easter-Day

'CHRIST the Lord is risen today',
Sons of men and angels say!
Raise your joys and triumphs high,
Sing, ye heav'ns, and earth reply.

2 Love's redeeming work is done,
Fought the fight, the battle won,
Lo! our Sun's eclipse is o'er,
Lo! he sets in blood no more.

3 Vain the stone, the watch, the seal;
Christ has burst the gates of hell!
Death in vain forbids his rise,
Christ has opened paradise!

4*Lives again our glorious King;
Where, O death, is now thy sting?
Dying once, he all doth save;
Where thy victory, O grave?

5 Soar we now, where Christ has led?
Following our exalted Head,
Made like him, like him we rise,
Ours the cross—the grave—the skies!

6 Hail, the Lord of earth and heaven!
Praise to thee by both be given:
Thee we greet triumphant now;
Hail, the Resurrection-Thou!

Charles Wesley (1707-88)

The Lord Jesus Christ:

105 VULPIUS 8 8 8.4

Melody from M. VULPIUS's *Gesangbuch* (1609)
Harmonized by HENRY G. LEY (1887-1962)

Al - le - lu - ia, Al - le - lu - ia, Al - le - lu - ia!

GOOD Christian men, rejoice and sing!
Now is the triumph of our King!
To all the world glad news we bring:
Alleluia!

2 The Lord of Life is risen for aye;
Bring flowers of song to strew his way;
Let all mankind rejoice and say:
Alleluia!

3 Praise we in songs of victory
That Love, that Life which cannot die,
And sing with hearts uplifted high:
Alleluia!

4 Thy name we bless, O risen Lord,
And sing to-day with one accord
The life laid down, the Life restored:
Alleluia!

C. A. Alington (1872-1955)

106 VRUECHTEN 67.67.D   Dutch melody, 17th century

Had Christ, that once was slain, Ne'er bursts his three-day pri - son,

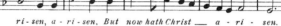

Our faith had been in vain: But now hath Christ a - ri - sen, a -

ri - sen, a - ri - sen, But now hath Christ ___ a - ri - sen.

THIS joyful Eastertide,
   Away with sin and sorrow!
My Love, the Crucified,
   Hath sprung to life this morrow:

   Had Christ, that once was slain,
      Ne'er burst his three-day prison,
   Our faith had been in vain:
      But now hath Christ arisen.

2 My flesh in hope shall rest,
      And for a season slumber:
   Till trump from east to west
      Shall wake the dead in number:

3 Death's flood hath lost his chill,
      Since Jesus crossed the river:
   Lover of souls, from ill
      My passing soul deliver:

                    G. R. Woodward (1848-1934)

The Lord Jesus Christ:

107 JESU, MEINE ZUVERSICHT 78.78.77.

From J. S. Bach's arrangements of a melody
in J. Crüger's *Praxis Pietatis Melica*
(1653)

His Resurrection

JESUS lives! No longer now
  Can thy terrors, Death, appal me;
Jesus lives! by this I know
  From the grave he will recall me:
Brighter scenes at death commence;
This shall be my confidence.

2*Jesus lives! to him the throne
  High o'er heav'n and earth is given:
I may go where he is gone,
  Live and reign with him in heaven:
God through Christ forgives offence;
This shall be my confidence.

3*Jesus lives! who now despairs,
  Spurns the Word which God hath spoken:
Grace to all that Word declares,
  Grace, whereby sin's yoke is broken:
Christ rejects not penitence;
This shall be my confidence.

4 Jesus lives! for me he died;
  Hence will I, to Jesus living,
Pure in heart and act abide,
  Praise to him and glory giving:
Freely God doth aid dispense;
This shall be my confidence.

5 Jesus lives! my heart knows well
  Naught from me his love shall sever:
Life, nor death, nor powers of hell,
  Part me now from Christ for ever:
God will be a sure defence;
This shall be my confidence.

6 Jesus lives! henceforth is death
  Entrance-gate of life immortal:
This shall calm my trembling breath
  When I pass its gloomy portal:
Faith shall cry, as fails each sense,
'Lord, thou art my Confidence'.

C. F. Gellert (1715-69)
Tr. F. E. Cox (1812-97)

The Lord Jesus Christ:

108 ST ALBINUS 78.78.4.

H. J. GAUNTLETT (1805-76)
(rhythm slightly altered)

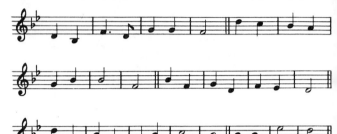

Al - le - lu - ia!

Jesus lebt!

JESUS lives! thy terrors now
    Can, O death, no more appal us:
Jesus lives! by this we know
    Thou, O grave, canst not enthral us.
        Alleluia!

2 Jesus lives! henceforth is death
    But the gate of life immortal:
This shall calm our trembling breath,
    When we pass its gloomy portal.
        Alleluia!

3 Jesus lives! for us he died:
    Then, alone to Jesus living,
Pure in heart may we abide,
    Glory to our Saviour giving.
        Alleluia!

4 Jesus lives! our hearts know well
    Naught from us his love shall sever;
Life nor death nor powers of hell
    Tear us from his keeping ever.
        Alleluia!

5 Jesus lives! to him the throne
    Over all the world is given:
May we go where he is gone,
    Rest and reign with him in heaven.
        Alleluia!

        C. F. Gellert (1715-69)
        Tr. adapted from Hymn 107

109 VICTORY 8 8 8.4.

Adapted by W. H. MONK (1823-89) from
a *Magnificat* by PALESTRINA (1591)

Al - le - lu - ia!

Finita iam sunt proelia

THE strife is o'er, the battle done;
Now is the Victor's triumph won;
O let the song of praise be sung:
Alleluia!

2 Death's mightiest powers have done their worst,
And Jesus hath his foes dispersed;
Let shouts of praise and joy outburst:
Alleluia!

3 On the third morn he rose again,
Glorious in majesty to reign;
O let us swell the joyful strain:
Alleluia!

4 He brake the age-bound chains of hell;
The bars from heav'n's high portals fell;
Let hymns of praise his triumph tell:
Alleluia!

5 Lord, by the stripes which wounded thee,
From death's dread sting thy servants free,
That we may live, and sing to thee:
Alleluia!

17th century.
Tr. F. Pott (1832-1909)

The Lord Jesus Christ:

FIRST TUNE

AVE VIRGO 76.76.D.

Melody as given in
J. HORN's *Gesangbuch* (1544)

SECOND TUNE

ST JOHN DAMASCENE 76.76.D.

A. H. BROWN (1830-1926)

His Resurrection

Αἴσωμεν πάντες λαοί

COME, ye faithful, raise the strain
    Of triumphant gladness;
God hath brought his Israel
    Into joy from sadness,
Loosed from Pharaoh's bitter yoke
    Jacob's sons and daughters,
Led them with unmoistened foot
    Through the Red Sea waters.

2 'Tis the spring of souls to-day;
    Christ hath burst his prison,
And from three days' sleep in death
    As a sun hath risen;
All the winter of our sins,
    Long and dark, is flying
From his light, to whom we give
    Laud and praise undying.

3 Now the queen of seasons, bright
    With the day of splendour,
With the royal feast of feasts,
    Comes its joy to render;
Comes to glad Jerusalem,
    Who with true affection
Welcomes in unwearied strains
    Jesu's Resurrection.

4 Neither might the gates of death,
    Nor the tomb's dark portal,
Nor the watchers, nor the seal,
    Hold thee as a mortal;
But to-day amidst thine own
    Thou didst stand, bestowing
That thy peace, which evermore
    Passeth human knowing.

St John of Damascus (died c. 750)
Tr. J. M. Neale† (1818-66)

The Lord Jesus Christ:

111 NUN LASST UNS 77.77.

Later form of a melody in
Selnecker's *Christliche Psalmen* (1587)
(as harmonized in *The English Hymnal*, 1906)

A BRIGHTER dawn is breaking,
And earth with praise is waking;
For thou, O King most highest,
The power of death defiest;

2 And thou hast come victorious,
With risen body glorious,
Who now for ever livest,
And life abundant givest.

3 O free the world from blindness,
And fill the world with kindness,
Give sinners resurrection,
Bring striving to perfection.

4 In sickness give us healing,
In doubt thy clear revealing,
That praise to thee be given
In earth as in thy heaven.

Percy Dearmer (1867-1936)

His Glory and Reign

112 METZLER'S REDHEAD   C.M.   R. REDHEAD (1820-1901)

Jesu, nostra redemptio

O CHRIST, our hope, our hearts' desire,
  Redemption's only spring;
Creator of the world art thou,
  Its Saviour and its King.

2 How vast the mercy and the love
    Which laid our sins on thee,
  And led thee to a cruel death
    To set thy people free.

3 But now the bonds of death are burst,
    The ransom has been paid:
  And thou art on thy Father's throne,
    In majesty arrayed.

4 O may thy mighty love prevail,
    Our sinful souls to spare!
  O may we come before thy throne,
    And find acceptance there!

5 O Christ, be thou our present joy,
    Our future great reward;
  Our only glory may it be
    To glory in the Lord.

Probably 7th or 8th century
Tr. J. Chandler† (1806-76)

The Lord Jesus Christ:

113 MOVILLE 76.76.D.

Irish Traditional Melody
Harmonized by C. H. KITSON (1874-1944)

1 Christ is the world's Re - deem - er, The lov - er of the pure,

The fount of heav'n-ly_ wis-dom, Our trust and hope se - cure;

The ar-mour of his sol-diers, The Lord _ of earth and sky;

Our health while we_ are_ liv-ing, Our life when we shall die.

His Glory and Reign

Christus Redemptor gentium

CHRIST is the world's Redeemer,
  The lover of the pure,
The fount of heav'nly wisdom,
  Our trust and hope secure;
The armour of his soldiers,
  The Lord of earth and sky;
Our health while we are living,
  Our life when we shall die.

2 Christ hath our host surrounded
  With clouds of martyrs bright,
Who wave their palms in triumph,
  And fire us for the fight.
For Christ the Cross ascended
  To save a world undone,
And, suffering for the sinful,
  Our full redemption won.

3 Down in the realm of darkness
  He lay a captive bound,
But at the hour appointed
  He rose, a Victor crowned;
And now, to heav'n ascended,
  He sits upon the throne,
In glorious dominion,
  His Father's and his own.

4 Glory to God the Father,
  The unbegotten One;
All honour be to Jesus,
  His sole-begotten Son;
And to the Holy Spirit—
  The perfect Trinity.
Let all the worlds give answer,
  'Amen—so let it be.'

Probably by St Columba (521-597)
Tr. Duncan MacGregor† (1854-1923)

The Lord Jesus Christ:

114 NEANDER 87.87.87. Melody from J. NEANDER's *Alpha und Omega* (1680)

His Glory and Reign

COME, ye faithful, raise the anthem,
  Cleave the skies with shouts of praise;
Sing to him who found the ransom,
  Ancient of eternal Days,
God of God, the Word incarnate,
  Whom the heav'n of heav'n obeys.

2 Ere he raised the lofty mountains,
  Formed the seas, or built the sky,
Love eternal, free, and boundless,
  Moved the Lord of Life to die,
Fore-ordained the Prince of Princes
  For the throne of Calvary.

3 There, for us and our redemption,
  See him all his life-blood pour!
There he wins our full salvation,
  Dies that we may die no more;
Then, arising, lives for ever,
  Reigning where he was before.

4 Yet this earth he still remembers,
  Still by him the flock are fed;
Yea, he gives them Food immortal,
  Gives himself, the living Bread;
Leads them where the precious fountain
  From the smitten rock is shed.

5 Trust him, then, ye fearful pilgrims;
  Who shall pluck you from his hand?
Pledged he stands for your salvation,
  Leads you to the Promised Land.
O that we, with all his true ones,
  There around his throne may stand!

*Adapted by J. M. Neale (1818-66) and others
from a hymn by J. Hupton (1762-1849)*

115 ST FULBERT C.M.   H. J. GAUNTLETT (1805-76)

THE eternal gates lift up their heads,
  The doors are opened wide,
The King of Glory is gone up
  Unto his Father's side.

2 Thou art gone up before us, Lord,
    To make for us a place,
  That we may be where now thou art,
    And look upon God's face.

3 And ever on our earthly path
    A gleam of glory lies,
  A light still breaks behind the cloud
    That veils thee from our eyes.

4 Lift up our hearts, lift up our minds,
    And let thy grace be given,
  That while we linger yet below
    Our treasure be in heaven;

5 That, where thou art at God's right hand,
    Our hope, our love may be:
  Dwell in us now, that we may dwell
    For evermore in thee.

                              Mrs C. F. Alexander (1818-95)

His Glory and Reign

ST MAGNUS   C.M.

Melody and bass (slightly altered)
probably by JEREMIAH CLARKE (c.1673-1707)

T HE head that once was crowned with thorns
    Is crowned with glory now;
A royal diadem adorns
    The mighty Victor's brow.

2 The highest place that heav'n affords
    Is his, is his by right,
The King of Kings and Lord of Lords
    And heav'n's eternal Light;

3 The joy of all who dwell above,
    The joy of all below,
To whom he manifests his love,
    And grants his name to know.

4 To them the Cross with all its shame,
    With all its grace, is given;
Their name an everlasting name,
    Their joy the joy of heav'n.

5 They suffer with their Lord below,
    They reign with him above,
Their profit and their joy to know
    The mystery of his love.

6 The Cross he bore is life and health,
    Though shame and death to him;
His people's hope, his people's wealth,
    Their everlasting theme.

Thomas Kelly (1769-1855)

The Lord Jesus Christ:

117 GOPSAL 66.66.88.   Melody and figured bass by G. F. HANDEL (1685-1759)

1 Re-joice, the Lord is King! Your Lord and King a-dore; Mor-tals, give thanks and sing, And tri-umph ev-er-more: *Lift up your heart, lift up your voice;* Re-joice, a-gain I__ say, re-joice.

LAST TWO LINES OF VERSE 5
(with realization of Handel's postlude)

We then shall hear th'Arch-an-gel's voice,

Org.

The trump of God shall sound, Re-joice!

His Glory and Reign

REJOICE, the Lord is King!
   Your Lord and King adore;
Mortals, give thanks and sing,
   And triumph evermore:

> *Lift up your heart, lift up your voice;*
> *Rejoice, again I say, rejoice.*

2 Jesus, the Saviour, reigns,
   The God of truth and love;
When he had purged our stains,
   He took his seat above:

3 His kingdom cannot fail,
   He rules o'er earth and heaven;
The keys of death and hell
   Are to our Jesus given:

4 He sits at God's right hand
   Till all his foes submit,
And bow to his command,
   And fall beneath his feet:

5 Rejoice in glorious hope;
   Jesus the Judge shall come,
And take his servants up
   To their eternal home:

> *We then shall hear th' Archangel's voice,*
> *The trump of God shall sound, Rejoice!*

Charles Wesley† (1707-88)

118 NATIVITY C.M.   H. LAHEE (1826-1912)

Christ Jesus worshipped by all the Creation

Come, let us join our cheerful songs
   With angels round the throne;
Ten thousand thousand are their tongues,
   But all their joys are one.

2 'Worthy the Lamb that died,' they cry,
      'To be exalted thus;'
   'Worthy the Lamb,' our lips reply,
      'For he was slain for us.'

3 Jesus is worthy to receive
      Honour and power divine;
   And blessings, more than we can give,
      Be, Lord, for ever thine.

4 Let all that dwell above the sky,
      And air and earth and seas,
   Conspire to lift thy glories high,
      And speak thine endless praise.

5 The whole creation join in one
      To bless the sacred name
   Of him that sits upon the throne,
      And to adore the Lamb.

                              Isaac Watts (1674-1748)
                              Based on Revelation 5. 11-13

119 LADYWELL D.C.M.   W. H. FERGUSON (1874-1950)

ALL hail the power of Jesu's name!
  Let angels prostrate fall;
Bring forth the royal diadem
  To crown him Lord of all.
Crown him, ye martyrs of your God,
  Who from his altar call;
Extol the Stem-of-Jesse's Rod,
  And crown him Lord of all.

2 Ye seed of Israel's chosen race,
    Ye ransomed of the fall,
  Hail him who saves you by his grace,
    And crown him Lord of all.
  Hail him, ye heirs of David's line,
    Whom David Lord did call;
  The God incarnate, man Divine,
    And crown him Lord of all.

3 Sinners, whose love can ne'er forget
    The wormwood and the gall,
  Go, spread your trophies at his feet,
    And crown him Lord of all.
  Let every tribe and every tongue
    To him their hearts enthral;
  Lift high the universal song,
    And crown him Lord of all.

                              E. Perronet‡ (1726-92)

The Lord Jesus Christ:

120 MILES LANE C.M.   Melody by WILLIAM SHRUBSOLE (1760-1806)

crown him,

crown him,   crown him,   crown him   Lord   of   all.

The note in brackets may be substituted if preferred.

His Glory and Reign

ALL hail the power of Jesu's name!
   Let angels prostrate fall;
Bring forth the royal diadem
   To crown him Lord of all.

2 Crown him, ye martyrs of your God,
   Who from his altar call;
Extol the Stem-of-Jesse's Rod,
   And crown him Lord of all.

3 Ye seed of Israel's chosen race,
   Ye ransomed of the fall,
Hail him who saves you by his grace,
   And crown him Lord of all.

4*Hail him, ye heirs of David's line,
   Whom David Lord did call;
The God incarnate, man Divine,
   And crown him Lord of all.

5 Sinners, whose love can ne'er forget
   The wormwood and the gall,
Go, spread your trophies at his feet,
   And crown him Lord of all.

6 Let every tribe and every tongue
   · To him their hearts enthral;
Lift high the universal song,
   And crown him Lord of all.

E. Perronet‡ (1726-92)

The Lord Jesus Christ:

121

DIADEMATA D.S.M.

G. J. ELVEY (1816-93)

SECOND TUNE

CORONA D.S.M.

C. HYLTON STEWART (1884-1932)

His Glory and Reign

CROWN him with many crowns,
The Lamb upon his throne;
Hark! how the heavenly anthem drowns
All music but its own.
Awake, my soul, and sing
Of him who died for thee,
And hail him as thy matchless King
Through all eternity.

2   Crown him the Son of God,
Before the worlds began;
And ye, who tread where he hath trod,
Crown him the Son of Man,
Who every grief hath known
That wrings the human breast,
And takes and bears them for his own,
That all in him may rest.

3   Crown him the Lord of Life,
Who triumphed o'er the grave,
And rose victorious in the strife
For those he came to save.
His glories now we sing,
Who died and rose on high;
Who died, eternal life to bring,
And lives that death may die.

4   Crown him the Lord of Peace,
Whose power a sceptre sways
From pole to pole, that wars may cease,
Absorbed in prayer and praise.
He reigns, the Lord of Years,
The Potentate of Time,
Creator of the rolling spheres,
Ineffably sublime.

5   Crown him the Lord of Heaven,
Enthroned in worlds above,
The King of Kings to whom is given
The wondrous name of Love.
All hail, Redeemer, hail!
For thou hast died for me;
Thy praise shall never, never fail
Throughout eternity.

Matthew Bridges† (1800-94) *and Godfrey Thring*† (1823-1903)

122

FIRST TUNE

IVYHATCH L.M.   B. LUARD SELBY (1853-1918)

SECOND TUNE

NIAGARA L.M.   R. JACKSON (1842-1914)

His Glory and Reign

THE Lord is King! lift up thy voice,
O earth, and all ye heav'ns, rejoice;
From world to world the joy shall ring,
'The Lord Omnipotent is King!'

2 The Lord is King! who then shall dare
Resist his will, distrust his care,
Or murmur at his wise decrees,
Or doubt his royal promises?

3 The Lord is King! O child of dust,
The Judge of all the earth is just;
Holy and true are all his ways,
Let every creature speak his praise.

4 He reigns; ye saints, exalt your strains;
Your God is King, your Father reigns;
And he is at the Father's side,
The Man of love, the Crucified.

5 *Alike pervaded by his eye
All parts of his dominion lie:
This world of ours and worlds unseen,
And thin the boundary between.

6 One Lord one empire all secures;
He reigns, and life and death are yours;
Through earth and heav'n one song shall ring,
'The Lord Omnipotent is King!'

J. Conder† (1789-1855)

The Lord Jesus Christ:

123

GALILEE L.M.

P. ARMES (1836-1908)

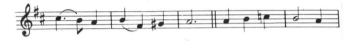

SECOND TUNE

TRURO L.M.

Melody from T. WILLIAMS's *Psalmodia Evangelica* (1789)

His Glory and Reign

Christ's Kingdom among the Nations

JESUS shall reign where'er the sun
Does his successive journeys run;
His kingdom stretch from shore to shore,
Till moons shall wax and wane no more.

2 To him shall endless prayer be made,
And praises throng to crown his head;
His name, like sweet perfume, shall rise
With ev'ry morning sacrifice;

3 People and realms of every tongue
Dwell on his love with sweetest song;
And infant-voices shall proclaim
Their early blessings on his name.

4 Blessings abound where'er he reigns;
The prisoner leaps to lose his chains;
The weary find eternal rest,
And all the sons of want are blest.

5 Let every creature rise and bring
Peculiar honours to our King;
Angels descend with songs again,
And earth repeat the long Amen.

Isaac Watts† (1674-1748)
Based on Psalm 72. 8-19

The Lord Jesus Christ:

124 CRÜGER 76.76.D.

Adapted by W. H. MONK (1823-89) from a melody
originally in J. CRÜGER's *Gesangbuch* (1640)
(harmony slightly altered)

His Glory and Reign

HAIL to the Lord's Anointed,
   Great David's greater Son!
Hail, in the time appointed,
   His reign on earth begun!
He comes to break oppression,
   To set the captive free,
To take away transgression,
   And rule in equity.

2 He shall come down like showers
   Upon the fruitful earth;
And love, joy, hope, like flowers,
   Spring in his path to birth:
Before him on the mountains,
   Shall peace the herald go,
And righteousness in fountains
   From hill to valley flow.

3 Kings shall fall down before him,
   And gold and incense bring;
All nations shall adore him,
   His praise all people sing;
To him shall prayer unceasing
   And daily vows ascend;
His kingdom still increasing,
   A kingdom without end.

4 O'er every foe victorious,
   He on his throne shall rest;
From age to age more glorious,
   All-blessing and all-blest;
The tide of time shall never
   His covenant remove;
His name shall stand for ever,
   His changeless name of Love.

James Montgomery (1771-1854)
Based on Psalm 72

The Lord Jesus Christ:

125 DARMSTADT 67.67.66.66.

Melody by A. FRITSCH (1679)
adapted and harmonized by J. S. BACH (1685-1750)

His Glory and Reign

CHRIST is the world's true Light,
  Its Captain of salvation,
The Daystar shining bright
  To every man and nation;
New life, new hope awakes,
  Where'er men own his sway:
Freedom her bondage breaks,
  And night is turned to day.

2 In Christ all races meet,
  Their ancient feuds forgetting,
The whole round world complete,
  From sunrise to its setting:
When Christ is throned as Lord,
  Men shall forsake their fear,
To ploughshare beat the sword,
  To pruning-hook the spear.

3 One Lord, in one great Name
  Unite us all who own thee;
Cast out our pride and shame
  That hinder to enthrone thee;
The world has waited long,
  Has travailed long in pain;
To heal its ancient wrong,
  Come, Prince of Peace, and reign.

G. W. Briggs (1875-1959)

The Lord Jesus Christ:

126 LALEHAM 10 10 10.4.

JOHN WILSON (1905-)

1 All praise to thee, for thou, O King di - vine,

Didst yield the glo - ry that of right was thine,

That in our dark-ened hearts thy grace might shine:

Al - le - lu - ia, Al - le - lu - ia!

His Glory and Reign

ALL praise to thee, for thou, O King divine,
Didst yield the glory that of right was thine,
That in our darkened hearts thy grace might shine:
Alleluia!

2 Thou cam'st to us in lowliness of thought;
   By thee the outcast and the poor were sought,
   And by thy death was God's salvation wrought:
   Alleluia!

3 Let this mind be in us which was in thee,
   Who wast a servant that we might be free,
   Humbling thyself to death on Calvary:
   Alleluia!

4 Wherefore, by God's eternal purpose, thou
   Art high exalted o'er all creatures now,
   And given the name to which all knees shall bow:
   Alleluia!

5 Let every tongue confess with one accord
   In heav'n and earth that Jesus Christ is Lord;
   And God the Father be by all adored:
   Alleluia!

F. Bland Tucker (1895-   )
Based on Philippians 2. 5-11

The Lord Jesus Christ:

127

FIRST TUNE

METZLER'S REDHEAD   C.M.   R. REDHEAD (1820-1901)

SECOND TUNE

NUN DANKET ALL   C.M.   Melody from J. CRÜGER's *Praxis Pietatis Melica*
(1647 edition)

His Continuing Love

Dulcis Jesu memoria

JESU, the very thought of thee
  With sweetness fills the breast;
But sweeter far thy face to see,
  And in thy presence rest.

2 No voice can sing, no heart can frame,
  Nor can the memory find
A sweeter sound than thy blest name,
  O Saviour of mankind!

3 O hope of every contrite heart,
  O joy of all the meek;
To those who fall how kind thou art,
  How good to those who seek!

4 But what to those who find? Ah, this
  Nor tongue nor pen can show;
The love of Jesus, what it is
  None but his loved ones know.

5 Jesu, our only joy be thou,
  As thou our prize wilt be;
In thee be all our glory now,
  And through eternity.

For Part II see overleaf.

127 (continued)

FIRST TUNE

METZLER'S REDHEAD   C.M.

R. REDHEAD (1820-1901)

SECOND TUNE

NUN DANKET ALL   C.M.

Melody from J. CRÜGER's *Praxis Pietatis Melica*
(1647 edition)

His Continuing Love

Jesu, Rex admirabilis

O JESU, King most wonderful,
    Thou Conqueror renowned,
Thou sweetness most ineffable,
    In whom all joys are found!

2 When once thou visitest the heart,
    Then truth begins to shine;
Then earthly vanities depart;
    Then kindles love divine.

3 May every heart confess thy name,
    And ever thee adore;
And, seeking thee, itself inflame
    To seek thee more and more.

4 Thee may our tongues for ever bless,
    Thee may we love alone;
And ever in our lives express
    The image of thine own.

5 Lord, grant us, while on earth we stay,
    Thy love to feel and know;
And, when from hence we pass away,
    To us thy glory show.

*From a Latin poem of c. 1200, probably
by an English Cistercian monk
Tr. E. Caswall† (1814-78)*

The Lord Jesus Christ:

128 JESU, MEINE FREUDE 665.665.786. Melody from J. CRÜGER's *Praxis Pietatis Melica* (1653), as arranged by J. S. BACH (1685-1750)

His Continuing Love

Jesu, meine Freude

JESU, priceless treasure,
Source of purest pleasure,
  Truest friend to me;
O how long and lonely,
Filled with thy love only,
  Yearns my heart for thee!
Thou art mine, and I am thine;
I will suffer naught to hide thee,
  Ask for naught beside thee.

2 In thine arm I rest me;
  Foes who would molest me
    Cannot reach me here;
  Though the earth be shaking,
  Every heart be quaking,
    God dispels our fear;
  Sin and hell in conflict fell
  With their heaviest storms assail us:
    Jesus will not fail us.

3 Hence, all thoughts of sadness!
  For the Lord of gladness,
    Jesus, enters in:
  Those who love the Father,
  Though the storms may gather,
    Still have peace within;
  Yea, whate'er we here must bear,
  Still in thee lies purest pleasure,
    Jesu, priceless treasure!

J. Franck (1618-77)
  Tr. C. Winkworth (1827-78) *and others*

The Lord Jesus Christ:

129 RATISBON 77.77.77.

Melody from WERNER's *Choralbuch* (Leipzig, 1815)
Harmony mostly by W. H. HAVERGAL (1793-1870)

CHRIST, whose glory fills the skies,
  Christ, the true, the only Light,
Sun of Righteousness, arise,
  Triumph o'er the shades of night:
Day-spring from on high, be near;
Day-star, in my heart appear.

2 Dark and cheerless is the morn
  Unaccompanied by thee;
Joyless is the day's return,
  Till thy mercy's beams I see;
Till they inward light impart,
Glad my eyes, and warm my heart.

3 Visit then this soul of mine,
  Pierce the gloom of sin and grief;
Fill me, Radiancy divine,
  Scatter all my unbelief;
More and more thyself display,
Shining to the perfect day.

Charles Wesley (1707-88)

His Continuing Love

FIRST TUNE

GLENFINLAS 65.65.

K. G. FINLAY (1882-   )

SECOND TUNE

LINTON 65.65.

W. K. STANTON (1891-   )

JESUS, stand among us
In thy risen power;
Let this time of worship
Be a hallowed hour.

2 Breathe the Holy Spirit
Into every heart;
Bid the fears and sorrows
From each soul depart.

3 Thus with quickened footsteps
We'll pursue our way,
Watching for the dawning
Of eternal day.

W. Pennefather† (1816-73)

The Lord Jesus Christ:

131 ST PETER C.M.

A. R. REINAGLE (1799-1877)

How sweet the name of Jesus sounds
In a believer's ear!
It soothes his sorrows, heals his wounds,
And drives away his fear.

2 It makes the wounded spirit whole,
And calms the troubled breast;
'Tis manna to the hungry soul,
And to the weary rest.

3 Dear name! the rock on which I build,
My shield and hiding-place,
My never-failing treasury filled
With boundless stores of grace.

4 Jesus! my Shepherd, Brother, Friend,
My Prophet, Priest, and King,
My Lord, my Life, my Way, my End,
Accept the praise I bring.

5 Weak is the effort of my heart,
And cold my warmest thought;
But when I see thee as thou art,
I'll praise thee as I ought.

6 Till then I would thy love proclaim
With every fleeting breath;
And may the music of thy name
Refresh my soul in death.

John Newton† (1725-1807)

132 PETERSFIELD 77.77.

WILL HARRIS 1883–

'Lovest thou Me?' (John 21.16)

HARK, my soul! it is the Lord;
'Tis thy Saviour, hear his word;
Jesus speaks, and speaks to thee,
'Say, poor sinner, lov'st thou me?

2 'I delivered thee when bound,
And, when wounded, healed thy wound;
Sought thee wandering, set thee right,
Turned thy darkness into light.

3 'Can a woman's tender care
Cease towards the child she bare?
Yes, she may forgetful be,
Yet will I remember thee.

4 'Mine is an unchanging love,
Higher than the heights above,
Deeper than the depths beneath,
Free and faithful, strong as death.

5 'Thou shalt see my glory soon,
When the work of grace is done;
Partner of my throne shalt be:
Say, poor sinner, lov'st thou me?'

6 Lord, it is my chief complaint
That my love is weak and faint;
Yet I love thee, and adore;
O for grace to love thee more!

William Cowper (1731-1800)

The Lord Jesus Christ:

FIRST TUNE

133

ABERYSTWYTH 77.77.D.

JOSEPH PARRY (1841-1903)

SECOND TUNE

HOLLINGSIDE 77.77.D.

J. B. DYKES (1823-76)

His Continuing Love

In Temptation

JESU, lover of my soul,
  Let me to thy bosom fly,
While the nearer waters roll,
  While the tempest still is high;
Hide me, O my Saviour, hide,
  Till the storm of life is past;
Safe into the haven guide,
  O receive my soul at last.

2 Other refuge have I none,
    Hangs my helpless soul on thee;
  Leave, ah! leave me not alone,
    Still support and comfort me:
  All my trust on thee is stayed,
    All my help from thee I bring;
  Cover my defenceless head
    With the shadow of thy wing.

3 ★Thou, O Christ, art all I want;
    More than all in thee I find;
  Raise the fallen, cheer the faint,
    Heal the sick, and lead the blind.
  Just and holy is thy name;
    I am all unrighteousness:
  False and full of sin I am;
    Thou art full of truth and grace.

4 Plenteous grace with thee is found,
    Grace to cover all my sin;
  Let the healing streams abound,
    Make and keep me pure within:
  Thou of life the fountain art;
    Freely let me take of thee;
  Spring thou up within my heart,
    Rise to all eternity.

Charles Wesley (1707-88)

The Lord Jesus Christ:

Traditional melody, found
both in Wales and in France

134 ARFON 87.87.D.

His Continuing Love

LOVE divine, all loves excelling,
  Joy of heav'n, to earth come down,
Fix in us thy humble dwelling,
  All thy faithful mercies crown.
Jesu, thou art all compassion,
  Pure unbounded love thou art;
Visit us with thy salvation,
  Enter every trembling heart.

2 Come, almighty to deliver,
    Let us all thy life receive;
  Suddenly return, and never,
    Never more thy temples leave.
  Thee we would be always blessing,
    Serve thee as thy hosts above,
  Pray, and praise thee, without ceasing,
    Glory in thy perfect love.

3 Finish then thy new creation,
    Pure and spotless let us be;
  Let us see thy great salvation,
    Perfectly restored in thee:
  Changed from glory into glory,
    Till in heav'n we take our place,
  Till we cast our crowns before thee,
    Lost in wonder, love, and praise!

Charles Wesley (1707-88)

135 LOVE DIVINE 87.87.   J. STAINER (1840-1901)

LOVE divine, all loves excelling,
   Joy of heav'n, to earth come down,
Fix in us thy humble dwelling,
   All thy faithful mercies crown.

2 Jesu, thou art all compassion,
      Pure unbounded love thou art;
   Visit us with thy salvation,
      Enter every trembling heart.

3 Come, almighty to deliver,
      Let us all thy life receive;
   Suddenly return, and never,
      Never more thy temples leave.

4 Thee we would be always blessing,
      Serve thee as thy hosts above,
   Pray, and praise thee, without ceasing,
      Glory in thy perfect love.

5 Finish then thy new creation,
      Pure and spotless let us be;
   Let us see thy great salvation,
      Perfectly restored in thee.

6 Changed from glory into glory,
      Till in heav'n we take our place,
   Till we cast our crowns before thee,
      Lost in wonder, love, and praise!

Charles Wesley (1707-88)

His Continuing Love

136 FRANCONIA S.M.

W. H. HAVERGAL (1793-1870), adapted from a tune
in KÖNIG'S *Harmonischer Liederschatz* (1738)
(harmony slightly altered)

BLEST are the pure in heart,
For they shall see our God;
The secret of the Lord is theirs,
Their soul is Christ's abode.

2 The Lord, who left the heavens
Our life and peace to bring,
To dwell in lowliness with men,
Their pattern and their King:

3 Still to the lowly soul
He doth himself impart,
And for his dwelling and his throne
Chooseth the pure in heart.

4 Lord, we thy presence seek;
May ours this blessing be:
Give us a pure and lowly heart,
A temple meet for thee.

Verses 1 & 3 by John Keble (1792-1866)
Verses 2 & 4 from W. J. Hall's 'Psalms & Hymns' (1836)

The Lord Jesus Christ:

First Tune

HARESFIELD C.M.
Broadly

J. DYKES BOWER (1905-   )

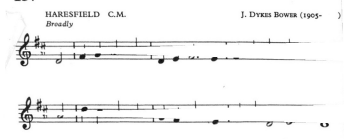

Second Tune

BISHOPTHORPE C.M.

Melody and bass from *Select Portions of
the Psalms* (published by H. GARDNER, c.1786)

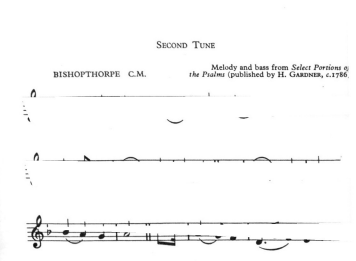

His Continuing Love

IMMORTAL Love, for ever full,
   For ever flowing free,
For ever shared, for ever whole,
   A never-ebbing sea!

2 Our outward lips confess the name
   All other names above;
Love only knoweth whence it came,
   And comprehendeth love.

3 Blow, winds of God, awake and blow
   The mists of earth away!
Shine out, O Light Divine, and show
   How wide and far we stray!

4 We may not climb the heav'nly steeps
   To bring the Lord Christ down:
In vain we search the lowest deeps,
   For him no depths can drown.

5*In joy of inward peace, or sense
   Of sorrow over sin,
He is his own best evidence,
   His witness is within.

6 The healing of his seamless dress
   Is by our beds of pain;
We touch him in life's throng and press,
   And we are whole again.

7 Alone, O Love ineffable,
   Thy saving name is given!
To turn aside from thee is hell,
   To walk with thee is heaven.

   J. G. Whittier (1807-92)
      From the poem 'Our Master'. (See also No. 138)

The Lord Jesus Christ:

138

FIRST TUNE

ST SWITHUN C.M.

SYDNEY WATSON (1903–

SECOND TUNE

WALSALL C.M.

Later form of a tune from W. ANCHOR
Choice Collection of Psalm-Tunes (c.172

His Continuing Love

O LORD and Master of us all,
 Whate'er our name or sign,
We own thy sway, we hear thy call,
 We test our lives by thine.

2 Our thoughts lie open to thy sight;
 And, naked to thy glance,
Our secret sins are in the light
 Of thy pure countenance.

3 Yet weak and blinded though we be,
 Thou dost our service own;
We bring our varying gifts to thee,
 And thou rejectest none.

4 To thee our full humanity,
 Its joys and pains belong;
The wrong of man to man on thee
 Inflicts a deeper wrong.

5 Who hates, hates thee; who loves, becomes
 Therein to thee allied;
All sweet accords of hearts and homes
 In thee are multiplied.

6 Apart from thee all gain is loss,
 All labour vainly done;
The solemn shadow of thy Cross
 Is better than the sun.

J. G. Whittier† (1807-92)
From the poem 'Our Master'. (See also No. 137)

The Lord Jesus Christ:

139 LAWES' PSALM 47 66.66.88.

Melody and bass by HENRY LAWES (1596-1662)
(rhythm of last two lines altered)

His Continuing Love

The Life Eternal that now is

Now is eternal life,
  If ris'n with Christ we stand,
In him to life reborn,
  And holden in his hand;
No more we fear death's ancient dread,
In Christ arisen from the dead.

2 Man long in bondage lay,
    Brooding o'er life's brief span;
  Was it, O God, for naught,
    For naught, thou madest man?
  Thou art our hope, our vital breath;
  Shall hope undying end in death?

3 And God, the living God,
    Stooped down to man's estate;
  By death destroying death,
    Christ opened wide life's gate.
  He lives, who died; he reigns on high;
  Who lives in him shall never die.

4 Unfathomed love divine,
    Reign thou within my heart;
  From thee nor depth nor height,
    Nor life nor death can part;
  My life is hid in God with thee,
  Now and through all eternity.

G. W. Briggs (1875-1959)

The Lord Jesus Christ:

140 JUDICIUM 888.D.   P. C. BUCK (1871-1947)

His Coming in Judgment

DIES irae, dies illa,
Solvet saeclum in favilla
Teste David cum Sibylla.

Quantus tremor est futurus
Quando iudex est venturus
Cuncta stricte discussurus!

2 Tuba mirum sparget sonum
Per sepulchra regionum:
Coget omnes ante thronum.

Mors stupebit et natura
Cum resurget creatura
Iudicanti responsura.

3*Liber scriptus proferetur
In quo totum continetur
Unde mundus iudicetur.

Iudex ergo cum sedebit
Quidquid latet apparebit:
Nil inultum remanebit.

4 Quid sum miser tunc dicturus?
Quem patronum rogaturus,
Dum vix iustus sit securus?

Rex tremendae maiestatis,
Qui salvandos salvas gratis,
Salva me, fons pietatis!

5 Recordare, Iesu pie,
Quod sum causa tuae viae:
Ne me perdas illa die.

Quaerens me sedisti lassus:
Redemisti crucem passus:
Tantus labor non sit cassus.

Attributed to Thomas of Celano, 12th century

See overleaf for translation.

The Lord Jesus Christ:

140 (continued)

TRANSLATION OF 'DIES IRAE'

1. That Day, the Day of Wrath, will dissolve the world into ashes, as David and the Sibyl testify. What a trembling will there be, when the judge will come, who will sternly examine all things!

2. The trumpet will scatter a wonderful sound through the tombs of all parts of the world; it will compel all men before the throne. Death and nature will be astonished when creation will arise to answer to him who judges.

3. The written book will be produced in which is contained the whole [record] from which the world will be judged. Therefore when the judge makes his review, whatever is hidden will come to light: nothing will remain unavenged.

4. What am I then to say, in my wretchedness? Whom shall I call upon as my defending counsel, seeing that the righteous man is scarcely safe? King of aweful majesty, who dost freely save those who are to be saved, save me, thou fount of pity!

5. Remember, kind Jesus, that I am the cause of thy journey: do not destroy me on that day. Thou didst sit in weariness when searching for me: thou didst redeem me by enduring the Cross. Let not all that labour be in vain.

This personal meditation on Death and Judgment, based on the 'Responsory' of the medieval Mass for the Dead, was adapted for liturgical use, and since the end of the 15th century it has been the Sequence (i.e. hymn sung before the Gospel) in the Requiem Mass of the Roman rite. The original poem contains 17 three-line stanzas, with some added lines to turn it into a prayer for the dead. Its probable author, Thomas of Celano, was a friend and biographer of St Francis of Assisi. It has been translated many times and into many languages, and has inspired authors such as Goethe and Sir Walter Scott, and composers such as Mozart, Berlioz, and Verdi.

His Coming in Judgment

141 ST STEPHEN C.M.

Melody, and almost all the harmony,
by WILLIAM JONES of Nayland (1726-1800)

THE Lord will come and not be slow,
   His footsteps cannot err;
Before him righteousness shall go,
   His royal harbinger.

2 Truth from the earth, like to a flower,
   Shall bud and blossom then;
And justice, from her heav'nly bower,
   Look down on mortal men.

3 Rise, God, judge thou the earth in might,
   This wicked earth redress;
For thou art he who shalt by right
   The nations all possess.

4 The nations all whom thou hast made
   Shall come, and all shall frame
To bow them low before thee, Lord,
   And glorify thy name.

5 For great thou art, and wonders great
   By thy strong hand are done:
Thou in thy everlasting seat
   Remainest God alone.

John Milton† (1608-74), from his
metrical versions of Psalms 82, 85 and 86

The Lord Jesus Christ:

142 HELMSLEY 87.87.47.

Later form of a melody in J. WESLEY'S
Select Hymns with Tunes Annext (1765)

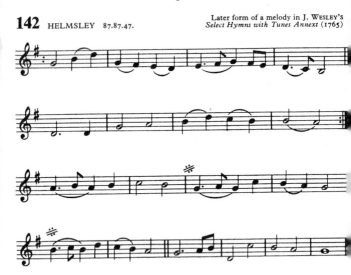

In the last line, the original rhythm may be used if preferred:

God ap - pears

His Coming in Judgment

Lo, he comes with clouds descending,
   Once for favoured sinners slain;
Thousand thousand saints attending
   Swell the triumph of his train:
      Alleluia!
   God appears on earth to reign.

2 Every eye shall now behold him
      Robed in dreadful majesty;
   Those who set at naught and sold him,
      Pierced and nailed him to the Tree,
         Deeply wailing,
      Shall the true Messiah see.

3 To his love and saving Passion
      All our happiness we owe:
   Pardon, holiness, salvation,
      Heav'n above and heav'n below:
         Grace and glory
      From that open fountain flow.

4 Yea, Amen, let all adore thee,
      High on thine eternal throne;
   Saviour, take the power and glory,
      Claim the kingdom for thine own:
         Alleluia!
      Thou shalt reign, and thou alone.

Charles Wesley‡ (1707-88)
(from two hymns on 'Thy Kingdom come')

The Lord Jesus Christ:

143 VISION 15 15 15.6.

WALFORD DAVIES (1869-1941)
(arranged by J. W.)

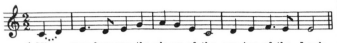

1 Mine eyes have seen the glo-ry of the com-ing of the Lord;

He is tramp-ling out the vin-tage where the grapes of wrath are stored;

He hath loosed the fate-ful light-ning of his ter-ri-ble swift sword:

(Small notes Org.)

His truth is march-ing on.

His Coming in Judgment

MINE eyes have seen the glory of the coming of the Lord;
He is trampling out the vintage where the grapes of wrath are stored;
He hath loosed the fateful lightning of his terrible swift sword:
     His truth is marching on.

2 I have read a fiery gospel writ in burnished rows of steel:
  'As ye deal with my contemners, so with you my grace shall deal;
Let the Hero, born of woman, crush the serpent with his heel!
     Since God is marching on'.

3 He has sounded forth the trumpet that shall never call retreat;
He is sifting out the hearts of men before his judgment-seat:
O be swift, my soul, to answer him; be jubilant, my feet!
     Our God is marching on.

4 He is coming like the glory of the morning on the wave;
He is wisdom to the mighty; he is succour to the brave:
So the world shall be his footstool, and the soul of time his slave:
     Our God is marching on.

Julia Ward Howe (1819-1910)

This poem, written in the first year of the American Civil War, was inspired by the writer's enthusiasm for the cause of Lincoln and the abolition of slavery. Intended at first for the popular tune of 'John Brown's Body', it soon became known as 'The Battle Hymn of the Republic'.

The Lord Jesus Christ:

144

GUARDA 7 7 7.5.   SYDNEY WATSON (1903-   )

SECOND TUNE

HUDDERSFIELD 7 7 7.5.   WALTER PARRATT (1841-1924)

His Coming in Judgment

LORD of all, to whom alone
All our hearts' desires are known,
When we stand before thy throne,
    Jesu, hear and save!

2 Son of Man, before whose eyes
Every secret open lies,
At thy great and last assize,
    Jesu, hear and save!

3 Son of God, whose angel host
(Thou hast said) rejoiceth most
O'er the sinner who was lost,
    Jesu, hear and save!

4 Saviour, who didst not condemn
Those who touched thy garments' hem,
Mercy show to us and them—
    Jesu, hear and save!

5 Lord, the Way to sinners shown,
Lord, the Truth by sinners known,
Love Incarnate on the throne,
    Jesu, hear and save!

C. A. Alington (1872-1955)

The Lord Jesus Christ:

145 NEWNHAM 87.87.887.   HERBERT HOWELLS (1892-   )

1 Lord   Christ, when first thou cam'st to men,   Up -
on   a Cross they bound thee,   And mocked thy sav-ing
king-ship then   By thorns with which they crowned thee: And
still our wrongs may weave thee now   New thorns to pierce that
stea - dy brow,   And robe of sor - row   round   thee.

His Coming in Judgment

LORD Christ, when first thou cam'st to men,
  Upon a Cross they bound thee,
And mocked thy saving kingship then
  By thorns with which they crowned thee:
And still our wrongs may weave thee now
New thorns to pierce that steady brow,
  And robe of sorrow round thee.

2*O aweful Love, which found no room
  In life where sin denied thee,
And, doomed to death, must bring to doom
  The power which crucified thee,
Till not a stone was left on stone,
And all a nation's pride, o'erthrown,
  Went down to dust beside thee!

3 New advent of the love of Christ,
  Shall we again refuse thee,
Till in the night of hate and war
  We perish as we lose thee?
From old unfaith our souls release
To seek the Kingdom of thy peace,
  By which alone we choose thee.

4 O wounded hands of Jesus, build
  In us thy new creation;
Our pride is dust, our vaunt is stilled,
  We wait thy revelation:
O Love that triumphs over loss,
We bring our hearts before thy Cross,
  To finish thy salvation.

W. Russell Bowie (1882-   )

The Holy Spirit

Simplified version (Mechlin, 1848)
of proper plainsong melody

146 VENI CREATOR L.M.

CONCLUSION OF VERSE 4

'Praise to thy e - ter - nal me - rit,

Fa - ther, Son, and Ho - ly Spi - rit. A - men'.

The Holy Spirit

Veni, Creator Spiritus

COME, Holy Ghost, our souls inspire,
And lighten with celestial fire;
Thou the anointing Spirit art,
Who dost thy sev'nfold gifts impart.

2 Thy blessèd unction from above
Is comfort, life, and fire of love;
Enable with perpetual light
The dullness of our blinded sight.

3 Anoint and cheer our soilèd face
With the abundance of thy grace:
Keep far our foes, give peace at home;
Where thou art guide no ill can come.

4 Teach us to know the Father, Son,
And thee, of both, to be but One;
That through the ages all along
This may be our endless song:

'Praise to thy eternal merit,
Father, Son, and Holy Spirit.   Amen'.

*9th century Latin, perhaps by
Rabanus Maurus (776-856)
Paraphrased by John Cosin (1594-1672)*

For a closer translation of the original Latin, see No. 147.

The Holy Spirit

FIRST TUNE

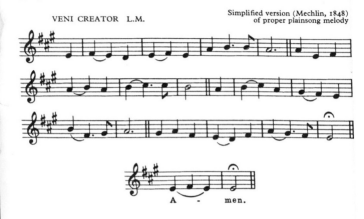

VENI CREATOR L.M.

Simplified version (Mechlin, 1848)
of proper plainsong melody

A - men.

SECOND TUNE

DULCIS MEMORIA L.M.
In free rhythm

P. C. BUCK (1871-1947)

1 Cre - a - tor Spi - rit, all - di - vine, Come vi - sit

ev-ery soul of thine, And fill with thy ce - les - tial

flame The hearts which thou thy - self ____ didst frame.

A - men.

The Holy Spirit

Veni, Creator Spiritus

CREATOR Spirit, all-divine,
Come visit every soul of thine,
And fill with thy celestial flame
The hearts which thou thyself didst frame.

2 O Comforter, to thee we cry,
To thee, the gift of God most high,
The fount of life and fire and love,
The soul's anointing from above.

3 The sev'nfold gifts of grace are thine,
O Finger of the hand divine;
True promise of the Father thou,
Who dost the tongue with speech endow.

4 Thy light to every sense impart,
And shed thy love in every heart;
The weakness of our mortal state
With deathless might invigorate.

5 Drive far away our mortal foe,
And grant us thy true peace to know;
So we, led by thy guidance still,
May safely pass through every ill.

6 To us, through thee, may grace be shown
To know the Father and the Son;
And, Spirit of them both, may we
For ever rest our faith in thee.   Amen.

9th century Latin, perhaps by
Rabanus Maurus (776-856)
Tr. J. D. Aylward (1813-72) and others

The Holy Spirit

148 VENI, SANCTE SPIRITUS 777.D.

Melody by S. WEBBE the elder (1740-1816)
Harmonized by W. H. MONK (1823-89)

The Holy Spirit

Veni, Sancte Spiritus

COME, thou Holy Spirit, come,
And from thy celestial home
   Thine unclouded light impart.
Come, thou Father of the poor,
All good gifts are from thy store,
   Come, illumine every heart.

2 Thou of comforters the best,
  Thou the soul's most welcome guest,
    Sweet refreshment here below;
  Who in toil art rest complete,
  Tempered coolness in the heat,
    Solace in the midst of woe.

3 O most blessèd Light divine,
  Shine within these hearts of thine
    And our inmost being fill;
  Where thou art not, man hath naught,
  Nothing good in deed or thought,
    Nothing free from taint of ill.

4 Heal our wounds; our strength renew;
  On our dryness pour thy dew;
    Wash the stains of guilt away:
  Bend the stubborn heart and will;
  Melt the frozen, warm the chill;
    Guide the steps that go astray.

5 On the faithful, who adore
  And confess thee, evermore
    In thy sev'nfold gifts descend;
  Give them virtue's sure reward,
  Give them thy salvation, Lord,
    Give them joys that never end.

13th century Latin 'Sequence'
Tr. E. Caswall (1849), Compilers of
'Hymns A. & M.', and others

The Holy Spirit

149 TEMPLE 66.84.

WALFORD DAVIES (1869-1941)

Βασιλεῦ οὐράνιε, Παράκλητε

O KING enthroned on high,
Thou Comforter divine,
Blest Spirit of all truth, be nigh
And make us thine.

2   Thou art the Source of life,
Thou art our treasure-store;
Give us thy peace, and end our strife
For evermore.

3   Descend, O heavenly Dove,
Abide with us alway;
And in the fullness of thy love
Cleanse us, we pray.

A hymn of the Eastern Church, c. 8th century
Tr. J. Brownlie (1859-1925)

The Holy Spirit

150   THOMAS TALLIS (c.1505-1585)

O Fons amoris, Spiritus

O HOLY Spirit, Lord of grace,
  Eternal Fount of love,
Inflame, we pray, our inmost hearts
  With fire from heaven above.

2 As thou in bond of love dost join
  The Father and the Son,
So fill us all with mutual love,
  And knit our hearts in one.

3 All glory to the Father be,
  All glory to the Son,
All glory, Holy Ghost, to thee,
  While endless ages run.

C. Coffin (1676-1749)
Tr. J. Chandler (1806-76) and others

The Holy Spirit

151 SALVE FESTA DIES Irreg.

R. Vaughan Williams (1872-1958)

Salve, festa dies, toto venerabilis aevo

With vigour

Verse 1 (*repeated as a Refrain after each verse*)

1 *Hail thee, Fes-ti-val Day! blest day that art hal-lowed for e - ver;*

Day where-in God from heav'n shone on the world with his grace.

Verses 2 and 4

2 Lo! in the like-ness of fire, on them that a-wait his ap-pear-ing,
4 Hark! in a hun-dred_ tongues Christ's own, his cho-sen A-post-les,

Repeat Refrain

He whom the Lord fore-told, sud-den-ly,_ swift-ly de-scends
Preach to a_ hun-dred tribes Christ and his won-der-ful works.

The Holy Spirit

VERSES 3 and 5

3 Forth from the Fa - ther he comes with his sev'n - fold
5 Praise to the Spi - rit of life, all praise to the

mys - ti - cal dow - ry, Pour - ing on hu - man
Fount of our be - ing, Light that dost light - en

Repeat Refrain.

souls in - fi - nite ri - ches of God.
all, Life that in all dost a - bide.

c. 14th century. (York Processional).
Tr. G. G. S. Gillett (1873-1948)

The Holy Spirit

FIRST TUNE

DOWN AMPNEY 66.11.D.   R. VAUGHAN WILLIAMS (1872-1958)

SECOND TUNE

NORTH PETHERTON 66.11.D.   WILLIAM H. HARRIS (1883-

The Holy Spirit

Discendi, Amor santo

COME down, O Love divine,
Seek thou this soul of mine,
And visit it with thine own ardour glowing;
O Comforter, draw near,
Within my heart appear,
And kindle it, thy holy flame bestowing.

2   O let it freely burn,
Till earthly passions turn
To dust and ashes in its heat consuming;
And let thy glorious light
Shine ever on my sight,
And clothe me round, the while my path illuming.

3   Let holy charity
Mine outward vesture be,
And lowliness become mine inner clothing;
True lowliness of heart,
Which takes the humbler part,
And o'er its own shortcomings weeps with loathing.

4   And so the yearning strong,
With which the soul will long,
Shall far outpass the power of human telling;
For none can guess its grace,
Till he become the place
Wherein the Holy Spirit makes his dwelling.

Bianco da Siena (d. 1434)
Tr. R. F. Littledale (1833-90)

The Holy Spirit

153

MARKENHORN 86.84.   LEONARD BLAKE (1907-

SECOND TUNE

ST CUTHBERT 86.84.   J. B. DYKES (1823-76

The Holy Spirit

OUR blest Redeemer, ere he breathed
   His tender last farewell,
A Guide, a Comforter, bequeathed
   With us to dwell.

2 He came in tongues of living flame,
   To teach, convince, subdue;
All-powerful as the wind he came,
   As viewless too.

3 He came sweet influence to impart,
   A gracious, willing guest,
While he can find one humble heart
   Wherein to rest.

4 And his that gentle voice we hear,
   Soft as the breath of ev'n,
That checks each fault, that calms each fear,
   And speaks of heav'n.

5 And every virtue we possess,
   And every victory won,
And every thought of holiness,
   Are his alone.

6 Spirit of purity and grace,
   Our weakness, pitying, see:
O make our hearts thy dwelling-place,
   And worthier thee.

Harriet Auber (1773-1862)

The Holy Spirit

154

FIRST TUNE

KINGSGATE 777.5.

GEORGE DYSON (1883-1964)

SECOND TUNE

CAPETOWN 777.5.

Adapted from a tune in
F. FILITZ's *Choralbuch* (1847)

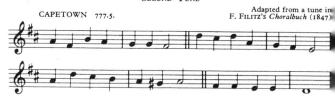

GRACIOUS Spirit, Holy Ghost,
Taught by thee, we covet most,
Of thy gifts at Pentecost,
 Holy, heav'nly love.

2 Love is kind, and suffers long,
Love is meek, and thinks no wrong,
Love than death itself more strong;
 Therefore give us love.

3 Prophecy will fade away,
Melting in the light of day;
Love will ever with us stay;
 Therefore give us love.

4 Faith will vanish into sight;
Hope be emptied in delight;
Love in heav'n will shine more bright;
 Therefore give us love.

5 Faith and hope and love we see
Joining hand in hand agree;
But the greatest of the three,
 And the best, is love.

C. Wordsworth (1807-85)
Based on 1 Corinthians 13

The Holy Spirit

55

WIRKSWORTH S.M.

Later form of a melody from
J. CHETHAM's *Psalmody* (1718)
Harmonized by S. S. WESLEY (1810-76)

SECOND TUNE

ST GEORGE S.M.

H. J. GAUNTLETT (1805-76)

BREATHE on me, Breath of God,
Fill me with life anew,
That I may love what thou dost love,
And do what thou wouldst do.

2   Breathe on me, Breath of God,
Until my heart is pure,
Until with thee I will one will,
To do and to endure.

3   Breathe on me, Breath of God,
Blend all my soul with thine,
Until this earthly part of me
Glows with thy fire divine.

4   Breathe on me, Breath of God;
So shall I never die,
But live with thee the perfect life
Of thine eternity.

E. Hatch (1835-89)

The Holy Spirit

156 SONG 22 10 10.10 10.

Melody & bass by
ORLANDO GIBBONS (1583-1625)

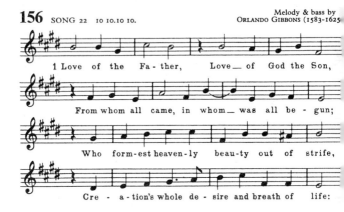

1 Love of the Fa - ther, Love— of God the Son,

From whom all came, in whom— was all be - gun;

Who form-est heaven-ly beau-ty out of strife,

Cre - a - tion's whole de - sire and breath of life:

The Holy Spirit

LOVE of the Father, Love of God the Son,
From whom all came, in whom was all begun;
Who formest heavenly beauty out of strife,
Creation's whole desire and breath of life:

2 Thou the All-holy, thou supreme in might,
Thou dost give peace, thy presence maketh right;
Thou with thy favour all things dost enfold,
With thine all-kindness free from harm wilt hold.

3*Hope of all comfort, splendour of all aid,
That dost not fail nor leave the heart affray'd:
To all that cry thou dost all help accord,
The angels' armour, and the saints' reward.

4 Purest and highest, wisest and most just,
There is no truth save only in thy trust;
Thou dost the mind from earthly dreams recall,
And bring, through Christ, to him for whom are all.

5 Eternal Glory, all men thee adore,
Who art and shalt be worshipped evermore:
Us whom thou madest, comfort with thy might,
And lead us to enjoy thy heavenly light.

Robert Bridges (1844-1930)
Based on Amor Patris et Filii, *12th centu*

The Holy Spirit

57 SALISBURY 87.87.D.   HERBERT HOWELLS (1892–   )
Sustained, but moving

Org.

1 Ho-ly Spi-rit, e-ver dwell-ing In the ho-liest realms of light; Ho-ly Spi-rit, e-ver brood-ing O'er a world of gloom and night; Ho-ly Spi-rit, e-ver rai-sing Sons of earth to thrones on high;— Liv-ing, life - im-part-ing Spi - rit, Thee we praise___ and mag-ni-fy.

2 Ho-ly Spi-rit, e-ver liv-ing As the Church's ve-ry life; Ho-ly Spi-rit, e-ver striv-ing Through her in a cease-less strife; Ho-ly Spi-rit, e-ver form-ing In the Church the mind of Christ;— Thee we praise___ with end-less wor - ship For thy fruit and gifts un-priced.___

3 Ho-ly Spi-rit, e-ver work-ing Through the Church's mi-nis-try; Quick-'ning, strength-'ning and ab-sol-ving, Set-ting cap-tive sin-ners free; Ho-ly Spi-rit, e-ver bind-ing Age to age, and soul to soul,— In a fel - low-ship un-end-ing— Thee we wor-ship and ex-tol.___

Timothy Rees (1874-1939)

The Holy Trinity

FIRST TUNE

O PATER SANCTE 11 11 11.5.   Plainsong Melody, Mode iv

1 Fa-ther most ho-ly, mer-ci-ful and lov-ing,

Je-sus, Re-deem-er, ev-er to be wor-shipped,

Life-giv-ing Spi-rit, Com-fort-er most gra-cious,

God ev-er-last-ing;   A   -   men.

SECOND TUNE

COELITES PLAUDANT 11 11 11.5.   Melody from the *Rouen Antiphoner* (1728)

The Holy Trinity

O Pater Sancte

FATHER most holy, merciful and loving,
Jesus, Redeemer, ever to be worshipped,
Life-giving Spirit, Comforter most gracious,
    God everlasting;

2 Three in a wondrous unity unbroken,
  One perfect Godhead, love that never faileth,
  Light of the angels, succour of the needy,
    Hope of all living;

3 All thy creation serveth its Creator;
  Thee every creature praiseth without ceasing;
  We too would sing thee psalms of true devotion;
    Hear, we beseech thee.

4 Lord God Almighty, unto thee be glory,
  One in Three Persons, over all exalted;
  Thine, as is meet, be honour, praise, and blessing,
    Now and for ever. (Amen)*

10th century or earlier
Tr. A. E. Alston (1862-1927)

* To be sung when the First Tune is used.

The Holy Trinity

159 ST PATRICK D.L.M.
For Verses 1, 2, 3 and 5.

Traditional Irish Melody
Harmonized by C. V. STANFORD (1852-1924)

V. 1 ends here.

The Holy Trinity

'*St Patrick's Breastplate*'

Atomriug indiu niurt tren

I BIND unto myself today
  The strong name of the Trinity,
By invocation of the same,
  The Three in One, and One in Three.

2 I bind unto myself today
  The virtues of the star-lit heav'n,
The glorious sun's life-giving ray,
  The whiteness of the moon at ev'n,
The flashing of the lightning free,
  The whirling wind's tempestuous shocks,
The stable earth, the deep salt sea
  Around the old eternal rocks.

3 I bind unto myself today
  The power of God to hold and lead,
His eye to watch, his might to stay,
  His ear to hearken to my need;
The wisdom of my God to teach,
  His hand to guide, his shield to ward,
The word of God to give me speech,
  His heav'nly host to be my guard.

(see overleaf for tune)
4*Christ be with me, Christ within me,
  Christ behind me, Christ before me,
Christ beside me, Christ to win me,
  Christ to comfort and restore me;
Christ beneath me, Christ above me,
  Christ in quiet, Christ in danger,
Christ in hearts of all that love me,
  Christ in mouth of friend and stranger.

5 I bind unto myself the name,
  The strong name of the Trinity,
By invocation of the same,
  The Three in One, and One in Three,
Of whom all nature hath creation,
  Eternal Father, Spirit, Word.
Praise to the Lord of my salvation:
  Salvation is of Christ the Lord.   (Amen)*

Attributed to St Patrick (372-466)
Tr. Mrs C. F. Alexander (1818-95)

* *To be sung when the Alternative Setting of Verse 5 is used.*

The Holy Trinity

159 (*continued*)

FOR VERSE 4

DEIRDRE 88.88.

Adapted from a
Traditional Irish Melody

4 Christ be with me, Christ with-in me, Christ be-hind me, Christ be-fore me,

Christ be-side me, Christ to win me, Christ to com-fort and re-store me;

Christ be-neath me, Christ a-bove me, Christ in qui-et, Christ in dan-ger,

Christ in hearts of all that love me, Christ in mouth of friend and stran-ger

The Holy Trinity

ALTERNATIVE SETTING OF VERSE 5

C. V. STANFORD (1852-1924)

5 I bind un-to— my-self the name, The strong name of— the Tri-ni-ty, By in-vo-ca-tion of the same, The Three in One, and One in Three,— Of whom all na-ture hath cre-a-tion, E-ter-nal Fa-ther, Spi-rit, Word. Praise to— the Lord of my sal-va-tion: Sal-va-tion is— of Christ the Lord.— A-men.—

The Holy Trinity

HOLY, Holy, Holy! Lord God Almighty!
  Early in the morning our song shall rise to thee:
Holy, Holy, Holy! merciful and mighty!
  God in Three Persons, blessèd Trinity!

2 Holy, Holy, Holy! all the saints adore thee,
    Casting down their golden crowns around the glassy sea,
  Cherubim and Seraphim falling down before thee,
    Which wert, and art, and evermore shalt be.

3 Holy, Holy, Holy! though the darkness hide thee,
    Though the eye of sinful man thy glory may not see,
  Only thou art holy; there is none beside thee,
    Perfect in power, in love, and purity.

4 Holy, Holy, Holy! Lord God Almighty!
    All thy works shall praise thy name in earth and sky and sea
  Holy, Holy, Holy! merciful and mighty!
    God in Three Persons, blessèd Trinity!

R. Heber (1783-1826)
Based on Revelation 4. 8-11

The Holy Trinity

Melody by F. GIARDINI (1716-96)

THOU, whose almighty Word
Chaos and darkness heard,
    And took their flight,
Hear us, we humbly pray,
And, where the Gospel-day
Sheds not its glorious ray,
    Let there be light!

Thou, who didst come to bring
On thy redeeming wing
    Healing and sight,
Health to the sick in mind,
Sight to the inly blind,
O now, to all mankind,
    Let there be light!

3 Spirit of truth and love,
Life-giving, holy Dove,
    Speed forth thy flight;
Move o'er the waters' face,
Bearing the lamp of grace,
And, in earth's darkest place,
    Let there be light!

4 Holy and blessèd Three,
Glorious Trinity,
    Wisdom, Love, Might;
Boundless as ocean's tide
Rolling in fullest pride,
Through the world, far and wide,
    Let there be light!

J. Marriott‡ (1780-1825)
Based on Genesis 1. 3

The Holy Trinity

162 OTTERY ST MARY 87.87.   HENRY G. LEY (1887-1962)

FIRMLY I believe and truly
  God is Three, and God is One;
And I next acknowledge duly
  Manhood taken by the Son.

2 And I trust and hope most fully
  In that Manhood crucified;
And each thought and deed unruly
  Do to death, as he has died.

3 Simply to his grace and wholly
  Light and life and strength belong,
And I love supremely, solely,
  Him the holy, him the strong.

4 And I hold in veneration,
  For the love of him alone,
Holy Church as his creation,
  And her teachings as his own.

5 Adoration aye be given,
  With and through the angelic host,
To the God of earth and heaven,
  Father, Son, and Holy Ghost.

J. H. Newman (1801-90)
from 'The Dream of Gerontius'

The Holy Trinity

FIRST TUNE

WESTMINSTER C.M.   J. TURLE (1802-82)

SECOND TUNE

ST MARY C.M.
Melody from E. PRYS's *Llyfr y Psalmau* (1621)
Harmony based on setting in PLAYFORD's *Psalms* (1677)

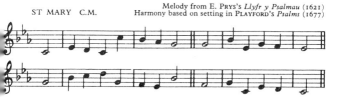

MOST ancient of all mysteries,
  Before thy throne we lie;
Have mercy now, most merciful,
  Most holy Trinity.

2 When heav'n and earth were yet unmade,
  When time was yet unknown,
Thou in thy bliss and majesty
  Didst live and love alone.

3 Thou wert not born; there was no fount
  From which thy being flowed;
There is no end which thou canst reach:
  But thou art simply God.

4 How wonderful creation is,
  The work which thou didst bless!
And O what then must thou be like,
  Eternal loveliness!

5 Most ancient of all mysteries,
  Still at thy throne we lie;
Have mercy now, most merciful,
  Most holy Trinity.

                      F. W. Faber (1814-63)

The Holy Trinity

164 GROVE HILL 887.D.   LEONARD BLAKE (1907-   )

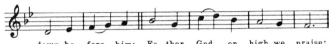

1 Praise the Lord, let earth a - dore him, Stars of heav'n bow

down be - fore him; Fa - ther, God on high we praise:

Sing his song, cry out his glo - ry, Told by men in

an - cient sto - ry, God of ev - er - last - ing days.

The Holy Trinity

PRAISE the Lord, let earth adore him,
Stars of heav'n bow down before him;
    Father, God on high we praise:
Sing his song, cry out his glory,
Told by men in ancient story,
    God of everlasting days.

2 Son of God, thy death has bought us,
    Thou the life of God hast taught us,
        Life that with thy Cross began.
    Guard us when our foes assail us,
    Guide us, though our goodness fail us,
        Lord of life, and Son of man.

3 Holy Spirit, wise and healing,
    Soul of God in Christ revealing
        Love that captures, love that binds:
    This we know, that man for ever
    By thy light and his endeavour
        Wisdom, hope, and comfort finds.

4 Through the years mankind doth ponder
    On the great and changeless wonder,
        God mysterious, God alone.
    Yet though foes may scorn our seeking,
    We, through countless voices speaking,
        Claim and know thee for our own.

H. C. A. Gaunt (1902-   )

165

DUNDEE C.M.

Melody from *Scottish Psalter* (1615)
Harmony from RAVENSCROFT'S *Psalmes* (1621)

SECOND VERSION
(with later form of rhythm)

DUNDEE C.M.

LET saints on earth in concert sing
With those whose work is done;
For all the servants of our King
In heaven and earth are one.

2 One family we dwell in him,
    One Church, above, beneath,
Though now divided by the stream,
    The narrow stream of death.

3 One army of the living God,
    To his command we bow;
Part of his host have crossed the flood,
    And part are crossing now.

4 E'en now to their eternal home
    There pass some spirits blest;
While others to the margin come,
    Waiting their call to rest.

5 Jesu, be thou our constant guide;
    Then, when the word is given,
Bid Jordan's narrow stream divide,
    And bring us safe to heaven.

Charles Wesley (1707-88) *and others*

Its Unity and Fellowship

166 WHITEHALL L.M.

Melody and bass by HENRY LAWES (1596-1662)
(rhythm slightly altered)

HE wants not friends that hath thy love,
    And may converse and walk with thee,
And with thy saints here and above,
    With whom for ever I must be.

2 In the communion of thy saints
    Is wisdom, safety, and delight;
And when my heart declines and faints,
    It's raisèd by their heat and light.

3 As for my friends, they are not lost;
    The several vessels of thy fleet,
Though parted now, by tempests tossed,
    Shall safely in the haven meet.

4 Still we are centred all in thee,
    Members, though distant, of one Head;
In the same family we be,
    By the same faith and spirit led.

5 Before thy throne we daily meet
    As joint-petitioners to thee;
In spirit we each other greet,
    And shall again each other see.

6 The heav'nly hosts, world without end,
    Shall be my company above;
And thou, my best and surest Friend,
    Who shall divide me from thy love?

Richard Baxter† (1615-91)

Richard Baxter, the Anglican Puritan divine, was driven to Nonconformity by the passing of the Act of Uniformity in 1662. These verses are from a poem he wrote in 1663, headed 'The Resolution. Psalm 119. 96. Written when I was silenced and cast out'.

167

Melody and bass by ORLANDO GIBBONS (1583-1625)
(rhythm simplified)

SONG 13   77.77.

SECOND TUNE

DA CHRISTUS GEBOREN WAR   77.77.   Melody, and almost all the harmony, from
J. F. DOLES's *Choralbuch* (Leipzig, 1785)

JESUS, Lord, we look to thee,
Let us in thy name agree;
Show thyself the Prince of Peace;
Bid our jarring conflicts cease.

2 By thy reconciling love,
Every stumbling-block remove;
Each to each unite, endear;
Come, and spread thy banner here.

3 Make us of one heart and mind,
Courteous, pitiful, and kind,
Lowly, meek in thought and word,
Altogether like our Lord.

4 Let us for each other care,
Each the other's burden bear,
To thy Church the pattern give,
Show how true believers live.

5 Free from anger and from pride,
Let us thus in God abide;
All the depths of love express,
All the heights† of holiness.

Charles Wesley† (1707-88)

168 BINCHESTER C.M.

Melody and bass by DR WILLIAM CROFT (1678-1727)
(his harmony slightly amplified)

O quam iuvat fratres

HAPPY are they, they that love God,
  Whose hearts have Christ confest,
Who by his Cross have found their life,
  And 'neath his yoke their rest.

2 Glad is the praise, sweet are the songs,
    When they together sing;
  And strong the prayers, that bow the ear
    Of heaven's eternal King.

3 Christ to their homes giveth his peace,
    And makes their loves his own:
  But ah, what tares the evil one
    Hath in his garden sown.

4 Sad were our lot, evil this earth,
    Did not its sorrows prove
  The path whereby the sheep may find
    The fold of Jesu's love.

5 Then shall they know, they that love him,
    How all their pain is good;
  And death itself cannot unbind
    Their happy brotherhood.

Robert Bridges (1844-1930)
  Based on the Latin of C. Coffin (1676-1749)

169 WARRINGTON L.M.

R. HARRISON (1748-1810)
(Original harmony, except in last 2 bars)

Alternative Tune, WAREHAM, 316

JESUS, where'er thy people meet,
There they behold thy mercy-seat;
Where'er they seek thee thou art found,
And every place is hallowed ground.

2 For thou, within no walls confined,
Inhabitest the humble mind;
Such ever bring thee where they come,
And going, take thee to their home.

3 Dear Shepherd of thy chosen few,
Thy former mercies here renew;
Here to our waiting hearts proclaim
The sweetness of thy saving name.

4 Here may we prove the power of prayer,
To strengthen faith and sweeten care,
To teach our faint desires to rise,
And bring all heav'n before our eyes.

5 Lord, we are few, but thou art near,
Nor short thine arm, nor deaf thine ear;
O rend the heav'ns, come quickly down,
And make a thousand hearts thine own!

William Cowper (1731-1800)

---

*This hymn and No. 170 were both written for the opening of a new and larger Prayer-meeting Room
at Olney, where Cowper and Newton worked. (See §7 of the Introductory Essay.)*

Its Unity and Fellowship

FIRST TUNE

WETHERBY C.M.

S. S. WESLEY (1810-76)

SECOND TUNE

HERMON C.M.

Melody, and most of the bass,
by JEREMIAH CLARKE (*c.*1673-1707)

GREAT Shepherd of thy people, hear,
  Thy presence now display;
As thou hast giv'n a place for prayer,
  So give us hearts to pray.

2 Within these walls let holy peace
    And love and concord dwell;
  Here give the troubled conscience ease,
    The wounded spirit heal.

3 May we in faith receive thy word,
    In faith present our prayers,
  And in the presence of our Lord
    Unburden all our cares.

4 The hearing ear, the seeing eye,
    The humble mind, bestow;
  And shine upon us from on high,
    That we in grace may grow.

John Newton‡ (1725-1807)

When the Second Tune is used, the last line of each verse is sung twice.

171 YORK C.M.

Melody from *Scottish Psalter* (1615)
Harmony adapted from J. MILTON (senior) in
RAVENSCROFT'S *Psalmes* (1621)

PRAY that Jerusalem may have
    Peace and felicity:
Let them that love thee and thy peace
    Have still prosperity.

2 Behold how good a thing it is,
    And how becoming well,
Together such as brethren are
    In unity to dwell.

3 Therefore I wish that peace may still
    Within thy walls remain,
And ever may thy palaces
    Prosperity retain.

4 Now, for my friends' and brethren's sake,
    Peace be in thee, I'll say;
And for the house of God our Lord
    I'll seek thy good alway.

Scottish Psalter (1650)
From Psalm 122. 6-9 and Psalm 133. 1

72 GOTT DES HIMMELS 87.87.

Adapted by C. STEGGALL (1826-1905)
from J. S. BACH's setting of a melody
by H. ALBERT (1604-51)

MAY the grace of Christ our Saviour,
   And the Father's boundless love,
With the Holy Spirit's favour,
   Rest upon us from above.

2 Thus may we abide in union
   With each other and the Lord,
And possess, in sweet communion,
   Joys which earth cannot afford.

John Newton (1725-1807)

The Church:

173 ISTE CONFESSOR 11 11 11.5   Melody from *Poitiers Antiphoner* (1746)

Its Unity and Fellowship

Christe du Beistand

LORD of our life, and God of our salvation,
Star of our night, and hope of every nation,
Hear and receive thy Church's supplication,
  Lord God Almighty.

2 See round thine ark the hungry billows curling;
 See how thy foes their banners are unfurling;
 Lord, while their darts envenomed they are hurling,
   Thou canst preserve us.

3 Lord, thou canst help when earthly armour faileth,
 Lord, thou canst save when deadly sin assaileth;
 Christ, o'er thy Rock nor death nor hell prevaileth;
   Grant us thy peace, Lord.

4 Peace in our hearts, our evil thoughts assuaging;
 Peace in thy Church, where brothers are engaging;
 Peace, when the world its busy war is waging;
   Calm thy foes' raging.

5 Grant us thy help till backward they are driven,
 Grant them thy truth, that they may be forgiven;
 Grant peace on earth, and, after we have striven,
   Peace in thy heaven.

*P. Pusey† (1799-1855), based on the German
of M. A. von Löwenstern (1594-1648)*

*n making this paraphrase, Philip Pusey had in mind the state of the Church of England in 1834—
ıssailed from without, enfeebled and distracted within, but on the eve of a great awakening'.*

The Church:

AURELIA 76.76.D.   S. S. WESLEY (1810-76)

Its Unity and Fellowship

THE Church's one foundation
  Is Jesus Christ, her Lord;
She is his new creation
  By water and the word:
From heaven he came and sought her
  To be his holy bride,
With his own blood he bought her,
  And for her life he died.

2 Elect from every nation,
  Yet one o'er all the earth,
Her charter of salvation
  One Lord, one faith, one birth;
One holy name she blesses,
  Partakes one holy food,
And to one hope she presses
  With every grace endued.

3*Though with a scornful wonder
  Men see her sore oppressed,
By schisms rent asunder,
  By heresies distressed,
Yet saints their watch are keeping,
  Their cry goes up, 'How long?'
And soon the night of weeping
  Shall be the morn of song.

4 'Mid toil and tribulation,
  And tumult of her war,
She waits the consummation
  Of peace for evermore;
Till with the vision glorious
  Her longing eyes are blest,
And the great Church victorious
  Shall be the Church at rest.

5 Yet she on earth hath union
  With God the Three in One,
And mystic sweet communion
  With those whose rest is won:
O happy ones and holy!
  Lord, give us grace that we
Like them, the meek and lowly,
  On high may dwell with thee.

S. J. Stone (1839-1900)

Verse 3 refers to the controversy raised in the Church in the 1860s by the advanced views of Bishop Colenso of Natal.

The Church:

175 SONG 1 10 10.10 10.10 10.

Melody and bass by
ORLANDO GIBBONS (1583-1625)

1 E - ter - nal Ru - ler of the cease - less round
Of cir - cling pla - nets sing - ing on their way;
Guide of the na - tions from the night pro - found
In - to the glo - ry of the per - fect day;
Rule in our hearts, that we may ev - er be
Gui - ded and streng-thened and up-held by thee.

Its Unity and Fellowship

ETERNAL Ruler of the ceaseless round
   Of circling planets singing on their way;
Guide of the nations from the night profound
   Into the glory of the perfect day;
Rule in our hearts, that we may ever be
Guided and strengthened and upheld by thee.

2 We are of thee, the children of thy love,
   The brothers of thy well-belovèd Son;
Descend, O Holy Spirit, like a dove,
   Into our hearts, that we may be as one:
As one with thee, to whom we ever tend;
As one with him, our Brother and our Friend.

3 We would be one in hatred of all wrong,
   One in our love of all things sweet and fair,
One with the joy that breaketh into song,
   One with the grief that trembles into prayer,
One in the power that makes thy children free
To follow truth, and thus to follow thee.

4 O clothe us with thy heavenly armour, Lord,
   Thy trusty shield, thy sword of love divine;
Our inspiration be thy constant word,
   We ask no victories that are not thine:
Give or withhold, let pain or pleasure be,
Enough to know that we are serving thee.

J. W. Chadwick (1840-1904)

The Church:

Its Unity and Fellowship

SON of God, eternal Saviour,
  Source of life and truth and grace,
Son of Man, whose birth incarnate
  Hallows all our human race;
Thou, our Head, who, throned in glory,
  For thine own dost ever plead,
Fill us with thy love and pity;
  Heal our wrongs and help our need.

2 Bind us all as one together
  In thy Church's sacred fold,
Weak and healthy, poor and wealthy,
  Sad and joyful, young and old.
Is there want or pain or sorrow?
  Make us all the burden share.
Are there spirits crushed and broken?
  Teach us, Lord, to soothe their care.

3 As thou, Lord, hast lived for others,
  So may we for others live;
Freely have thy gifts been granted,
  Freely may thy servants give.
Thine the gold and thine the silver,
  Thine the wealth of land and sea,
We but stewards of thy bounty,
  Held in solemn trust for thee.

4 Come, O Christ, and reign among us,
  King of love, and Prince of peace,
Hush the storm of strife and passion,
  Bid its cruel discords cease;
Thou who prayedst, thou who willest
  That thy people should be one,
Grant, O grant our hope's fruition:
  Here on earth thy will be done.

S. C. Lowry (1855-1932)

The Church:

FIRST TUNE

McKEE   C.M.
With dignity

Negro Melody, adapted by
HARRY T. BURLEIGH (1866-1949)

SECOND TUNE

KILMARNOCK   C.M.

Melody, and almost all the harmony
by NEIL DOUGALL (1776-1862)

Its Unity and Fellowship

IN Christ there is no East or West,
    In him no South or North,
But one great fellowship of love
    Throughout the whole wide earth.

2 In him shall true hearts everywhere
    Their high communion find,
His service is the golden cord
    Close-binding all mankind.

3 Join hands, then, brothers of the faith,
    Whate'er your race may be;
Who serves my Father as a son
    Is surely kin to me.

4 In Christ now meet both East and West,
    In him meet South and North,
All Christlike souls are one in him,
    Throughout the whole wide earth.

John Oxenham† (1852-1941)

The Church:

178 CRUCIFER 10 10. & Refrain

Verse 1 (to be repeated as a Refrain)

S. H. NICHOLSON (1875-1947)

1 *Lift   high   the   Cross,   the   love   of Christ pro - claim*

Till   all   the   world___   a - dore___   his   sa - cred   name.

Verses 2-12

D.

Its Unity and Fellowship

LIFT high the Cross, the love of Christ proclaim
Till all the world adore his sacred name.

2 Come, brethren, follow where our Captain trod,
Our King victorious, Christ the Son of God:

3*Led on their way by this triumphant sign,
The hosts of God in conquering ranks combine:

4*Each new-born soldier of the Crucified
Bears on his brow the seal of him who died:

5*This is the sign which Satan's legions fear
And angels veil their faces to revere:

6 Saved by this Cross whereon their Lord was slain,
The sons of Adam their lost home regain:

7 From north and south, from east and west they raise
In growing unison their song of praise:

8 O Lord, once lifted on the glorious Tree,
As thou hast promised, draw men unto thee:

9*Let every race and every language tell
Of him who saves our souls from death and hell:

10*From farthest regions let them homage bring,
And on his Cross adore their Saviour King:

11 Set up thy throne, that earth's despair may cease
Beneath the shadow of its healing peace:

12 For thy blest Cross which doth for all atone
Creation's praises rise before thy throne:

M. R. Newbolt (1874-1956),
based on G. W. Kitchin (1827-1912)

179 HAREWOOD 66.66.44.44.   S. S. WESLEY (1810-76)

Its Witness and Mission

Angularis fundamentum

CHRIST is our Corner-stone,
　On him alone we build;
With his true saints alone
　The courts of heav'n are filled;
　　On his great love
　　　Our hopes we place
　　　Of present grace
　　And joys above.

2 O then with hymns of praise
　These hallowed courts shall ring;
Our voices we will raise
　The Three in One to sing;
　　And thus proclaim
　　　In joyful song,
　　　Both loud and long,
　　That glorious name.

3 Here, gracious God, do thou
　For evermore draw nigh;
Accept each faithful vow,
　And mark each suppliant sigh;
　　In copious shower
　　　On all who pray
　　　Each holy day
　　Thy blessings pour.

4 Here may we gain from heav'n
　Thy grace which we implore;
And may that grace, once giv'n,
　Be with us evermore,
　　Until that day
　　　When all the blest
　　　To endless rest
　　Are called away.

　　　　　　7th or 8th century
　　　　　　Tr. J. Chandler† (1806-76)

For another translation, see No. 180

The Church:

FIRST TUNE

ORIEL 87.87.87.

From C. ETT, *Cantica Sacra* (1840)
Harmony revised by W. H. MONK (1823-89)

SECOND TUNE

WESTMINSTER ABBEY 87.87.87.

Adapted from an anthem
of HENRY PURCELL (*c.*1659-1695)

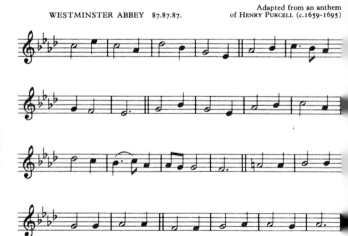

ᷣ

Angularis fundamentum

CHRIST is made the sure Foundation,
    Christ the Head and Corner-stone,
Chosen of the Lord, and precious,
    Binding all the Church in one,
Holy Zion's help for ever,
    And her confidence alone.

2 All that dedicated city,
    Dearly loved of God on high,
In exultant jubilation,
    Pours perpetual melody,
God the One in Three adoring
    In glad hymns eternally.

3 To this temple, where we call thee,
    Come, O Lord of Hosts, today;
With thy wonted loving-kindness
    Hear thy servants as they pray;
And thy fullest benediction
    Shed within its walls alway.

4 Here vouchsafe to all thy servants
    What they ask of thee to gain,
What they gain from thee for ever
    With the blessèd to retain,
And hereafter in thy glory
    Evermore with thee to reign.

7th or 8th century
Tr. J. M. Neale‡ (1818-66)

For another translation, see No. 179

The Church:

181 PSALM 36(68) 887.887.D.

Version from *Genevan Psalter* (1542) of a melody
by M. GREITER (*Strassburger Kirchenampt*, 1525)
Harmony from *The English Hymnal* (1906)

1 Faith of our Fa-thers, taught of old By faith-ful
2 Our fa-thers held the faith re-ceived, By saints de-

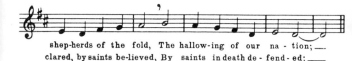

shep-herds of the fold, The hallow-ing of our na - tion; ___
clared, by saints be-lieved, By saints in death de - fend-ed; ___

Thou wast through many a weal-thy year, Through many a
Through pain of doubt and bit - ter-ness, Through pain of

dark-ened day of fear, The rock of our sal - va - tion. ___
trea-son and dis-tress, They for the right con-tend-ed. ___

Its Witness and Mission

A - rise, a - rise, good Chris-tian men, Your glo-rious
A - rise, a - rise, good Chris-tian men, Your glo-rious

stan-dard raise a - gain, The Cross of Christ who calls you; —
stan-dard raise a - gain, The Cross of Christ who bought you; —

Who bids you live and bids you die For his great
Who leads you forth in this new age, With long - en -

cause, and stands on high To wit-ness what be - falls you.
dur - ing hearts to wage The war-fare he has taught you.

T. A. Lacey† (1853-1931)

182 THORNBURY 76.76.D.
Slow

BASIL HARWOOD (1859-1949)

Its Witness and Mission

THY hand, O God, has guided
　　Thy flock, from age to age;
The wondrous tale is written,
　　Full clear, on every page;
Our fathers owned thy goodness,
　　And we their deeds record;
And both of this bear witness:
　　One Church, one Faith, one Lord.

2 Thy heralds brought glad tidings
　　To greatest, as to least;
They bade men rise, and hasten
　　To share the great King's feast;
And this was all their teaching,
　　In every deed and word,
To all alike proclaiming
　　One Church, one Faith, one Lord.

3 Through many a day of darkness,
　　Through many a scene of strife,
The faithful few fought bravely,
　　To guard the nation's life.
Their Gospel of redemption,
　　Sin pardoned, man restored,
Was all in this enfolded:
　　One Church, one Faith, one Lord.

4 Thy mercy will not fail us,
　　Nor leave thy work undone;
With thy right hand to help us,
　　The vict'ry shall be won;
And then, by men and angels,
　　Thy name shall be adored,
And this shall be their anthem:
　　One Church, one Faith, one Lord.

E. H. Plumptre (1821-91)

The Church:

183 HYFRYDOL 87.87.D.

Melody by R. H. PRICHARD (1811-87)

Its Witness and Mission

YE that know the Lord is gracious,
  Ye for whom a Corner-stone
Stands, of God elect and precious,
  Laid that ye may build thereon,
See that on that sure foundation
  Ye a living temple raise,
Towers that may tell forth salvation,
  Walls that may re-echo praise.

2 Living stones, by God appointed
  Each to his allotted place,
Kings and priests, by God anointed,
  Shall ye not declare his grace?
Ye, a royal generation,
  Tell the tidings of your birth,
Tidings of a new creation
  To an old and weary earth.

3 Tell the praise of him who called you
  Out of darkness into light,
Broke the fetters that enthralled you,
  Gave you freedom, peace and sight:
Tell the tale of sins forgiven,
  Strength renewed and hope restored,
Till the earth, in tune with heaven,
  Praise and magnify the Lord!

C. A. Alington (1872-1955)
Based on 1 *Peter* 2. 4-10

The Church:

184 OLD 104TH   10 10. 11 11.

Melody (with 4th line adapted), and most of the harmony, from T. RAVENSCROFT'S *Psalmes* (1621)

*ALTERNATIVE VERSION OF LAST LINE

NOTE—*The two versions of the last line are different adaptations of the following original:*

Its Witness and Mission

Supreme, quales, Arbiter

DISPOSER Supreme and Judge of the earth,
  Who choosest for thine the weak and the poor;
To frail earthen vessels, and things of no worth,
  Entrusting thy riches which aye shall endure;

2 Those vessels soon fail, though full of thy light,
  And at thy decree are broken and gone;
Then brightly appeareth the arm of thy might,
  As through the clouds breaking the lightnings have shone.

3*Like clouds are they borne to do thy great will,
  And swift as the winds about the world go:
All full of thy Godhead, while earth lieth still,
  They thunder, they lighten, the waters o'erflow.

4 Their sound goeth forth, 'Christ Jesus the Lord!'
  Then Satan doth fear, his citadels fall,
As when the dread trumpets went forth at thy word,
  And one long blast shattered the Canaanites' wall.

5 O loud be thy trump, and stirring the sound,
  To rouse us, O Lord, from sin's deadly sleep;
May lights which thou kindlest in darkness around
  Each dull soul awaken her vigils to keep!

6 All honour and praise, dominion and might,
  To thee, Three in One, eternally be,
Who pouring around us thy glorious light,
  Dost call us from darkness thy glory to see.

J-B. de Santeuil (1630-97)
Tr. I. Williams‡ (1802-65)

185 MARCHING 87. 87   MARTIN SHAW (1875-1958)

Igjennem Nat og Trængsel

THROUGH the night of doubt and sorrow
    Onward goes the pilgrim band,
Singing songs of expectation,
    Marching to the Promised Land.

2 Clear before us through the darkness
    Gleams and burns the guiding light;
Brother clasps the hand of brother,
    Stepping fearless through the night.

3 One the light of God's own presence
    O'er his ransomed people shed,
Chasing far the gloom and terror,
    Brightening all the path we tread;

4 One the object of our journey,
    One the faith which never tires,
One the earnest looking forward,
    One the hope our God inspires:

5 One the strain that lips of thousands
   Lift as from the heart of one;
 One the conflict, one the peril,
   One the march in God begun;

6 One the gladness of rejoicing
   On the far eternal shore,
 Where the one almighty Father
   Reigns in love for evermore.

7 Onward, therefore, pilgrim brothers,
   Onward with the Cross our aid;
 Bear its shame, and fight its battle,
   Till we rest beneath its shade.

8 Soon shall come the great awaking,
   Soon the rending of the tomb;
 Then the scatt'ring of all shadows,
   And the end of toil and gloom.

B. S. Ingemann (1789-1862)
Tr. from the Danish by
S. Baring-Gould (1834-1924)

186 MILTON ABBAS 664. 6664.

ERIC H. THIMAN (1900-

1 Christ for the world! we sing, The world to Christ we

bring, With one ac - cord; With us the work to

share, With us re - proach to dare, With

us the cross to bear, — For Christ our Lord.

CHRIST for the world! we sing,
The world to Christ we bring,
    With one accord;
With us the work to share,
With us reproach to dare,
With us the cross to bear,
    For Christ our Lord.

2 Christ for the world! we sing,
    The world to Christ we bring,
        With fervent prayer;
    The wayward and the lost,
    By restless passions tossed,
    Redeemed at countless cost
        From dark despair.

3 Christ for the world! we sing,
    The world to Christ we bring,
        With joyful song;
    The new-born souls, whose days,
    Reclaimed from error's ways,
    Inspired with hope and praise,
        To Christ belong.

Samuel Wolcott (1813-86)

The Church:

187

FIRST TUNE

CRUCIS VICTORIA C.M.   M. B. FOSTER (1851-1922)

SECOND TUNE

BROMSGROVE C.M.   H. A. DYER (1878-1918)

L<small>IFT</small> up your heads, ye gates of brass;
    Ye bars of iron, yield;
And let the King of Glory pass;
    The Cross is in the field.

2 That banner, brighter than the star
    That leads the train of night,
Shines on their march, and guides from far
    His servants to the fight.

3 A holy war those servants wage;
    In that mysterious strife
The powers of heav'n and hell engage
    For more than death or life.

4 Ye armies of the living God,
    Ye warriors of Christ's host,
Where hallowed footsteps never trod
    Take your appointed post.

5 Though few and small and weak your bands,
    Strong in your Captain's strength,
Go to the conquest of all lands:
    All must be his at length.

6 Then fear not, faint not, halt not now;
    Quit you like men, be strong:
To Christ shall all the nations bow,
    And sing the triumph song:

7 'Uplifted are the gates of brass,
    The bars of iron yield;
Behold the King of Glory pass:
    The Cross hath won the field.'

James Montgomery‡ (1771-1854)

The Church:

188 LITTLE CORNARD 66. 66. 88. MARTIN SHAW (1875-1958)

Hills of the North, rejoice,
    River and mountain-spring,
Hark to the advent voice,
    Valley and lowland, sing:
Though absent long, your Lord is nigh;
He judgment brings and victory.

2   Isles of the Southern seas,
       Deep in your coral caves
    Pent be each warring breeze,
       Lulled be your restless waves:
He comes to reign with boundless sway,
And makes your wastes his great highway.

3   Lands of the East, arise,
       Yours is the first bright dawn:
    Open the seeing eyes,
       Greet you the world's true morn.
The God of all, whom you would know
And seek on high, seeks you below.

4   Shores of the utmost West,
       See the full journey done:
    Prairie and lake are blest
       Bright with the setting sun.
Far spreads the word that Jesus died,
Yet lives and reigns—the Crucified!

5   Shout, while ye journey home!
       Songs be in every mouth!
    Lo, from the North we come,
       From East, and West, and South:
City of God, the bond are free;
We come to live and reign in thee!

C. E. Oakley (1832-65) *and others*

The Church:

189 BENSON Irreg. MILLICENT D. KINGHAM (composed c.1894)

1 God is work-ing his pur-pose out as
2* From ut-most East to ut-most West wher-
3 What can we do to work God's work, to
4 March we forth in the strength of God with the
5 All we can do is no-thing worth un -

1 year suc-ceeds to year, God is work-ing his
2* e'er man's foot hath trod, By the mouth of ma-ny
3 pros-per and in-crease The bro-ther-hood of
4 ban-ner of Christ un-furled, That the light of the glo-rious
5 less God blesses the deed; Vain-ly we hope for the

1 pur-pose out and the time is draw-ing near;
2* mes-sen-gers goes forth the voice of God: 'Giv
3 all man-kind, the reign of the Prince of Peace?
4 gos-pel of truth may shine through-out the world;
5 har-vest-tide till God gives life to the seed; Yet

Its Witness and Mission

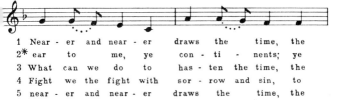

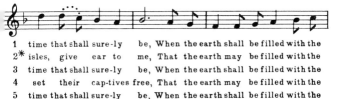

1 Near - er and near - er draws the time, the
2* ear to me, ye con - ti - nents; ye
3 What can we do to has - ten the time, the
4 Fight we the fight with sor - row and sin, to
5 near - er and near - er draws the time, the

1 time that shall sure-ly be, When the earth shall be filled with the
2* isles, give ear to me, That the earth may be filled with the
3 time that shall sure-ly be, When the earth shall be filled with the
4 set their cap-tives free, That the earth may be filled with the
5 time that shall sure-ly be, When the earth shall be filled with the

1 glo - ry of God, as the wa - ters co - ver the sea;
2* glo - ry of God, as the wa - ters co - ver the sea'.
3 glo - ry of God, as the wa - ters co - ver the sea?
4 glo - ry of God, as the wa - ters co - ver the sea.
5 glo - ry of God, as the wa - ters co - ver the sea.

A. C. Ainger (1841-1919)
Based on Habakkuk 2.14

The Church:

190 NORTHBROOK 11 10. 11 10.   R. S. THATCHER (1888-1957)

1 Thy love, O God, has all man - kind cre - a - ted,

And led thy peo - ple to this pre - sent hour:

In Christ we see love's glo - ry con - sum - ma - ted;

Thy Spi - rit ma - ni - fests his liv - ing power.

THY love, O God, has all mankind created,
  And led thy people to this present hour:
In Christ we see love's glory consummated;
  Thy Spirit manifests his living power.

2*We bring thee, Lord, in fervent intercession
  The children of thy world-wide family:
With contrite hearts we offer our confession,
  For we have sinned against thy charity.

3 From out the darkness of our hope's frustration;
  From all the broken idols of our pride;
We turn to seek thy truth's illumination;
  And find thy mercy waiting at our side.

4 In pity look upon thy children's striving
  For life and freedom, peace and brotherhood;
Till, at the fullness of thy truth arriving,
  We find in Christ the crown of every good.

5 Inspire thy Church, mid earth's discordant voices,
  To preach the gospel of her Lord above;
Until the day this warring world rejoices
  To hear the mighty harmonies of love.

6 Until the tidings men have long awaited,
  From north to south, from east to west shall ring;
And all mankind, by Jesus liberated,
  Proclaims in jubilation, Christ is King!

Albert F. Bayly (1901-   )

The Church:

191 DIADEMATA D.S.M.

G. J. ELVEY (1816-93)

The Holy Scriptures

A Hymn of the Bible Reading Fellowship

WORD of the living God,
  Lighting the souls of men,
With heavenly wisdom from on high
  Inspiring lips and pen!
  Their hearts athirst for truth
  With truth did God inspire;
In words of men God spake the word,
  His word a burning fire.

2 Ages and empires passed;
    The word was still the same;
  Still from the ancient beacon-fires
    Men caught the living flame;
    Unchanged the truth of God,
    Unchanged his righteousness,
  His hand stretched out to judge the world,
    His arms outstretched to bless.

3 Still burns the fire of God,
    From age to following age;
  New mornings break, new light is thrown
    Upon the hallowed page;
    Still sounds the trumpet-call,
    Still speaks the living word,
  Rings out, as in the ancient days,
    The cry, 'Thus saith the Lord'.

G. W. Briggs (1875-1959)

The Church:

Adapted by W. H. MONK (1861) from a melody
in M. WEISSE'S *Gesengbuchlen* (1531)
(harmony slightly altered)

'Thy word is a lantern unto my feet . . .'

LORD, thy word abideth,
And our footsteps guideth;
Who its truth believeth
Light and joy receiveth.

2 When our foes are near us,
Then thy word doth cheer us,
Word of consolation,
Message of salvation.

3 When the storms are o'er us,
And dark clouds before us,
Then its light directeth,
And our way protecteth.

4 Who can tell the pleasure,
Who recount the treasure,
By thy word imparted
To the simple-hearted?

5 Word of mercy, giving
Succour to the living;
Word of life, supplying
Comfort to the dying!

6 O that we discerning
Its most holy learning,
Lord, may love and fear thee,
Evermore be near thee!

H. W. Baker (1821-77)

Holy Communion

193 STONOR 11 10. 11 10.   SYDNEY WATSON (1903-   )

O JOY of God, that comest in the morning,
   For thee, unsunned, we wait and eastward gaze,
Lift on our dark the splendours of thy dawning,
   Flood all our being in the feast of praise.

2 O life of God, for whom our spirits hunger,
   Except we eat and drink indeed of thee,
With love and faith renewed and hope grown younger
   Send us out hence thy saving health to see.

3 O peace of God, that passest understanding,
   Guard thou our heart through every fretting day:
In him who is our Peace, our wills commanding,
   Direct our path and perfect all our way.

C. H. Boutflower (1863-1942)

The Church:

FIRST TUNE

LES COMMANDEMENS 98. 98.

Melody from *La Forme des Prieres et*
Chantz Ecclesiastiques (Strasbourg, 1545)

NOTE—*A regular crotchet beat should be maintained in the first line. The following simpler rhythm may be used if preferred:*

Holy Communion

PADSTOW 98. 98.   C. S. Lang (1891–   )

FATHER, we thank thee who hast planted
  Thy holy name within our hearts.
Knowledge and faith and life immortal
  Jesus thy Son to us imparts.

2 Thou, Lord, didst make all for thy pleasure,
    Didst give man food for all his days,
  Giving in Christ the bread eternal;
    Thine is the power, be thine the praise.

3 Watch o'er thy Church, O Lord, in mercy,
    Save it from evil, guard it still,
  Perfect it in thy love, unite it,
    Cleansed and conformed unto thy will.

4 As grain, once scattered on the hillsides,
    Was in this broken bread made one,
  So from all lands thy Church be gathered
    Into thy kingdom by thy Son.

From prayers in the 'Didache', probably 2nd century
Tr. F. Bland Tucker (1895–   )

The Church:

195 STONER HILL 10 10. 10 10.   WILLIAM H. HARRIS (1883-   )

1 Come, ri - sen Lord, and deign to be___ our guest;

Nay, let us be thy guests: the feast is thine;

Thy-self at thine own board make ma - ni - fest,

In thine own sac - ra - ment of bread and wine.

Holy Communion

COME, risen Lord, and deign to be our guest;
   Nay, let us be thy guests: the feast is thine;
Thyself at thine own board make manifest,
   In thine own sacrament of bread and wine.

2 We meet, as in that upper room they met;
   Thou at the table, blessing, yet dost stand:
'This is my body': so thou givest yet:
   Faith still receives the cup as from thy hand.

3 One body we, one body who partake,
   One Church united in communion blest;
One name we bear, one bread of life we break,
   With all thy saints on earth and saints at rest.

4 One with each other, Lord, for one in thee,
   Who art one Saviour and one living Head;
Then open thou our eyes, that we may see;
   Be known to us in breaking of the bread.

G. W. Briggs (1875-1959)

The Church:

SONG 1   10 10. 10 10. 10 10.

Melody and bass by
ORLANDO GIBBONS (1583-1625)

1 O thou, who at thy Eu-cha-rist didst pray

That all thy Church might be for ev - er one,

Grant us at ev - ery Eu-cha-rist to say

With long-ing heart and soul, 'Thy will be done':

O may we all one Bread, one Bo - dy be,

One through this Sac - ra - ment of u - ni - ty.

Holy Communion

O THOU, who at thy Eucharist didst pray
  That all thy Church might be for ever one,
Grant us at every Eucharist to say
  With longing heart and soul, 'Thy will be done':
O may we all one Bread, one Body be,
One through this Sacrament of unity.

2 For all thy Church, O Lord, we intercede;
    Make thou our sad divisions soon to cease;
  Draw us the nearer each to each, we plead,
    By drawing all to thee, O Prince of Peace:
  Thus may we all one Bread, one Body be,
  One through this Sacrament of unity.

3 We pray thee too for wanderers from thy fold;
    O bring them back, Good Shepherd of the sheep,
  Back to the faith which saints believed of old,
    Back to the Church which still that faith doth keep:
  Soon may we all one Bread, one Body be,
  One through this Sacrament of unity.

4 So, Lord, at length when sacraments shall cease,
    We may be one with all thy Church above,
  One with thy saints in one unbroken peace,
    One with thy saints in one unbounded love:
  More blessèd still, in peace and love to be
  One with the Trinity in Unity.

W. H. Turton‡ (1856-1938)

The Church:

PEARSALL 76. 76.D.   R. L. PEARSALL (1795-1856)

SECOND TUNE

DIES DOMINICA 76. 76.D.   J. B. DYKES (1823-76)

Holy Communion

WE pray thee, heavenly Father,
  To hear us in thy love,
And pour upon thy children
  The unction from above;
That so in love abiding,
  From all defilement free,
We may in pureness offer
  Our Eucharist to thee.

2 Be thou our guide and helper,
    O Jesu Christ, we pray;
  So may we well approach thee,
    If thou wilt be the Way:
  Thou, very Truth, hast promised
    To help us in our strife,
  Food of the weary pilgrim,
    Eternal source of life.

3 And thou, Creator Spirit,
    Look on us, we are thine;
  Renew in us thy graces,
    Upon our darkness shine;
  That, with thy benediction
    Upon our souls outpoured,
  We may receive in gladness
    The body of the Lord.

4 O Trinity of Persons,
    O Unity most high,
  To thy tremendous worship
    Thy servants would draw nigh:
  Unworthy in our weakness,
    On thee our hope is stayed,
  And, blessed by thy forgiveness,
    We will not be afraid.

V. S. S. Coles (1845-1929)

The Church:

198 PICARDY 87. 87. 87.

French Carol Melody, as harmonized
in *The English Hymnal* (1906)

Σιγησάτω πᾶσα σὰρξ βροτεία

Let all mortal flesh keep silence, and with fear and trembling stand;
Ponder nothing earthly-minded, for with blessing in his hand
Christ our God to earth descendeth, our full homage to demand.

2 King of Kings, yet born of Mary, as of old on earth he stood,
Lord of Lords, in human vesture—in the body and the blood—
He will give to all the faithful his own self for heav'nly food.

3 Rank on rank the host of heaven spreads its vanguard on the way,
As the Light of Light descendeth from the realms of endless day,
That the powers of hell may vanish as the darkness clears away.

4 At his feet the six-winged seraph; cherubim with sleepless eye
Veil their faces to the Presence, as with ceaseless voice they cry—
Alleluia, Alleluia, Alleluia, Lord most high!

From the Liturgy of St James
Tr. G. Moultrie (1829-85)

This prayer, used in Eastern Churches in the 5th century or earlier, was said by the Priest at the place in the Eucharist corresponding to the Offertory in the Western Church.

Holy Communion

SONG 46   10 10.

Melody and bass by
ORLANDO GIBBONS (1583-1625)
(first strain of his *Song 46*)

Sancti, venite, Christi corpus sumite

DRAW nigh and take the body of the Lord,
And drink with faith the blood for you outpoured.

2 Offered was he for greatest and for least,
Himself the Victim, and himself the Priest.

3 He that his saints in this world rules and shields
To all believers life eternal yields.

4 He feeds the hungry with the bread of heaven,
And living streams to those who thirst are given.

5 Approach ye then with faithful hearts sincere,
And take the pledges of salvation here.

7th century
Tr. J. M. Neale (1818-66) and others

200 VERBUM SUPERNUM L.M. Plainsong melody (Mechlin version), Mode vii

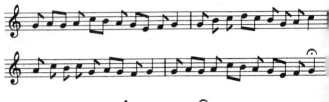

A - men. ——

Verbum supernum prodiens

THE Héav'nly Wórd, procéeding forth
   Yet leaving nót the Father's side,
Accomplishing his wórk on earth
   Had réached at léngth life's éventide.

2 By fálse disciple tó be giv'n
   To foemen fór his life athirst,
Himself, the very Bréad of heav'n,
   He gáve to hís disciples first.

3 He gáve himsélf in eíther kind,
   He gave his flésh, he gave his blood;
In love's own fullness thús designed
   Of thé whole mán to bé the food.

4 O sáving Víctim, ópening wide
   The gate of héav'n to man below,
Our foes press hard on év'ry side;
   Thine áid supplý, thy stréngth bestow.

5 All práise and thánks to thée ascend
   For evermóre, blest One in Three;
O grant us life that sháll not end
   In oúr true nátive lánd with thee.
                              ²Amèn.

St Thomas Aquinas (1227-74)
Tr. J. M. Neale, E. Caswall, and others

A small figure indicates the number of notes to a syllable

Holy Communion

Melody from *Chants Ordinaires de l'Office Divin* (Paris, 1881)

01 GRAFTON 87.87.87.

Verbum caro panem verum

WORD made flesh, by word he maketh
  Very bread his flesh to be;
Man in wine Christ's blood partaketh:
  And if senses fail to see,
Faith alone the true heart waketh
  To behold the mystery.

2 Therefore we, before him bending,
    This great sacrament revere;
  Types and shadows have their ending,
    For the newer rite is here;
  Faith, our outward sense befriending,
    Makes the inward vision clear.

St Thomas Aquinas (1227-74)
Tr. J. M. Neale (1818-66) *and others*

202

FIRST TUNE

NÜRNBERG L.M.

From an original hymn-tune by J. S. BACH
in SCHEMELLI's *Gesang-Buch* (1736)
(shortened and adapted by J.W.)

SECOND TUNE

MEON L.M.

SYDNEY WATSON (1903–

Holy Communion

Jesu, dulcedo cordium

JESUS, thou joy of loving hearts,
    Thou fount of life, thou light of men,
From the best bliss that earth imparts
    We turn unfilled to thee again.

2 Thy truth unchanged hath ever stood;
    Thou savest those that on thee call:
To them that seek thee thou art good,
    To them that find thee, all in all.

3 We taste thee, O thou living bread,
    And long to feast upon thee still;
We drink of thee, the fountain-head,
    And thirst our souls from thee to fill.

4 Our restless spirits yearn for thee,
    Where'er our changeful lot is cast,
Glad when thy gracious smile we see,
    Blest when our faith can hold thee fast.

5 O Jesus, ever with us stay:
    Make all our moments calm and bright;
Chase the dark night of sin away;
    Shed o'er the world thy holy light.

Cento from the poem 'Jesu, dulcis memoria'
Tr. R. Palmer (1808-87). (See No. 127)

The Church:

203 SCHMÜCKE DICH D.L.M.

Melody from J. CRÜGER's
Geistliche Kirchen-Melodien (1649)

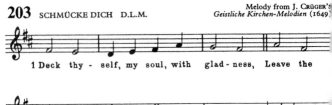

1 Deck thy - self, my soul, with glad - ness, Leave the

gloom of sin and sad-ness; Come in - to the day-light's splen-dour,

There with joy thy prais-es ren - der Un - to him whose grace un-

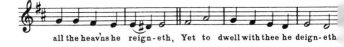

bound-ed Hath this wond-rous ban-quet found-ed: High o'er

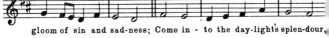

all the heav'ns he reign-eth, Yet to dwell with thee he deign-eth

Holy Communion

Schmücke dich

Deck thyself, my soul, with gladness,
Leave the gloom of sin and sadness;
Come into the daylight's splendour,
There with joy thy praises render
Unto him whose grace unbounded
Hath this wondrous banquet founded:
High o'er all the heav'ns he reigneth,
Yet to dwell with thee he deigneth.

2 Sun, who all my life dost brighten,
Light, who dost my soul enlighten,
Joy, the sweetest man e'er knoweth,
Fount, whence all my being floweth,
At thy feet I cry, my Maker,
Let me be a fit partaker
Of this blessèd food from heaven,
For our good, thy glory, given.

3 Jesus, Bread of Life, I pray thee,
Let me gladly here obey thee;
Never to my hurt invited,
Be thy love with love requited:
From this banquet let me measure,
Lord, how vast and deep its treasure;
Through the gifts thou here dost give me,
As thy guest in heav'n receive me.

J. Franck (1618-77)
Tr. C. Winkworth† (1827-78)

204 NICHT SO TRAURIG   77.77.77.

J. S. BACH (1685-1750)
(from *Vierstimmige Choralgesänge*, 1769)

BREAD of heav'n, on thee we feed,
For thy flesh is meat indeed;
Ever may our souls be fed
With this true and living bread,
Day by day with strength supplied
Through the life of him who died.

2 Vine of heav'n, thy blood supplies
This blest cup of sacrifice;
'Tis thy wounds our healing give;
To thy Cross we look and live:
Thou our life! O let us be
Rooted, grafted, built on thee.

J. Conder† (1789-1855)

Holy Communion

205 RENDEZ À DIEU 98.98.D.

Melody from *La Forme des Prieres et Chantz Ecclesiastiques* (Strasbourg, 1545) (2nd line as in *Genevan Psalter* of 1551)

Bread of the world in mer - cy bro - ken, Wine of the soul in mer - cy shed, By whom the words of life were spo - ken, And in whose death our sins are dead: Look on the heart by sor - row bro - ken, Look on the tears by sin - ners shed, And be thy feast to us the to - ken That by thy grace our souls are fed.

R. Heber (1783-1826)

The Church:

FIRST TUNE

RAVENDALE 10 10.10 10.10 10. JOHN WILSON (1905-)

1 And now, O Fa-ther, mind-ful of the love That

bought us, once for all, on Cal-vary's Tree, And hav-ing with us

him that pleads a - bove, We here pre-sent, we here spread forth to

thee, That on - ly off'-ring per - fect in thine eyes,

The one true, pure, im - mor - tal sac - ri - fice.

Holy Communion

UNDE ET MEMORES 10 10.10 10.10 10.   W. H. MONK (1823-89)

AND now, O Father, mindful of the love
   That bought us, once for all, on Calvary's Tree,
And having with us him that pleads above,
   We here present, we here spread forth to thee,
That only offering perfect in thine eyes,
The one true, pure, immortal sacrifice.

2 Look, Father, look on his anointed face,
   And only look on us as found in him;
Look not on our misusings of thy grace,
   Our prayer so languid, and our faith so dim:
For lo, between our sins and their reward
We set the Passion of thy Son our Lord.

W. Bright (1824-1901)

207

FARLEY CASTLE   10 10.10 10.

Melody, and most of the bass,
by HENRY LAWES (1596-1662)

SECOND TUNE

LONGWOOD   10 10.10 10.

J. BARNBY (1838-96)

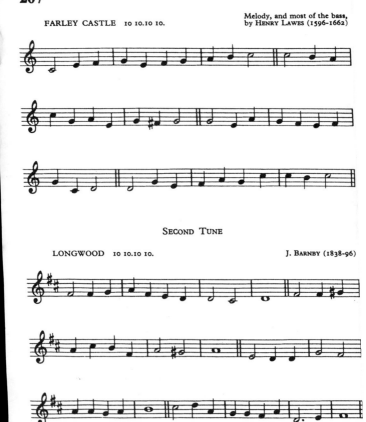

Holy Communion

·HERE, O my Lord, I see thee face to face;
 Here would I touch and handle things unseen;
Here grasp with firmer hand the eternal grace,
 And all my weariness upon thee lean.

2 Here would I feed upon the bread of God;
 Here drink with thee the royal wine of heaven;
Here would I lay aside each earthly load,
 Here taste afresh the calm of sin forgiven.

3 This is the hour of banquet and of song;
 This is the heav'nly table spread for me;
Here let me feast, and feasting, still prolong
 This hallowed hour of fellowship with thee.

4 Too soon we rise; the symbols disappear;
 The feast, though not the love, is past and gone;
The bread and wine remove, but thou art here,
 Nearer than ever, still my shield and sun.

5 I have no help but thine; nor do I need
 Another arm save thine to lean upon:
It is enough, my Lord, enough indeed;
 My strength is in thy might, thy might alone.

Horatius Bonar† (1808-89)

208 GWEEDORE 66.66.88.   S. S. WESLEY (1810-76)

AUTHOR of life divine,
 Who hast a table spread,
Furnished with mystic wine
 And everlasting bread,
Preserve the life thyself hast given,
And feed and train us up for heaven.

2   Our needy souls sustain
 With fresh supplies of love,
Till all thy life we gain,
 And all thy fullness prove,
And, strengthened by thy perfect grace,
Behold without a veil thy face.

From 'Hymns on the Lord's Supper'
by John and Charles Wesley (1745)

Holy Communion

209 SOUTHWELL (IRONS) C.M.   H. S. IRONS (1834-1905)

ONCE, only once, and once for all,
  His precious life he gave;
Before the Cross our spirits fall,
  And own it strong to save.

2 'One offering, single and complete',
  With lips and heart we say;
But what he never can repeat
  He shows forth day by day.

3 For as the priest of Aaron's line
  Within the holiest stood,
And sprinkled all the mercy-shrine
  With sacrificial blood;

4 So he who once atonement wrought,
  Our Priest of endless power,
Presents himself for those he bought
  In that dark noontide hour.

5 His Manhood pleads where now it lives
  On heaven's eternal throne,
And where in mystic rite he gives
  Its presence to his own.

6 And so we show thy death, O Lord,
  Till thou again appear;
And feel, when we approach thy board,
  We have an altar here.

W. Bright (1824-1901)
Based on Hebrews 10. 1-14

210 HYFRYDOL 87.87.D.   Melody by R. H. PRICHARD (1811-87)

Holy Communion

ALLELUIA! sing to Jesus,
    His the sceptre, his the throne;
Alleluia! his the triumph,
    His the victory alone:
Hark! the songs of peaceful Zion
    Thunder like a mighty flood;
Jesus, out of every nation,
    Hath redeemed us by his blood.

2*Alleluia! not as orphans
    Are we left in sorrow now;
Alleluia! he is near us,
    Faith believes, nor questions how;
Though the cloud from sight received him
    When the forty days were o'er,
Shall our hearts forget his promise,
    'I am with you evermore'?

3 Alleluia! bread of angels,
    Thou on earth our food, our stay;
Alleluia! here the sinful
    Flee to thee from day to day:
Intercessor, friend of sinners,
    Earth's Redeemer, plead for me,
Where the songs of all the sinless
    Sweep across the crystal sea.

4 Alleluia! King eternal,
    Thee the Lord of Lords we own;
Alleluia! born of Mary,
    Earth thy footstool, heav'n thy throne:
Thou within the veil hast entered,
    Robed in flesh, our great High Priest;
Thou on earth both priest and victim
    In the Eucharistic feast.

W. Chatterton Dix (1837-98)

211

FIRST TUNE

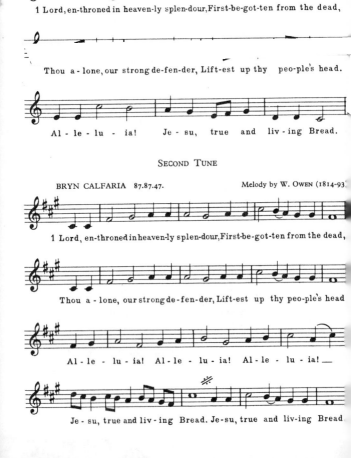

KINGLEY VALE 87.87.47.   H. P. ALLEN (1869-1946)

1 Lord, en-throned in heaven-ly splen-dour, First-be-got-ten from the dead,

Thou a-lone, our strong de-fen-der, Lift-est up thy peo-ple's head.

Al - le - lu - ia!   Je - su,   true   and   liv-ing Bread.

SECOND TUNE

BRYN CALFARIA 87.87.47.   Melody by W. OWEN (1814-93)

1 Lord, en-throned in heaven-ly splen-dour, First-be-got-ten from the dead,

Thou a-lone, our strong de-fen-der, Lift-est up thy peo-ple's head

Al - le - lu - ia! Al - le - lu - ia! Al - le - lu - ia! __

Je - su, true and liv - ing Bread. Je-su, true and liv-ing Bread

Holy Communion

LORD, enthroned in heavenly splendour,
First-begotten from the dead,
Thou alone, our strong defender,
Liftest up thy people's head.
Alleluia!
Jesu, true and living Bread.

2 Here our humblest homage pay we;
Here in loving reverence bow;
Here for faith's discernment pray we,
Lest we fail to know thee now.
Alleluia!
Thou art here, we ask not how.

3 Though the lowliest form doth veil thee
As of old in Bethlehem,
Here as there thine angels hail thee,
Branch and Flower of Jesse's stem.
Alleluia!
We in worship join with them.

4*Paschal Lamb, thine offering, finished
Once for all when thou wast slain,
In its fullness undiminished
Shall for evermore remain,
Alleluia!
Cleansing souls from every stain.

5 Life-imparting heav'nly Manna,
Stricken Rock with streaming side,
Heaven and earth with loud hosanna
Worship thee, the Lamb who died,
Alleluia!
Risen, ascended, glorified!

G. H. Bourne (1840-1925)

The Church:

TANTUM ERGO   87.87.87.

Melody from *An Essay on
the Church Plain Chant* (1782)

Holy Communion

STRENGTHEN, Lord, for loving service
    Hands which took thy mysteries here;
Be the ears which heard thy praises
    Shielded from the voice of fear;
May the eyes that saw thy mercy
    See thy blessèd hope appear.

2 May the tongues which chanted 'Holy'
    Ever unto truth incline;
Grant the feet which trod thy temple
    In the land of light to shine;
Bodies by thy body nourished
    Quicken thou with life divine.

3 With thy worshippers abide thou;
    May thy light direct our ways;
Hear the prayers we lift before thee,
    And accept our thankful praise;
May thy grace and mercy keep us
    Safe from harm through all our days.

4*In the hour of thine appearing
    May we stand before thy face;
Raise we ever glad hosannas
    For the wonder of thy grace,
And the love which stooped to save us,
    Rescuing our fallen race.

5 Lord, who knowest our offences,
    Yet dost pardon and restore,
Grant us grace to own thy Godhead
    And in lowliest faith adore,
To thy majesty uplifting
    Praise and blessing evermore.

From the Liturgy of Malabar (South India),
and based on a poem by St Ephraim the Syrian, 4th century
    Tr. Jack C. Winslow (1882-   )

The Church:

From a tune by A. EWING (1830-95)

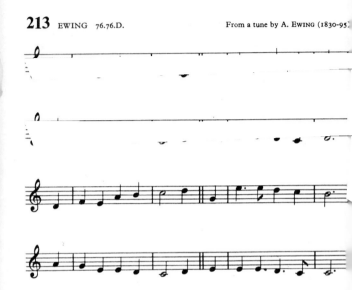

The Church Triumphant

Urbs Sion aurea

JERUSALEM the golden,
  With milk and honey blessed,
Beneath thy contemplation
  Sink heart and voice oppressed.
I know not, O I know not
  What joys await us there,
What radiancy of glory,
  What light beyond compare.

2 They stand, those halls of Zion,
    Conjubilant with song,
  And bright with many an angel,
    And all the martyr throng;
  The Prince is ever in them,
    The daylight is serene:
  The pastures of the blessèd
    Are decked in glorious sheen.

3 There is the throne of David,
    And there, from care released,
  The shout of them that triumph,
    The song of them that feast;
  And they who, with their Leader,
    Have conquered in the fight,
  For ever and for ever
    Are clad in robes of white.

4 Jerusalem the glorious,
    The home of God's elect;
  O dear and future vision
    That eager hearts expect!
  Jesu, in mercy bring us
    To that dear land of rest,
  Who art, with God the Father,
    And Spirit, ever blest.

Bernard of Cluny (12th century)
Tr. J. M. Neale‡ (1818-66)

214 REGENT SQUARE 87.87.87.   HENRY SMART (1813-79)

Jerusalem luminosa

LIGHT'S abode, Celestial Salem,
  Vision whence true peace doth spring,
Brighter than the heart can fancy,
  Mansion of the highest King;
O how glorious are the praises
  Which of thee the prophets sing!

2 There for ever and for ever
    Alleluia is outpoured;
  For unending, for unbroken,
    Is the feast-day of the Lord:
  All is pure, and all is holy,
    That within thy walls is stored.

3 Eye hath never seen the glory;
    Ear hath never heard the song;
  Heart of man can never image
    What good things to them belong,
  Who have loved the Lord of beauty
    While they dwelt in this world's throng.

4 Wherefore, man, take heart and courage,
    Whatsoe'er thy present pain;
  Such untold reward through suffering
    Thou may'st merit to attain,
  And for ever in his glory
    With the Light of Light to reign.

> From a group of 15th century Latin poems on
> 'The Glory of the Heavenly Jerusalem'.
> Tr. J. M. Neale (1818-66)

The Church Triumphant

215 ALL SAINTS 87.87.77.

Adapted by W. H. MONK (1823-89) from a melody
in *Geistreiches Gesangbuch* (Darmstadt, 1698)
(harmony slightly altered)

Wer sind die vor Gottes Throne?

WHO are these, like stars appearing,
  These, before God's throne who stand?
Each a golden crown is wearing;
  Who are all this glorious band?
    Alleluia! hark, they sing,
    Praising loud their heavenly King.

2 These are they who have contended
    For their Saviour's honour long,
  Wrestling on till life was ended,
    Following not the sinful throng;
      These, who well the fight sustained,
      Triumph through the Lamb have gained.

3 These are they whose hearts were riven,
    Sore with woe and anguish tried,
  Who in prayer full oft have striven
    With the God they glorified;
      Now, their painful conflict o'er,
      God has bid them weep no more.

4 These like priests have watched and waited,
    Offering up to Christ their will,
  Soul and body consecrated,
    Day and night to serve him still:
      Now, in God's most holy place
      Blest they stand before his face.

H. T. Schenk (1656-1727). Tr. F. E. Cox (1812-97)
Based on Revelation 7. 13-17

The Church:

216 HADLOW 84.84.44.44.   JOHN WILSON (1905-)
Not too fast

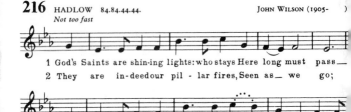

1 God's Saints are shin-ing lights: who stays Here long must pass
2 They are in-deed our pil - lar fires, Seen as we go;

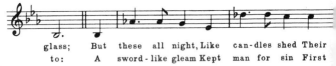

O'er dark hills, swift streams, and steep ways As smooth as
They are that Ci - ty's shin - ing spires We tra - vel

glass; But these all night, Like can-dles shed Their
to: A sword - like gleam Kept man for sin First

beams, and light Us in - to bed.
out; this beam Will guide him in.

GOD'S Saints are shining lights: who stays
    Here long must pass
O'er dark hills, swift streams, and steep ways
    As smooth as glass;
    But these all night,
    Like candles, shed
    Their beams, and light
    Us into bed.

2 They are indeed our pillar fires,
    Seen as we go;
They are that City's shining spires
    We travel to:
    A swordlike gleam
    Kept man for sin
    First out; this beam
    Will guide him in.

From a poem by Henry Vaughan (1622-95)

The Church Triumphant

FIRST TUNE

ST HELENA S.M.

Adapted by W. H. Monk
from a tune by B. Milgrove (1789)

SECOND TUNE

WINDERMERE S.M.

Arthur Somervell (1863-1937)

For all thy Saints, O Lord,
Who strove in thee to live,
Who followed thee, obeyed, adored,
Our grateful hymn receive.

2 For all thy Saints, O Lord,
Accept our thankful cry,
Who counted thee their great reward,
And strove in thee to die.

3 They all in life and death,
With thee, their Lord, in view,
Learned from thy Holy Spirit's breath
To suffer and to do.

4 For this thy name we bless,
And humbly beg that we
May follow them in holiness,
And live and die in thee:

5 With them the Father, Son,
And Holy Ghost to praise,
As in the ancient time was done,
And shall through endless days.

R. Mant† (1776-1848)

The Church:

SINE NOMINE 10 10 10.4.
Verses 1, 2, 3, 7 and 8

R. VAUGHAN WILLIAMS (1872-1958)

2

1 For all the Saints who from their la-bours rest, Who
2 Thou wast their rock, their for-tress, and their might;
3 O may thy sol - diers, faith - ful, true, and bold,

7 But lo! there breaks a yet more glo-rious day; The
8 From earth's wide bounds, from o - cean's far-thest coast, Through

1 thee by faith be - fore the world con - fest,
2 Thou, Lord, their cap - tain in the well-fought fight;
3 Fight as the Saints who no - bly fought of old,

7 Saints tri - um - phant rise in bright ar - ray:
8 gates of pearl streams in the count - less host,

1 Thy name, O Je - su, be for ev - er blest:
2 Thou, in the dark - ness, still their one true light:
3 And win, with them, the vic - tor's crown of gold:

7 The King of Glo - ry pass - es on his way:
8 Sing - ing to Fa - ther, Son, and Ho - ly Ghost:

Al -

- le - lu - ia! Al - le - lu - ia!

Verses 4, 5 and 6 are opposite

W. Walsham How (1823-97)

The Church Triumphant

Verses 4, 5, and 6

4 O blest com - mu - nion! fel - low-ship di - vine!
5 And when the strife is fierce, the war - fare long,
6 The gol - den eve - ning bright-ens in the west;

4 We fight, as they did, 'neath the ho - ly sign;
5 Steals on the ear the dis - tant tri - umph - song,
6 Soon, soon to faith - ful war - riors com - eth rest;

4 And all are one in thee, for all are thine:
5 And hearts are brave a - gain, and arms are strong: } *Al -*
6 — Sweet is the calm of pa - ra - dise the blest:

Return to previous page for vv. 7 and 8

- le - lu - ia! Al - le - lu - ia!

Verses 4 and 6 may be sung by the Choir alone

The Church:

218 *(continued)*   SECOND TUNE

ENGELBERG 10 10 10.4.   C. V. STANFORD (1852-1924)

1 For all the Saints who from their la-bours rest, —
2 Thou wast their rock, their fort-ress, and their might; —
3 O may thy sol-diers, faith-ful, true, and bold, —

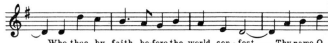

Who thee by faith be-fore the world con-fest, — Thy name, O
Thou, Lord, their cap-tain in the well-fought fight; — Thou, in the
Fight as the Saints who no-bly fought of old, — And win, with

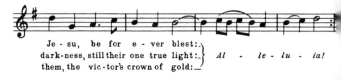

Je-su, be for e-ver blest: ⎫
dark-ness, still their one true light: ⎬ Al - le - lu - ia!
them, the vic-tor's crown of gold: ⎭

Choir
mf

4 O blest com-mu-nion! fel-low-ship di-vine! —

— We fight, as they did, 'neath the ho-ly sign; — And all are

one in thee, for all are thine: — Al - le - lu - ia!

The Church Triumphant

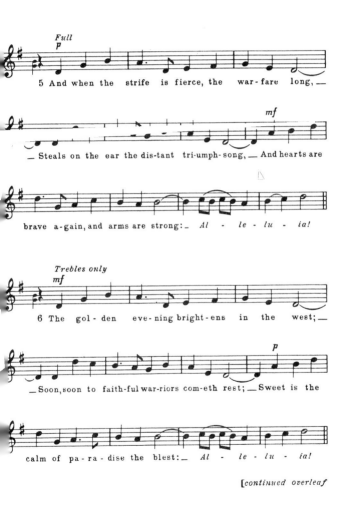

5 And when the strife is fierce, the war-fare long, — — Steals on the ear the dis-tant tri-umph-song, — And hearts are brave a-gain, and arms are strong:— *Al - le - lu - ia!*

6 The gol - den eve-ning bright-ens in the west; — — Soon, soon to faith-ful war-riors com-eth rest; — Sweet is the calm of pa-ra-dise the blest:— *Al - le - lu - ia!*

[continued overleaf

218 *(continued)*

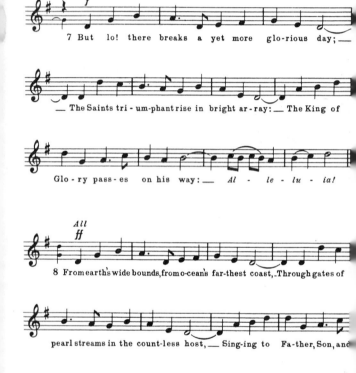

All (except Trebles)
f
7 But lo! there breaks a yet more glo-rious day;—

— The Saints tri-um-phant rise in bright ar-ray:— The King of

Glo-ry pass-es on his way:— *Al - le - lu - ia!*

All
ff
8 From earth's wide bounds, from o-cean's far-thest coast,— Through gates of

pearl streams in the count-less host,— Sing-ing to Fa-ther, Son, and

Ho-ly Ghost:— *Al - le - lu - ia.* A - men.

W. Walsham How (1823-97)

The Church Triumphant

219 WOLVESEY 87.87.87.   E. T. SWEETING (1863-1930)

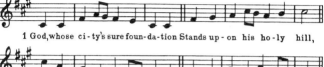

1 God, whose ci-ty's sure foun-da-tion Stands up-on his ho-ly hill,

By his migh-ty in-spi-ra-tion Chose of old and choos-eth still

Men of ev-ery race and na-tion His good plea-sure to ful-fil.

GOD, whose city's sure foundation
    Stands upon his holy hill,
By his mighty inspiration
    Chose of old and chooseth still
Men of every race and nation
    His good pleasure to fulfil.

2 Here before us through the ages,
    While the Christian years went by,
Saints, confessors, martyrs, sages,
    Strong to live and strong to die,
Wrote their names upon the pages
    Of God's blessèd company.

3 Some there were like lamps of learning
    Shining in a faithless night,
Some on fire with love, and burning
    With a flaming zeal for right,
Some by simple goodness turning
    Souls from darkness unto light.

4 As we now with high thanksgiving
    Their triumphant names record,
Grant that we, like them, believing
    In the promise of thy word,
May, like them, in all good living
    Praise and magnify the Lord.

C. A. Alington† (1872-1955)

220 BEACON 66.66.44.44. LEONARD BLAKE (1907-   )

1 Glo-ry to thee, O God, For all thy Saints in light, Who

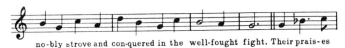

no-bly strove and con-quered in the well-fought fight. Their prais-es

sing, Who life out-poured By fire and sword for Christ their King.

GLORY to thee, O God,
For all thy Saints in light,
Who nobly strove and conquered in the well-fought fight.
Their praises sing,
Who life outpoured
By fire and sword for Christ their King.

2 Thanks be to thee, O Lord,
For saints thy Spirit stirred
In humble paths to live thy life and speak thy word.
Unnumbered they,
Whose candles shine
To lead our footsteps after thine.

3 Lord God of Truth and Love,
'Thy kingdom come!' we pray;
Give us thy grace to know thy truth and walk thy way:
That here on earth
Thy will be done,
Till saints in earth and heaven are one.

H. C. A. Gaunt (1902-   )

The Church Triumphant

221 EVANGELISTS 887.D.
(ALLES IST AN GOTTES SEGEN)

Adapted from J. S. BACH's version of a
chorale by J. LÖHNER (1691) and others

The Four Evangelists

COME, pure hearts, in sweetest measures
Sing of those who spread the treasures
  In the holy Gospels shrined:
Blessèd tidings of salvation,
Peace on earth, their proclamation,
  Love from God to lost mankind.

2 See the Rivers Four that gladden
  With their streams the better Eden
    Planted by our Lord most dear:
  Christ the fountain, these the waters;
  Drink, O Zion's sons and daughters,
    Drink and find salvation here.

3 O that we, thy truth confessing
  And thy holy word possessing,
    Jesu, may thy love adore;
  Unto thee our voices raising,
  Thee with all thy ransomed praising
    Ever and for evermore.

R. Campbell (1814-68) and others,
based on 12th century Latin Sequences

222 AETERNA CHRISTI MUNERA L.M.   Late form of plainsong melody, as given in GUIDETTI's *Directorium Chori* (1582)

1 Th'e - ter - nal gifts of Christ _____ the King.

Th'A - post - les' glo - ry, let us sing;

With joy - ful heart and mind to - day _____

Our debt of ho - mage du - - ly pay.

The Church Triumphant

The Apostles

Aeterna Christi munera

Tʜ' ETERNAL gifts of Christ the King,
Th' Apostles' glory, let us sing;
With joyful heart and mind to-day
Our debt of homage duly pay.

2 For they the Church's princes are,
Triumphant leaders in the war,
In heavèn's hall a soldier band,
True lights that lighten ev'ry land.

3 Theirs was the steadfast faith of saints,
Th' unconquered hope that never faints,
The perfect love of Christ to know,
That lays the prince of this world low.

4 In them the Father's glory shone,
In them the Spirit's will was done;
The Son's glad praise to them is giv'n,
With joy resound the courts of heav'n.

5 To thee, Redeemer, now we cry,
That with this glorious band on high,
Through endless ages, by thy grace,
Thy servants too may find a place.

Probably 5th century, in the style of St. Ambrose
Tr. J. M. Neale (1818-66) and others

A small figure indicates the number of notes to a syllable.

The Church:

223

TRISAGION 10 10.10 10.

HENRY SMART (1813–79)

SECOND TUNE

QUEDLINBURG 10 10.10 10.

From a Chorale by
J. C. KITTEL (1732–1809)

The Church Triumphant

Φωστῆρες τῆς αὔλου

Sᴛᴀʀs of the morning, so gloriously bright,
Filled with celestial resplendence and light,
These that, where night never followeth day,
Raise the 'Thrice Holy' for ever and aye:

2 These are thy ministers, these dost thou own,
Lord God of Hosts, ever nearest thy throne;
These are thy messengers, these dost thou send,
Help of the helpless ones, man to defend.

3*These keep the guard amid Salem's dear bowers;
Thrones, Principalities, Virtues, and Powers;
Where, with the Living Ones, mystical Four,
Cherubim, Seraphim bow and adore.

4 'Who like the Lord?' thunders Michael the chief;
Raphael, 'the Cure of God', comforteth grief;
And, as at Nazareth, prophet of peace,
Gabriel, 'the Might of God', bringeth release.

5 Then, when the earth was first poised in mid-space,
Then, when the planets first sped on their race,
Then, when were ended the six days' employ,
Then all the Sons of God shouted for joy.

6 Still let them succour us; still let them fight,
Lord of angelic hosts, battling for right;
Till, where their anthems they ceaselessly pour,
We with the Angels may bow and adore.

*J. M. Neale† (1818-66), based on the Greek
of St Joseph the Hymnographer (d. 883)*

The Church:

224

FIRST TUNE

ST PAUL'S S.M.   J. STAINER (1840-1901)

SECOND TUNE

FRANCONIA S.M.   W. H. HAVERGAL (1793-1870), adapted from a tune
in KÖNIG's *Harmonischer Liederschatz* (1738)
(harmony slightly altered)

The Church Triumphant

The Annunciation (March 25th)

PRAISE we the Lord this day,
  This day so long foretold,
Whose promise shone with cheering ray
  On waiting saints of old.

2   The prophet gave the sign
      For faithful men to read:
  A Virgin, born of David's line,
      Shall bear the promised Seed.

3   Ask not how this should be,
      But worship and adore;
  Like her, whom heaven's majesty
      Came down to shadow o'er.

4   Meekly she bowed her head
      To hear the gracious word,
  Mary, the pure and lowly maid,
      The favoured of the Lord.

5   Blessèd shall be her name
      In all the Church on earth,
  Through whom that wondrous mercy came,
      The incarnate Saviour's birth.

                    Anonymous (1847)

The Christian Life:

FIRST TUNE

ST KEVERNE 14 14.14 15.

C. S. LANG (1891-)

1 From glo-ry to glo-ry ad - vanc-ing, we praise thee, O Lord;
2 Thanks-giv-ing, and glo-ry and wor-ship, and bless-ing and love,

Thy name with the Fa-ther and Spi-rit be ev-er a-dored.
One heart and one song have the saints up-on earth and a - bove.

From strength un-to strength we go for-ward on Zi-on's high-way,
O_ Lord, ev-er-more to thy ser-vants thy pre-sence be nigh;

Verse 1

To ap-pear be-fore God in the ci-ty of in-fi-nite day.

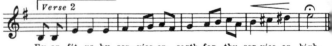

Verse 2

Ev-er fit us by ser-vice on earth for thy ser-vice on high.

Praise and Worship

SECOND TUNE

SHEEN 14 14.14 15.   GUSTAV HOLST (1874-1934)

Slower ad lib.

'Ἀπὸ δόξης εἰς δόξαν ποοευόμενοι

FROM glory to glory advancing, we praise thee, O Lord;
Thy name with the Father and Spirit be ever adored.
From strength unto strength we go forward on Zion's highway,
To appear before God in the city of infinite day.

2 Thanksgiving, and glory and worship, and blessing and love,
One heart and one song have the saints upon earth and above.
O Lord, evermore to thy servants thy presence be nigh;
Ever fit us by service on earth for thy service on high.

From the Liturgy of St James
Tr. C. W. Humphreys† (1840-1921)

The Liturgy of St James originated in the Church of Jerusalem before the 5th century. This hymn s based on the concluding prayer of the Eucharist.

226 MARTINS 10 10.7.   P. C. Buck (1871-1947)

An end-less Al - le-lu - ia.

A - men.

Alleluia piis edite laudibus

Sing Alleluia forth in loyal praise,
Ye citizens of heav'n, and sweetly raise
    An endless Alleluia.

2 City of God, eternal and supreme,
  On earth begin, in heav'n complete the theme:

3 Ye spirits blest, God's own victorious band,
  Re-echo through your starry fatherland:

4 Thus, in one great acclaim shall ever ring
  Blithe strains which tell the virtue of our King:

5 Thee, O Creator of the world, we praise,
  And thrilling we tell out our joyous lays:

6 To thee, O Word, our merry hearts we bring;
  O Holy Spirit, jubilant we sing
          An endless Alleluia. Amen.

Latin, 10th century or earlier
Tr. J. Ellerton (1865) and P. Dearmer (1932)

Praise and Worship

227   AUSTRIA   87.87.D.   J. HAYDN (1732-1809)

PRAISE the Lord! Ye heavens, adore him;
    Praise him, angels, in the height;
Sun and moon, rejoice before him;
    Praise him, all ye stars and light:
Praise the Lord, for he hath spoken;
    Worlds his mighty voice obeyed;
Laws, which never shall be broken,
    For their guidance hath he made.

2 Praise the Lord, for he is glorious!
    Never shall his promise fail;
God hath made his saints victorious;
    Sin and death shall not prevail.
Praise the God of our salvation;
    Hosts on high, his power proclaim;
Heaven and earth, and all creation,
    Laud and magnify his name!

3 Worship, honour, glory, blessing,
    Lord, we offer to thy name;
Young and old, their praise expressing,
    Join thy goodness to proclaim.
As the hosts of heaven adore thee,
    We would bow before thy throne;
As thine angels serve before thee,
    So on earth thy will be done.

Verses 1 & 2 from Foundling Hospital Collection
of c. 1796, based on Psalm 148
Verse 3 by Edward Osler (1798-1863)

The Christian Life:

228   DARWALL'S 148th   66.66.44.44.   Melody by J. DARWALL (1731-89)

Praise and Worship

YE holy angels bright,
  Who wait at God's right hand,
Or through the realms of light
  Fly at your Lord's command,
    Assist our song,
      Or else the theme
      Too high doth seem
    For mortal tongue.

2 Ye blessèd souls at rest,
  Who ran this earthly race,
And now, from sin released,
  Behold the Saviour's face,
    His praises sound,
      As in his sight
      With sweet delight
    Ye do abound.

3 Ye saints, who toil below,
  Adore your heavenly King,
And onward as ye go
  Some joyful anthem sing;
    Take what he gives,
      And praise him still
      Through good and ill,
    Who ever lives.

4 My soul, bear thou thy part,
  Triumph in God above,
And with a well-tuned heart
  Sing thou the songs of love.
    Let all thy days
      Till life shall end,
      Whate'er he send,
    Be filled with praise.

*J. H. Gurney (1802-62), based on a
poem by Richard Baxter (1615-91)*

The Christian Life:

FIRST TUNE

NORTHAMPTON 77.77.   C. J. KING (1859-1934)

SECOND TUNE

CULBACH 77.77.

German melody of 17th century or earlier
adapted by W. H. HAVERGAL (1793-1870)
(harmony slightly altered)

SONGS of praise the angels sang,
Heaven with alleluias rang,
When creation was begun,
When God spake and it was done.

2 Songs of praise awoke the morn
When the Prince of Peace was born;
Songs of praise arose when he
Captive led captivity.

3 Heaven and earth must pass away,
Songs of praise shall crown that day;
God will make new heavens, new earth,
Songs of praise shall hail their birth.

4 And can man alone be dumb
Till that glorious kingdom come?
No! the Church delights to raise
Psalms and hymns and songs of praise.

5 Saints below, with heart and voice,
Still in songs of praise rejoice,
Learning here, by faith and love,
Songs of praise to sing above.

6 Borne upon their latest breath,
Songs of praise shall conquer death;
Then, amidst eternal joy,
Songs of praise their powers employ.

James Montgomery† (1771-1854)

230

FIRST TUNE

LAUDES DOMINI 666.666.
In quick time

J. BARNBY (1838-96)

SECOND TUNE

LUDGATE 666.666.

J. DYKES BOWER (1905-

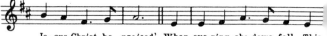

1 When morn-ing gilds the skies, My heart a-wak-ing cries, 'May

Je-sus Christ be praised'. When eve-ning sha-dows fall, This

rings my cur-few call, 'May Je-sus Christ be praised'.

Praise and Worship

Beim frühen Morgenlicht

WHEN morning gilds the skies,
My heart awaking cries,
  'May Jesus Christ be praised'.
When evening shadows fall,
This rings my curfew-call,
  'May Jesus Christ be praised'.

2 When mirth for music longs,
  This is my song of songs,
    'May Jesus Christ be praised'.
  God's holy house of prayer
  Hath none that can compare
    With 'Jesus Christ be praised'.

3 This greeting of great joy,
  I ne'er have found it cloy,
    'May Jesus Christ be praised'.
  When sorrow would molest,
  Then sing I undistrest,
    'May Jesus Christ be praised'.

4 No lovelier antiphon
  In all high heav'n is known
    Than 'Jesus Christ be praised'.
  There to the Eternal Word
  The eternal psalm is heard,
    'O Jesus Christ be praised'.

5 Ye nations of mankind,
  In this your concord find,
    'May Jesus Christ be praised'.
  Let all the earth around
  Ring joyous with the sound
    'May Jesus Christ be praised'.

6 Sing, suns and stars of space,
  Sing, ye that see his face,
    Sing 'Jesus Christ be praised'.
  God's whole creation o'er,
  For aye and evermore,
    Shall Jesus Christ be praised.

Anonymous German hymn, early 19th century
Tr. Robert Bridges (1844-1930)

The Christian Life:

231 LASST UNS ERFREUEN
88.44.88 and Alleluias

Melody from *Geistliche Kirchengesang*, Cologne, 1623
Arranged by R. VAUGHAN WILLIAMS (1872-1958)

Al - le - lu - ia, Al - le -
lu - ia, Al - le - lu - ia, Al - le - lu - ia, Al - le - lu - ia!

Y<small>E</small> watchers and ye holy ones,
Bright Seraphs, Cherubim, and Thrones,
   Raise the glad strain, Alleluia!
Cry out, Dominions, Princedoms, Powers,
Virtues, Archangels, Angels' choirs,
    Alleluia!

2 O higher than the Cherubim,
  More glorious than the Seraphim,
    Lead their praises, Alleluia!
  Thou Bearer of the eternal Word,
  Most gracious, magnify the Lord:

3 Respond, ye souls in endless rest,
  Ye Patriarchs and Prophets blest,
    Alleluia! Alleluia!
  Ye holy Twelve, ye Martyrs strong,
  All Saints triumphant raise the song:

4 O friends, in gladness let us sing,
  Supernal anthems echoing,
    Alleluia! Alleluia!
  To God the Father, God the Son,
  And God the Spirit, Three in One:

Athelstan Riley (1858-1945)

---

*In verse 1 the names are those of different orders (or 'choirs') of Angels. Verse 2 is addressed to the
Virgin Mary. Verses 3 and 4 speak of the Church Triumphant in heaven, and the Church Militant
on earth.*

232 LAUDATE DOMINUM (PARRY) 10 10.11 11. C. HUBERT H. PARRY (1848-1918)
Vigorously

O PRAISE ye the Lord! praise him in the height;
Rejoice in his word, ye angels of light;
Ye heavens, adore him, by whom ye were made,
And worship before him, in brightness arrayed.

2 O praise ye the Lord! praise him upon earth,
In tuneful accord, ye sons of new birth;
Praise him who hath brought you his grace from above,
Praise him who hath taught you to sing of his love.

3 O praise ye the Lord, all things that give sound;
Each jubilant chord re-echo around;
Loud organs, his glory forth tell in deep tone,
And, sweet harp, the story of what he hath done.

4 O praise ye the Lord! thanksgiving and song
To him be outpoured all ages along:
For love in creation, for heaven restored,
For grace of salvation, O praise ye the Lord!
(Amen)*

H. W. Baker (1821-77)
Based on Psalms 148 and 150

* *To be sung when the Alternative Harmonization is used.*

Praise and Worship

ALTERNATIVE HARMONIZATION OF VERSE 4

(C. HUBERT H. PARRY)

4 O praise ye the Lord! thanks - giv - ing and

song To him be out - poured all a - ges a -

long: For love in cre - a - tion, for_ hea - ven re -

stored, For grace of sal - va - tion, O praise ye the Lord!

A - men, _ A - men.

233 PRAISE, MY SOUL 87.87.87.   J. GOSS (1800-80)

PRAISE, my soul, the King of heaven;
   To his feet thy tribute bring.
Ransomed, healed, restored, forgiven,
   Who like me his praise should sing?
      Praise him! Praise him!
   Praise the everlasting King!

2 Praise him for his grace and favour
   To our fathers in distress;
Praise him still the same for ever,
   Slow to chide, and swift to bless.
      Praise him! Praise him!
   Glorious in his faithfulness.

3 Father-like, he tends and spares us;
   Well our feeble frame he knows;
In his hands he gently bears us,
   Rescues us from all our foes.
      Praise him! Praise him!
   Widely as his mercy flows.

4 Angels, help us to adore him;
   Ye behold him face to face;
Sun and moon, bow down before him,
   Dwellers all in time and space.
      Praise him! Praise him!
   Praise with us the God of grace!

                    H. F. Lyte (1793-1847)
                    Based on Psalm 103

234 OLD HUNDREDTH L.M.

Melody of Psalm 134 in *Genevan Psalter* (1551),
with English (1563) form of rhythm in last line

Psalm 100

ALL people that on earth do dwell,
    Sing to the Lord with cheerful voice;
Him serve with fear, his praise forth tell,
    Come ye before him, and rejoice.

2 The Lord, ye know, is God indeed;
    Without our aid he did us make;
We are his folk, he doth us feed,
    And for his sheep he doth us take.

3 O enter then his gates with praise,
    Approach with joy his courts unto;
Praise, laud, and bless his name always,
    For it is seemly so to do.

4 For why? the Lord our God is good;
    His mercy is for ever sure;
His truth at all times firmly stood,
    And shall from age to age endure.

5 To Father, Son, and Holy Ghost,
    The God whom heaven and earth adore,
From men and from the angel-host
    Be praise and glory evermore.

William Kethe (died 1594)
(Verse 5 added c. 1861)

235 OLD HUNDREDTH L.M.   Melody of Psalm 134 in *Genevan Psalter* (1551), with English (1563) form of rhythm in last line

Psalm 100

SING to the Lord with joyful voice;
  Let every land his name adore;
Serve him, and in your hearts rejoice;
  Tell forth his praise from shore to shore.

2 Nations, attend before his throne
    With solemn fear, with sacred joy;
  Know that the Lord is God alone;
    He can create, and he destroy.

3 His sovereign power without our aid
    Made us of clay, and formed us men;
  And when like wandering sheep we strayed,
    He brought us to his fold again.

4*We are his people, we his care,
    Our souls and all our mortal frame:
  What lasting honours shall we rear,
    Almighty Maker, to thy name?

5 We'll crowd thy gates with thankful songs,
    High as the heav'ns our voices raise;
  And earth with her ten thousand tongues
    Shall fill thy courts with sounding praise.

6 Wide as the world is thy command,
    Vast as eternity thy love;
  Firm as the rock thy truth shall stand,
    When rolling years shall cease to move.

Isaac Watts† (1674-1748)

236 LUCKINGTON 10 4.66.66.10 4.   BASIL HARWOOD (1859-1949)
Cheerfully

LET all the world in ev'ry corner sing,
My God and King!
The heav'ns are not too high,
His praise may thither fly;
The earth is not too low,
His praises there may grow.
Let all the world in ev'ry corner sing,
My God and King!

2 Let all the world in ev'ry corner sing,
My God and King!
The Church with psalms must shout,
No door can keep them out;
But above all, the heart
Must bear the longest part.
Let all the world in ev'ry corner sing,
My God and King!

George Herbert (1593-1633)

See No. 237 for another setting, which preserves the original form of the poem.

The Christian Life:

237 AUGUSTINE

ERIK ROUTLEY (1917-   )

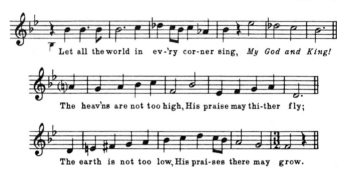

Let all the world in ev'ry cor-ner sing, *My God and King!*

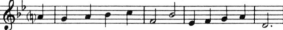

The heav'ns are not too high, His praise may thi-ther fly;

The earth is not too low, His prai-ses there may grow.

Let all the world in ev-'ry cor-ner sing, *My God and King!*

The Church with psalms must shout, No door can keep them out; —

But a-bove all, the heart Must bear the long-est part.

Let all the world in ev-'ry cor-ner sing, *My God and King!*

238 ST GEORGE'S, WINDSOR 77.77.D.   G. J. ELVEY (1816-93)

COME, O come, in pious lays
Sound we God Almighty's praise:
Hither bring, in one concent,
Heart and voice and instrument.
Let those things which do not live
In still music praises give;
Nor a creature dumb be found,
That hath either voice or sound.

2 Come, ye sons of human race,
In this chorus take your place;
And amid the mortal throng
Be you masters of the song.
Let, in praise of God, the sound
Run a never-ending round,
That our song of praise may be
Everlasting, as is he.

3 So this huge, wide orb we see
Shall one choir, one temple be,
And our song shall overclimb
All the bounds of space and time,
And ascend from sphere to sphere
To the great Almighty's ear.
Then, O come, in pious lays
Sound we God Almighty's praise!

Adapted from a poem by George Wither (1588-1667)

The Christian Life:

239 LOBE DEN HERREN 14 14.4 7.8. Melody from *Praxis Pietatis Melica* (1668 edition), as set in *The Chorale Book for England* (1863)

Praise and Worship

Lobe den Herren

PRAISE to the Lord! the Almighty, the King of creation!
O my soul, praise him, for he is thy health and salvation!
　　　All ye who hear,
　　　Now to his temple draw near,
　　Joining in glad adoration.

2 Praise to the Lord, who o'er all things so wondrously reigneth,
　Shelters thee under his wings, yea, so gently sustaineth:
　　　Hast thou not seen?
　　　All that is needful hath been
　　Granted in what he ordaineth.

3 Praise to the Lord, who doth prosper thy work and defend thee;
　Surely his goodness and mercy here daily attend thee:
　　　Ponder anew
　　　What the Almighty can do,
　　If with his love he befriend thee.

4 Praise to the Lord! O let all that is in me adore him!
　All that hath life and breath, come now with praises before him!
　　　Let the Amen
　　　Sound from his people again:
　　Gladly for aye we adore him!

J. Neander (1650-80), *based on Psalms* 103 & 150
Tr. C. Winkworth† (1827-78)

The Christian Life:

240 DEO LAUS ET GLORIA 87.87.887.

Melody and figured bass by J. S. BACH
in SCHEMELLI's *Gesang-Buch* (1736)

With breadth

1 Sing praise to God who reigns a-bove, The God of all cre-a - tion,

The God of pow'r, the God of love, The God of our sal - va - tion;

With heal - ing balm my soul he fills, And ev'-ry faith-less

mur-mur stills: *To God all praise and glo - ry!*

Praise and Worship

SING praise to God who reigns above,
    The God of all creation,
The God of pow'r, the God of love,
    The God of our salvation;
With healing balm my soul he fills,
And ev'ry faithless murmur stills:
    To God all praise and glory!

2 What God's almighty pow'r hath made,
    His gracious mercy keepeth;
By morning glow or evening shade
    His watchful eye ne'er sleepeth:
Within the kingdom of his might
Lo! all is just, and all is right:
    To God all praise and glory!

3*Then all my gladsome way along
    I sing aloud thy praises,
That men may hear the grateful song
    My voice unwearied raises:
Be joyful in the Lord, my heart!
Both soul and body, bear your part!
    To God all praise and glory!

4 O ye who name Christ's holy name,
    Give God all praise and glory!
All ye who own his pow'r, proclaim
    Aloud the wondrous story!
Cast each false idol from his throne,
The Lord is God, and he alone:
    To God all praise and glory!

J. J. Schütz (1640-90)
Tr. F. E. Cox (1812-97)

The Christian Life:

241 ST BARTHOLOMEW L.M.   HENRY DUNCALF (18th century)
(from W. RILEY's *Parochial Harmony*, 1762)

The Greatness of God

MY God, my King, thy various praise
Shall fill the remnant of my days;
Thy grace employ my humble tongue,
Till death and glory raise the song.

2 The wings of every hour shall bear
Some thankful tribute to thine ear,
And every setting sun shall see
New works of duty done for thee.

3 Thy truth and justice I'll proclaim;
Thy bounty flows, an endless stream;
Thy mercy swift; thine anger slow,
But dreadful to the stubborn foe.

4 Let distant times and nations raise
The long succession of thy praise;
And unborn ages make my song
The joy and labour of their tongue.

5 But who can speak thy wondrous deeds?
Thy greatness all our thoughts exceeds;
Vast and unsearchable thy ways,
Vast and immortal be thy praise.

Isaac Watts (1674-1748)
Based on Psalm 145

242 LAUDATE DOMINUM (GAUNTLETT)
10 10.11 11.

H. J. GAUNTLETT (1805-76)
(harmony slightly altered)

Y<small>E</small> servants of God, your Master proclaim,
And publish abroad his wonderful name:
The name all-victorious of Jesus extol;
His kingdom is glorious, and rules over all.

2 God ruleth on high, almighty to save;
And still he is nigh, his presence we have.
The great congregation his triumph shall sing,
Ascribing salvation to Jesus our King.

3 'Salvation to God who sits on the throne',
Let all cry aloud, and honour the Son.
The praises of Jesus the angels proclaim,
Fall down on their faces, and worship the Lamb.

4 Then let us adore, and give him his right:
All glory and power, all wisdom and might,
And honour and blessing, with angels above,
And thanks never-ceasing, and infinite love.

Charles Wesley† (1707-88)

The Christian Life:

243 CHRISTCHURCH 66.66.44.44.   C. STEGGALL (1826-1905)

Praise and Worship

Longing for the House of God

LORD of the worlds above,
  How pleasant and how fair
The dwellings of thy love,
  Thy earthly temples, are!
    To thine abode
      My heart aspires
      With warm desires
    To see my God.

2 O happy souls that pray
  Where God appoints to hear!
O happy men that pay
  Their constant service there!
    They praise thee still;
      And happy they
      That love the way
    To Zion's hill.

3 They go from strength to strength,
  Through this dark vale of tears,
Till each arrives at length,
  Till each in heaven appears:
    O glorious seat,
      When God our King
      Shall thither bring
    Our willing feet!

4 God is our sun and shield,
  Our light and our defence;
With gifts his hands are filled,
  We draw our blessings thence.
    Thrice happy he,
      O God of Hosts,
      Whose spirit trusts
    Alone in thee.

Isaac Watts (1674-1748)
Based on Psalm 84

244 DURHAM   C.M.

Melody and bass from
T. Ravenscroft's *Psalmes* (1621)
Mean parts adapted by S. S. Wesley (1872)

From Psalm 84

How lovely are thy dwellings fair!
  O Lord of Hosts, how dear
Thy pleasant tabernacles are,
  Where thou dost dwell so near!

2 Happy who in thy house reside,
    Where thee they ever praise!
  Happy whose strength in thee doth bide,
    And in their hearts thy ways!

3 They journey on from strength to strength
    With joy and gladsome cheer,
  Till all before our God at length
    In Zion do appear.

4 For God, the Lord, both sun and shield,
    Gives grace and glory bright;
  No good from them shall be withheld
    Whose ways are just and right.

John Milton† (1608-74)

245 ARTHOG 85.85.843.   G. THALBEN-BALL (1896-   )

1 Lord, we know that thou re-joi-cest O'er each work of thine;

Thou didst ears and hands and voi-ces For thy praise com-bine;

Crafts-man's art and mu-sic's mea-sure For thy plea-sure Didst de - sign.

LORD, we know that thou rejoicest
    O'er each work of thine;
Thou didst ears and hands and voices
    For thy praise combine;
Craftsman's art and music's measure
      For thy pleasure
        Didst design.

2 In thy house, O God, we offer
    Of thine own to thee;
And for thine acceptance proffer,
    All unworthily,
Hearts and minds and hands and voices,
      In our choicest
        Melody.

3 Honour, glory, might, and merit
    Thine shall ever be,
Father, Son, and Holy Spirit,
    Blessèd One in Three!
Of the best that thou hast given,
      Earth and Heaven
        Render thee.

Francis Pott† (1832-1909)

The Christian Life:

FIRST TUNE

GWALCHMAI 74.74.D.   J. D. JONES (1827-70)

SECOND TUNE

BEMERTON 74.74.D.   JOHN WILSON (1905-   )

Praise and Worship

Praise

Kɪɴɢ of Glory, King of Peace,
    I will love thee;
And, that love may never cease,
    I will move thee.
Thou hast granted my request,
    Thou hast heard me;
Thou didst note my working breast,
    Thou hast spared me.

2 Wherefore with my utmost art
    I will sing thee,
And the cream of all my heart
    I will bring thee.
Though my sins against me cried,
    Thou didst clear me,
And alone, when they replied,
    Thou didst hear me.

3 Sev'n whole days, not one in sev'n,
    I will praise thee;
In my heart, though not in heav'n,
    I can raise thee.
Small it is, in this poor sort
    To enrol thee;
E'en eternity's too short
    To extol thee.

George Herbert (1593-1633)

Verse 2   when they replied]   *when my sins again clamoured*
Verse 3   to enrol]   *to honour*

The Christian Life:

FIRST TUNE

OXFORD NEW   C.M.

By 'Mr Coombes' in *Twenty Psalm Tunes* (*c.*1775);
probably GEORGE COOMBES of Bristol (*d.*1769)
(melody slightly simplified)

SECOND TUNE

RICHMOND   C.M.

Melody by T. HAWEIS (1734-1820),
as adapted by S. WEBBE the younger (*c.*1770-1843)

Praise and Worship

O FOR a thousand tongues to sing
My great Redeemer's praise,
The glories of my God and King,
The triumphs of his grace!

2 Jesus—the name that charms our fears,
That bids our sorrows cease;
'Tis music in the sinner's ears,
'Tis life, and health, and peace.

3*He breaks the power of cancelled sin,
He sets the prisoner free;
His blood can make the foulest clean;
His blood availed for me.

4 He speaks: and, listening to his voice,
New life the dead receive;
The mournful, broken hearts rejoice;
The humble poor believe.

5 Hear him, ye deaf; his praise, ye dumb,
Your loosened tongues employ;
Ye blind, behold your Saviour come;
And leap, ye lame, for joy.

6 My gracious Master and my God,
Assist me to proclaim,
To spread through all the earth abroad
The honours of thy name.

Charles Wesley† (1707-88)

Charles Wesley wrote this hymn in 1739 on the first anniversary of his conversion. It has been the first hymn in every edition of the Methodist Hymn Book since 1780.

248 CARLISLE S.M.

Melody, and most of the harmony,
by C. LOCKHART (1745-1815)

STAND up, and bless the Lord,
Ye people of his choice:
Stand up, and bless the Lord your God
With heart and soul and voice.

2   Though high above all praise,
Above all blessing high,
Who would not fear his holy name,
And laud and magnify?

3   O for the living flame
From his own altar brought,
To touch our lips, our minds inspire,
And wing to heaven our thought!

4   God is our strength and song,
And his salvation ours;
Then be his love in Christ proclaimed
With all our ransomed powers.

5   Stand up, and bless the Lord,
The Lord your God adore;
Stand up, and bless his glorious name
Henceforth for evermore.

James Montgomery (1771-1854)

249 WAS LEBET, WAS SCHWEBET
13 10.13 10.

Melody from the 'Rheinhardt MS' (Üttingen, 1754),
as harmonized in *The English Hymnal* (1906)

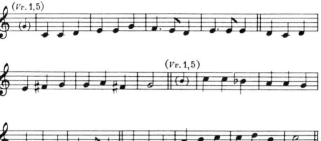

O WORSHIP the Lord in the beauty of holiness,
    Bow down before him, his glory proclaim;
With gold of obedience and incense of lowliness,
    Kneel and adore him: the Lord is his name.

2 Low at his feet lay thy burden of carefulness,
    High on his heart he will bear it for thee,
Comfort thy sorrows, and answer thy prayerfulness,
    Guiding thy steps as may best for thee be.

3 Fear not to enter his courts in the slenderness
    Of the poor wealth thou wouldst reckon as thine;
Truth in its beauty, and love in its tenderness,
    These are the offerings to lay on his shrine.

4 These, though we bring them in trembling and fearfulness,
    He will accept for the name that is dear;
Mornings of joy give for evenings of tearfulness,
    Trust for our trembling, and hope for our fear.

5 O worship the Lord in the beauty of holiness,
    Bow down before him, his glory proclaim;
With gold of obedience and incense of lowliness,
    Kneel and adore him: the Lord is his name.

J. S. B. Monsell (1811-75)

The Christian Life:

FIRST TUNE

GERONTIUS C.M.

J. B. DYKES (1823-76)

SECOND TUNE

RICHMOND   C.M.

Melody by T. HAWEIS (1734-1820),
as adapted by S. WEBBE the younger (c.1770-1843)

Praise and Worship

PRAISE to the Holiest in the height,
  And in the depth be praise;
In all his words most wonderful,
  Most sure in all his ways.

2 O loving wisdom of our God!
    When all was sin and shame,
  A second Adam to the fight
    And to the rescue came.

3 O wisest love! that flesh and blood,
    Which did in Adam fail,
  Should strive afresh against the foe,
    Should strive and should prevail;

4 And that a higher gift than grace
    Should flesh and blood refine,
  God's presence and his very self,
    And essence all-divine.

5 O generous love! that he, who smote
    In Man for man the foe,
  The double agony in Man
    For man should undergo;

6 And in the garden secretly,
    And on the Cross on high,
  Should teach his brethren, and inspire
    To suffer and to die.

7 Praise to the Holiest in the height,
    And in the depth be praise;
  In all his words most wonderful,
    Most sure in all his ways.

J. H. Newman (1801-90)
from 'The Dream of Gerontius'

251 CAROLYN 85.85.88.85.   HERBERT MURRILL (1909-52)

1 God of love and truth and beau-ty, Hal-lowed be thy name;

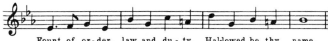

Fount of or-der, law, and du-ty, Hal-lowed be thy name.

As in heav'n thy hosts a-dore thee, And their fa-ces

veil be-fore thee, So on earth, Lord, we im-plore thee,

Hal-lowed be thy name.

Praise and Worship

GOD of love and truth and beauty,
    Hallowed be thy name;
Fount of order, law, and duty,
    Hallowed be thy name.
As in heaven thy hosts adore thee,
And their faces veil before thee,
So on earth, Lord, we implore thee,
    Hallowed be thy name.

2 Lord, remove our guilty blindness,
    Hallowed be thy name;
Show thy heart of lovingkindness,
    Hallowed be thy name.
By our heart's deep-felt contrition,
By our mind's enlightened vision,
By our will's complete submission,
    Hallowed be thy name.

3 In our worship, Lord most holy,
    Hallowed be thy name;
In our work, however lowly,
    Hallowed be thy name.
In each heart's imagination,
In the Church's adoration,
In the conscience of the nation,
    Hallowed be thy name.

Timothy Rees (1874-1939)

The Christian Life:

Later form of a melody in the
Bohemian Brethren's *Kirchengeseng*
(Berlin, 1566)

1 Let us em-ploy all notes of joy And_ praise that nev-er_

end-eth To God a-bove, whose might-y love Our_

hearts and minds de - fend-eth; Who by his grace, in

ev-ery place, To all who need and du - ly plead

His power and pre - sence lend - eth.

LET us employ all notes of joy
  And praise that never endeth
To God above, whose mighty love
  Our hearts and minds defendeth;
Who by his grace, in every place,
To all who need and duly plead
  His power and presence lendeth.

2 For, ere he died, the Crucified
    Wrought things eternal for us
  By bread and wine, which Love divine
    Hath given to assure us:
  O taste and see; find him to be
  Our great reward, our living Lord
    Most willing to restore us.

3 The word he spoke, the bread he broke
    Shall fill our lives with glory,
  If we are true and loving too
    And for our sins are sorry:
  O do his will, and praise him still,
  And still proclaim his glorious name
    And deathless Gospel story.

Adam Fox (1883-   )

253 HEATHLANDS 77.77.77.   HENRY SMART (1813-79)

Psalm 67

GOD of mercy, God of grace,
Show the brightness of thy face;
Shine upon us, Saviour, shine,
Fill thy Church with light divine;
And thy saving health extend
Unto earth's remotest end.

2 Let the people praise thee, Lord;
Be by all that live adored;
Let the nations shout and sing
Glory to their Saviour King;
At thy feet their tribute pay,
And thy holy will obey.

3 Let the people praise thee, Lord;
Earth shall then her fruits afford;
God to man his blessing give,
Man to God devoted live;
All below, and all above,
One in joy and light and love.

H. F. Lyte (1793-1847)

Faith and Aspiration

254 ST PETERSBURG L.M.   Melody by D. S. BORTNIANSKI (1752-1825)

The Christian Race

AWAKE, our souls; away, our fears;
  Let every trembling thought be gone;
Awake and run the heav'nly race,
  And put a cheerful courage on.

2 True, 'tis a strait and thorny road,
  And mortal spirits tire and faint;
But they forget the mighty God
  That feeds the strength of every saint:

3 Thee, mighty God! whose matchless power
  Is ever new and ever young,
And firm endures, while endless years
  Their everlasting circles run.

4 From thee, the overflowing spring,
  Our souls shall drink a fresh supply,
While such as trust their native strength
  Shall melt away, and drop, and die.

5 Swift as an eagle cuts the air,
  We'll mount aloft to thine abode;
On wings of love our souls shall fly,
  Nor tire amidst the heav'nly road.

Isaac Watts (1674-1748)
Based on Isaiah 40. 28-31

The Christian Life:

255 EIN' FESTE BURG 87.87.66.667.
From J. S. BACH's harmonizations of
MARTIN LUTHER's melody for this hymn (1529)

Faith and Aspiration

Ein' feste Burg

A FORTRESS sure is God our King,
　　A Shield that ne'er shall fail us;
His sword alone shall succour bring,
　　When evil doth assail us.
　　　　With craft and cruel hate
　　　　Doth Satan lie in wait,
　　　　And, armed with deadly power,
　　　　Seeks whom he may devour;
　　On earth where is his equal?

2　O who shall then our champion be,
　　　Lest we be lost for ever?
　One sent by God—from sin 'tis he
　　The sinner shall deliver;
　　　　And dost thou ask his name?
　　　　'Tis Jesus Christ—the same
　　　　Of Sabaoth the Lord,
　　　　The Everlasting Word;
　　'Tis he must win the battle.

3　God's word remaineth ever sure,
　　　To us his goodness showing;
　The Spirit's gifts, of sin the cure,
　　Each day he is bestowing.
　　　　Though naught we love be left,
　　　　Of all, e'en life, bereft,
　　　　Yet what shall Satan gain?
　　　　God's kingdom doth remain,
　And shall be ours for ever.

Martin Luther (1483-1546)
Tr. G. Thring† (1823-1903)

Verse 2] *Sabaoth: the Hebrew for* 'hosts'

The Christian Life:

256

FIRST TUNE

DONCASTER S.M.

Melody and bass by
SAMUEL WESLEY (1766-1837)

*Samuel Wesley, the composer of this tune, was a son of Charles Wesley the hymn-writer, and a
nephew of John Wesley (the translator of this hymn). He was also the father of the church-
musician S. S. Wesley, who is best known for his anthems and for the tune* AURELIA *(No. 174)*

SECOND TUNE

FOSTER S.M.

M. B. FOSTER (1851-1922)

Faith and Aspiration

Befiehl du deine Wege

COMMIT thou all thy griefs
And ways into his hands;
To his sure truth and tender care,
Who earth and heaven commands.

2   Who points the clouds their course,
Whom winds and seas obey;
He shall direct thy wandering feet,
He shall prepare thy way

3   Thou on the Lord rely;
So safe shalt thou go on;
Fix on his work thy steadfast eye,
So shall thy work be done.

4   Give to the winds thy fears;
Hope, and be undismayed;
God hears thy sighs, and counts thy tears,
God shall lift up thy head.

5* Leave to his sovereign sway
To choose and to command;
So shalt thou wondering own, his way
How wise, how strong his hand.

6* Far, far above thy thought
His counsel shall appear,
When fully he the work hath wrought,
That caused thy needless fear.

7   Father, thy ceaseless truth,
Thy everlasting love,
Sees all thy children's wants, and knows
What best for each will prove.

8   Let us in life, in death,
Thy steadfast truth declare,
And publish with our latest breath
Thy love and guardian care.

P. Gerhardt (1607-76), based on Psalm 37, v. 5
Tr. John Wesley† (1703-91)

The Christian Life:

Organ

1 Christ who knows all his sheep Will all in safe-ty keep:

He will not lose one soul, Nor ev - er fail us:

Nor we the pro - mised goal, What - e'er as - sail us.

Org.

Faith and Aspiration

The Life Eternal

CHRIST who knows all his sheep
Will all in safety keep:
He will not lose one soul,
  Nor ever fail us:
Nor we the promised goal,
  Whate'er assail us.

2 We know our God is just;
  To him we wholly trust
All that we have and claim,
    And all we hope for:
All's sure and seen to him,
    Which here we grope for.

3 Fear not the World of Light,
  Though out of mortal's sight;
There shall we know God more,
    Where all is holy:
There is no grief or care,
    No sin or folly.

4 O Blessèd Company,
  Where all in harmony
God's joyous praises sing,
    In love unceasing;
And all obey their King,
    With perfect pleasing!

Adapted from a poem by Richard Baxter (1615-91)

258 CHAPEL ROYAL 886. D.

Melody and figured bass by
DR WILLIAM BOYCE (c.1710-1779)

Supreme motor cordium

GREAT Mover of all hearts, whose hand
Doth all the secret springs command
    Of human thought and will,
Thou, since the world was made, dost bless
Thy saints with fruits of holiness,
    Their order to fulfil.

2 Faith, hope, and love here weave one chain;
But love alone shall then remain
    When this short day is gone:
O Love, O Truth, O endless Light,
When shall we see thy sabbath bright
    With all our labours done?

3 We sow 'mid perils here and tears;
There the glad hand the harvest bears,
    Which here in grief hath sown:
Great Three in One, the increase give;
Thy gifts of grace, by which we live,
    With heav'nly glory crown.

C. Coffin (1676-1749)
Tr. I. Williams† (1802-65)

Faith and Aspiration

ST JAMES C.M.

Melody, and most of the bass,
from *Select Psalms and Hymns* (1697)
Probably by R. COURTEVILLE

THOU art the Way: to thee alone
From sin and death we flee;
And he who would the Father seek
Must seek him, Lord, by thee.

2 Thou art the Truth: thy word alone
True wisdom can impart;
Thou only canst inform the mind,
And purify the heart.

3 Thou art the Life: the rending tomb
Proclaims thy conquering arm;
And those who put their trust in thee
Nor death nor hell shall harm.

4 Thou art the Way, the Truth, the Life;
Grant us that Way to know,
That Truth to keep, that Life to win,
Whose joys eternal flow.

G. W. Doane† (1799-1859)
Based on John 14.6

The Christian Life:

FIRST TUNE

CROSSINGS 89. 89. D.
In moderate time

C. ARMSTRONG GIBBS (1889-1960)

1 Thee will I love, my God and King, Thee will I
sing, my strength and tow-er: For ev-er-more thee
will I trust, O God most just of truth and pow-er:
Who all things hast in or-der placed, Yea, for thy plea-sure
hast cre-a-ted; And on thy throne un-seen, unknown, Reign-est a-lone in glo-ry seat-ed.

Faith and Aspiration

THEE will I love, my God and King,
Thee will I sing, my strength and tower:
　For evermore thee will I trust,
O God most just of truth and power:
　Who all things hast in order placed,
Yea, for thy pleasure hast created;
　And on thy throne unseen, unknown,
Reignest alone in glory seated.

2　Set in my heart thy love I find;
My wand'ring mind to thee thou leadest;
　My trembling hope, my strong desire
With heav'nly fire thou kindly feedest.
　Lo, all things fair thy path prepare,
Thy beauty to my spirit calleth,
　Thine to remain in joy or pain,
And count it gain whate'er befalleth.

3　O more and more thy love extend,
My life befriend with heav'nly pleasure;
　That I may win thy paradise,
Thy pearl of price, thy countless treasure.
　Since but in thee I can go free
From earthly care and vain oppression,
　This prayer I make for Jesu's sake,
That thou me take in thy possession.

Robert Bridges (1844-1930)

260 *(continued)*   SECOND TUNE

HAMBLEDEN 89.89. D.   W. K. STANTON (1891-)

1 Thee will I love, my God and King, Thee will I sing, my strength and tow-er: For ev-er-more thee will I trust, O God most just of truth and pow-er: Who all things hast in or-der placed, Yea, for thy plea-sure hast cre-a-ted; And on thy throne un-seen, un-known, Reign-est a-lone in glo-'ry seat-ed.

Faith and Aspiration

THEE will I love, my God and King,
Thee will I sing, my strength and tower:
   For evermore thee will I trust,
O God most just of truth and power:
   Who all things hast in order placed,
Yea, for thy pleasure hast created;
   And on thy throne unseen, unknown,
Reignest alone in glory seated.

2   Set in my heart thy love I find;
My wand'ring mind to thee thou leadest;
   My trembling hope, my strong desire
With heav'nly fire thou kindly feedest.
   Lo, all things fair thy path prepare,
Thy beauty to my spirit calleth,
   Thine to remain in joy or pain,
And count it gain whate'er befalleth.

3   O more and more thy love extend,
My life befriend with heav'nly pleasure;
   That I may win thy paradise,
Thy pearl of price, thy countless treasure.
   Since but in thee I can go free
From earthly care and vain oppression,
   This prayer I make for Jesu's sake,
That thou me take in thy possession.

Robert Bridges (1844-1930)

261 COME, MY WAY 77.77.   ALEXANDER BRENT SMITH (1889-1950)

Slow

1 Come, my Way, my Truth,— my Life: Such a
2 Come, my Light, my Feast,— my Strength: Such a
3 Come, my Joy, my Love,— my Heart: Such a

Way, as gives us breath; Such a Truth, as ends all
Light, as shows a feast; Such a Feast, as mends in
Joy, as none can move; Such a Love, as none can

strife; Such a Life,— as kill - eth death.
length; Such a Strength,— as makes his guest.
part; Such a Heart,— as joys in love.

The Call

COME, my Way, my Truth, my Life:
Such a Way, as gives us breath;
Such a Truth, as ends all strife;
Such a Life, as killeth death.

2 Come, my Light, my Feast, my Strength:
Such a Light, as shows a feast;
Such a Feast, as mends in length;
Such a Strength, as makes his guest.

3 Come, my Joy, my Love, my Heart:
Such a Joy, as none can move;
Such a Love, as none can part;
Such a Heart, as joys in love.

George Herbert (1593-1633)

Faith and Aspiration

262

FIRST TUNE

ST HUGH C.M.

E. J. HOPKINS (1818-1901)

SECOND TUNE

WIGTOWN C.M.

Melody, and most of the harmony,
from *Scottish Psalter* (1635)

LORD, it belongs not to my care
　Whether I die or live;
To love and serve thee is my share,
　And this thy grace must give.

2 If life be long, I will be glad
　That I may long obey:
If short, yet why should I be sad
　To welcome endless day?

3 Christ leads me through no darker rooms
　Than he went through before:
He that into God's Kingdom comes
　Must enter by this door.

4 Come, Lord, when grace hath made me meet
　Thy blessèd face to see;
For if thy work on earth be sweet,
　What will thy glory be!

5 Then I shall end my sad complaints
　And weary sinful days,
And join with those triumphant saints
　That sing Jehovah's praise.

6 My knowledge of that life is small,
　The eye of faith is dim;
But 'tis enough that Christ knows all,
　And I shall be with him.

Richard Baxter‡ (1615-91)

263 MARTYRDOM C.M.   Melody by Hugh Wilson (1766-1824)

Psalm 42, vv. 1-2, 14-15

A S pants the hart for cooling streams
　　When heated in the chase,
So longs my soul, O God, for thee,
　　And thy refreshing grace.

2 For thee, my God, the living God,
　　My thirsty soul doth pine:
O when shall I behold thy face,
　　Thou Majesty divine?

3 Why restless, why cast down, my soul?
　　Hope still, and thou shalt sing
The praise of him who is thy God,
　　Thy health's eternal spring.

4 To Father, Son, and Holy Ghost,
　　The God whom we adore,
Be glory, as it was, is now,
　　And shall be evermore.

N. Tate (1652-1715) and N. Brady (1659-1726)
in 'A New Version of the Psalms'

Faith and Aspiration

ABERDEEN (ST PAUL) C.M.

Melody from *Chalmers' Collection*
(Aberdeen, *c.*1749)

Hebrews 13, *vv.* 20-21

FATHER of peace, and God of love,
  We own thy power to save,
That power by which our Shepherd rose
  Victorious o'er the grave.

2 Him from the dead thou brought'st again,
  When, by his sacred blood,
Confirmed and sealed for evermore
  The eternal covenant stood.

3 O may thy Spirit seal our souls,
  And mould them to thy will,
That our weak hearts no more may stray,
  But keep thy precepts still;

4 That to perfection's sacred height
  We nearer still may rise,
And all we think, and all we do,
  Be pleasing in thine eyes.

Philip Doddridge (1702-51)
as in Scottish Paraphrases (1781)

FIRST TUNE

265

OCKLEY 66.66.　　　　　　　　　THOMAS FIELDEN (1882-　)

SECOND TUNE

SHARPENHURST 66.66.　　　　　　BRIAN HEAD (1936-　)

MY spirit longs for thee
    Within my troubled breast,
Though I unworthy be
    Of so divine a guest.

2 Of so divine a guest
    Unworthy though I be,
Yet has my heart no rest
    Unless it come from thee.

3 Unless it come from thee,
    In vain I look around;
In all that I can see
    No rest is to be found.

4 No rest is to be found
    But in thy blessèd love:
O let my wish be crowned,
    And send it from above!

John Byrom† (1692-1763)

Faith and Aspiration

266

SONG 20 S.M.

Melody and bass by
ORLANDO GIBBONS (1583-1625)
(rhythm slightly altered)

Second Tune

ST PAUL'S S.M.

J. STAINER (1840-1901)

My Lord, my Life, my Love,
To thee, to thee I call:
I cannot live if thou remove;
Thou art my joy, my all.

2 My only sun to cheer
The darkness where I dwell;
The best and only true delight
My song hath found to tell.

3 To thee in very heav'n
The angels owe their bliss,
To thee the saints, whom thou hast called
Where perfect pleasure is.

4 And how shall man, thy child,
Without thee happy be,
Who hath no comfort nor desire
In all the world but thee?

5 Return, my Love, my Life,
Thy grace hath won my heart;
If thou forgive, if thou return,
I will no more depart.

Robert Bridges (1844-1930)
Based on a hymn by Isaac Watts (1674-1748)

The Christian Life:

267 ICH HALTE TREULICH STILL D.S.M.

Melody and figured bass from
SCHEMELLI's *Gesang-Buch* (1736)
Probably by J. S. BACH

1 Je-sus, my strength, my hope, On thee I cast my care,
With hum-ble con-fi-dence look up And know thou hear'st my prayer.
Give me on thee to wait, Till I can all things do,
On thee, al-migh-ty to cre-ate, Al-migh-ty to re-new.

Faith and Aspiration

JESUS, my strength, my hope,
  On thee I cast my care,
With humble confidence look up
  And know thou hear'st my prayer.
  Give me on thee to wait,
  Till I can all things do,
On thee, almighty to create,
  Almighty to renew.

2   Give me a godly fear,
  A quick-discerning eye,
That looks to thee when sin is near,
  And sees the tempter fly:
  A spirit still prepared,
  And armed with jealous care,
For ever standing on its guard,
  And watching unto prayer.

3   Give me a true regard,
  A single, steady aim,
Unmoved by threatening or reward,
  To thee and thy great name;
  A jealous, just concern
  For thine immortal praise;
A pure desire that all may learn
  And glorify thy grace.

4   I rest upon thy word;
  Thy promise is for me;
My succour and salvation, Lord,
  Shall surely come from thee:
  But let me still abide,
  Nor from my hope remove,
Till thou my patient spirit guide
  Into thy perfect love.

Charles Wesley† (1707-88)

The Christian Life:

268

FIRST TUNE

CAERSALEM 87.87.47.

Melody by R. EDWARDS (1797-1862)

SECOND TUNE

CWM RHONDDA 87.87.47.

JOHN HUGHES (1873-1932)

Faith and Aspiration

Arglwydd arwain trwy'r anialwch

G UIDE me, O thou great Jehovah,
  Pilgrim through this barren land;
I am weak, but thou art mighty;
  Hold me with thy powerful hand;
    Bread of heaven,
  Feed me now and evermore.

2 Open now the crystal fountain,
    Whence the healing stream doth flow;
  Let the fire and cloudy pillar
    Lead me all my journey through;
      Strong Deliv'rer,
    Be thou still my strength and shield.

3 When I tread the verge of Jordan,
    Bid my anxious fears subside;
  Death of deaths, and hell's destruction,
    Land me safe on Canaan's side;
      Songs of praises
    I will ever give to thee.

From the Welsh of W. Williams (1716-91)
Tr. P. Williams† and others, c. 1771

269 SENNEN COVE C.M.   WILLIAM H. HARRIS (1883-)

FATHER, to thee my soul I lift,
My soul on thee depends,
Convinced that every perfect gift
From thee alone descends.

2 Mercy and grace are thine alone,
And power and wisdom too;
Without the Spirit of thy Son
We nothing good can do.

3 Thou all our works in us hast wrought,
Our good is all divine;
The praise of every virtuous thought,
And righteous word, is thine.

4 From thee, through Jesus, we receive
The power on thee to call,
In whom we are, and move, and live;
Our God is all in all.

Charles Wesley† (1707-88)
Based on Philippians 2.13

Faith and Aspiration

Melody by J. H. SCHEIN (1586-1630)
Harmony from settings by J. S. BACH (1685-1750)

DEAR Master, in whose life I see
All that I would, but fail to be,
Let thy clear light for ever shine,
To shame and guide this life of mine.

2 Though what I dream and what I do
In my weak days are always two,
Help me, oppressed by things undone,
O thou, whose deeds and dreams were one!

John Hunter (1848-1917)

The Christian Life:

271 EVENTIDE 10 10.10 10.   W. H. MONK (1823-89)

ABIDE with me: fast falls the eventide;
The darkness deepens; Lord, with me abide:
When other helpers fail, and comforts flee,
Help of the helpless, O abide with me.

2*Swift to its close ebbs out life's little day;
Earth's joys grow dim, its glories pass away;
Change and decay in all around I see;
O thou who changest not, abide with me.

3 I need thy presence every passing hour;
What but thy grace can foil the tempter's power?
Who like thyself my guide and stay can be?
Through cloud and sunshine, O abide with me.

4 I fear no foe, with thee at hand to bless;
Ills have no weight, and tears no bitterness.
Where is death's sting? where, grave, thy victory?
I triumph still, if thou abide with me.

5 Hold thou thy Cross before my closing eyes;
Shine through the gloom, and point me to the skies:
Heaven's morning breaks, and earth's vain shadows flee;
In life, in death, O Lord, abide with me.

H. F. Lyte† (1793-1847)

272 ST BOTOLPH C.M.   GORDON SLATER (1896-   )

ENTHRONE thy God within thy heart,
   Thy being's inmost shrine;
He doth to thee the power impart
   To live the life divine.

2 Seek truth in him with Christlike mind;
     With faith his will discern;
  Walk on life's way with him, and find
     Thy heart within thee burn.

3 With love that overflows thy soul
     Love him who first loved thee;
  Is not his love thy life, thy goal,
     Thy soul's eternity?

4 Serve him in his sufficing strength:
     Heart, mind, and soul employ;
  And he shall crown thy days at length
     With everlasting joy.

                          W. J. Penn (1875-1956)

The Christian Life:

273 GOD BE IN MY HEAD

WALFORD DAVIES (1869-1941)

Org.

God be in my head, and in my un-der-stand-ing;

God be in mine eyes, and in my look-ing; God be in my mouth, and in my

speak-ing;   God be in my heart, and in my think - ing;

God be at mine_ end,   and at my de - part - ing.

Book of Hours† (1514)

Prayer and Repentance

274 WIGTOWN C.M.

Melody, and most of the harmony,
from *Scottish Psalter* (1635)

What is Prayer?

PRAYER is the soul's sincere desire,
    Uttered or unexpressed;
The motion of a hidden fire
    That trembles in the breast.

2 Prayer is the simplest form of speech
    That infant-lips can try;
Prayer the sublimest strains that reach
    The Majesty on high.

3 Prayer is the Christian's vital breath,
    The Christian's native air,
His watchword at the gates of death:
    He enters heaven with prayer.

4 The saints in prayer appear as one
    In word, and deed, and mind,
While with the Father and the Son
    Sweet fellowship they find.

5*Nor prayer is made by man alone:
    The Holy Spirit pleads;
And Jesus, on the eternal throne,
    For sinners intercedes.

6 O thou by whom we come to God,
    The Life, the Truth, the Way,
The path of prayer thyself hast trod:
    Lord, teach us how to pray!

James Montgomery (1771-1854)

275 WALSALL C.M.

Later form of a tune from W. ANCHORS'
Choice Collection of Psalm-Tunes (c.1721)

LORD, teach us how to pray aright
With reverence and with fear;
Though dust and ashes in thy sight,
We may, we must, draw near.

2 We perish if we cease from prayer;
O grant us power to pray;
And, when to meet thee we prepare,
Lord, meet us by the way.

3 God of all grace, we bring to thee
A broken, contrite heart;
Give what thine eye delights to see,
Truth in the inward part;

4*Give deep humility; the sense
Of godly sorrow give;
A strong, desiring confidence
To hear thy voice and live;

5 Faith in the only sacrifice
That can for sin atone;
To cast our hopes, to fix our eyes,
On Christ, on Christ alone;

6 Give these, and then thy will be done;
Thus, strengthened with all might,
We, through thy Spirit and thy Son,
Shall pray, and pray aright.

James Montgomery (1771-1854)

276 WHITEHALL L.M.

Melody and bass by
HENRY LAWES (1596-1662)

(In Lent)

Audi, benigne Conditor

O MAKER of the world, give ear;
In pitying love vouchsafe to hear
The prayers our contrite spirits raise
In this our fast of forty days.

2 All hearts are open unto thee;
Thou knowest each infirmity;
Now, as we turn to seek thy face,
Pour down on us thy pardoning grace.

3 Help us to grow in self-control,
To make the body serve the soul:
So may thy loving-kindness bless
Our fast with fruits of holiness.

Before 11th century
Tr. C. S. Phillips (1883-1949)

The Christian Life:

FIRST VERSION

CHESHIRE C.M.

From T. Est's *Psalmes* (1592)
(Harmony slightly altered)

SECOND VERSION
(with later form of rhythm)

CHESHIRE C.M.

Harmonized by CHARLES WOOD (1866-1926)
in his *Passion according to St Mark*

Prayer and Repentance

LORD, when we bend before thy throne,
　　And our confessions pour,
Teach us to feel the sins we own,
　　And hate what we deplore.

2 Our broken spirits pitying see,
　　And penitence impart;
Then let a kindling glance from thee
　　Shed hope upon the heart.

3 When we disclose our wants in prayer,
　　May we our wills resign;
And may our hearts no longing share
　　That is not wholly thine.

4 Let faith each meek petition fill,
　　And raise it to the skies,
And teach our hearts 'tis goodness still
　　That grants it or denies.

J. D. Carlyle‡ (1758-1804)

The Christian Life:

Melody by ISAAC SMITH,
from his *Psalm Tunes* (*c.*1780)

'*And lead us not into temptation*'

BE thou my Guardian and my Guide,
    And hear me when I call;
Let not my slippery footsteps slide,
    And hold me lest I fall.

2 The world, the flesh, and Satan dwell
    Around the path I tread;
O save me from the snares of hell,
    Thou quickener of the dead.

3 And if I tempted am to sin,
    And outward things are strong,
Do thou, O Lord, keep watch within,
    And save my soul from wrong.

4 Still let me ever watch and pray,
    And feel that I am frail;
That if the tempter cross my way,
    Yet he may not prevail.

I. Williams‡ (1802-65)

Prayer and Repentance

279 MANNHEIM 87.87.87.

Melody adapted from a chorale
in F. FILITZ's *Choralbuch* (1847)
Harmony chiefly by LOWELL MASON (1853)

LEAD us, heavenly Father, lead us
O'er the world's tempestuous sea;
Guard us, guide us, keep us, feed us,
For we have no help but thee;
Yet possessing every blessing,
If our God our Father be.

2 Saviour, breathe forgiveness o'er us:
All our weakness thou dost know;
Thou didst tread this earth before us,
Thou didst feel its keenest woe;
Lone and dreary, faint and weary,
Through the desert thou didst go.

3 Spirit of our God, descending,
Fill our hearts with heavenly joy,
Love with every passion blending,
Pleasure that can never cloy:
Thus provided, pardoned, guided,
Nothing can our peace destroy.

J. Edmeston (1791-1867)

280 REPTON 86. 886.

C. HUBERT H. PARRY (1848-1918)
(from a song in his oratorio *Judith*)

DEAR Lord and Father of mankind,
　Forgive our foolish ways!
Re-clothe us in our rightful mind,
In purer lives thy service find,
　In deeper reverence praise.

2 In simple trust like theirs who heard,
　　Beside the Syrian sea,
　The gracious calling of the Lord,
　Let us, like them, without a word
　　Rise up and follow thee.

3 Drop thy still dews of quietness,
　　Till all our strivings cease;
　Take from our souls the strain and stress,
　And let our ordered lives confess
　　The beauty of thy peace.

4 Breathe through the heats of our desire
　　Thy coolness and thy balm;
　Let sense be dumb, let flesh retire;
　Speak through the earthquake, wind, and fire,
　　O still small voice of calm!

J. G. Whittier (1807-92)

281 HONITON C.M.   HENRY G. LEY (1887-1962)

The Friend of sinners

JESUS, whose all-redeeming love
　No penitent did scorn,
Who didst the stain of guilt remove,
　Till hope anew was born:

2 To thee, Physician of the soul,
　The lost, the outcast, came:
Thou didst restore and make them whole,
　Disburdened of their shame.

3 'Twas love, thy love, their bondage brake,
　Whose fetters sin had bound:
For faith to love did answer make,
　And free forgiveness found.

4 Thou didst rebuke the scornful pride
　That called thee 'sinners' friend',
Thy mercy as thy Father's wide,
　God's mercy without end.

5*Along life's desecrated way,
　Where man despairing trod,
Thy love all-pitying did display
　The pitying love of God.

6 Jesus, that pardoning grace to find,
　I too would come to thee:
O merciful to all mankind,
　Be merciful to me.

G. W. Briggs (1875-1959)

282 WINDSOR C.M.

Melody from DAMON's *Psalmes* (1591)
(rhythm simplified)

LORD, as to thy dear Cross we flee,
    And plead to be forgiven,
So let thy life our pattern be,
    And form our souls for heaven.

2 Help us, through good report and ill,
    Our daily cross to bear;
Like thee, to do our Father's will,
    Our brethren's griefs to share.

3 Let grace our selfishness expel,
    Our earthliness refine;
And in our hearts let kindness dwell,
    As free and true as thine.

4 Kept peaceful in the midst of strife,
    Forgiving and forgiven,
O may we lead the pilgrim's life,
    And follow thee to heaven.

J. H. Gurney† (1802-62)

283 INTERCESSOR 11 10.11 10.　　　　　C. HUBERT H. PARRY (1848-1918)

'Father, forgive them . . .'

O WORD of pity, for our pardon pleading,
　　Breathed in the hour of loneliness and pain;
O voice, which through the ages interceding
　　Calls us to fellowship with God again!

2 O word of comfort, through the silence stealing,
　　As the dread act of sacrifice began;
O infinite compassion, still revealing
　　The infinite forgiveness won for man!

3 O word of hope to raise us nearer heaven,
　　When courage fails us and when faith is dim!
The souls for whom Christ prays to Christ are given,
　　To find their pardon and their joy in him.

4 O Intercessor, who art ever living
　　To plead for dying souls that they may live,
Teach us to know our sin which needs forgiving,
　　Teach us to know the love which can forgive.

Ada R. Greenaway (1861-1937)

284 REDHEAD No. 76 77.77.77.

R. REDHEAD (1820-1901)

R OCK of Ages, cleft for me,
Let me hide myself in thee;
Let the water and the blood,
From thy riven side which flowed,
Be of sin the double cure,
Cleanse me from its guilt and power.

2 Not the labours of my hands
Can fulfil thy law's demands;
Could my zeal no respite know,
Could my tears for ever flow,
All for sin could not atone;
Thou must save, and thou alone.

3 Nothing in my hand I bring,
Simply to thy Cross I cling;
Naked, come to thee for dress;
Helpless, look to thee for grace;
Foul, I to the fountain fly;
Wash me, Saviour, or I die.

4 While I draw this fleeting breath,
When my eyelids close in death,
When I soar through tracts unknown,
See thee on thy judgment throne;
Rock of Ages, cleft for me,
Let me hide myself in thee.

A. M. Toplady† (1740-78)

Prayer and Repentance

285 LUTHER'S HYMN 87.87.887.
(NUN FREUT EUCH)

Later form of a melody in
Geistliche Lieder (1533 or earlier)

O GOD of mercy, love, and power,
  O Life in all abounding,
O hidden Presence hour by hour
  Thy children's way surrounding,
Whose dwelling is in heaven apart,
And in the lowly contrite heart,
  O Heavenly Father, hear us.

2 Deliver us from evil, Lord,
  Whom here thy bounty blesses,
From pride of soul and boasting word,
  And lure of low successes;
In times of wealth that tempt to wrong
O bid our halting wills be strong;
  In mercy, Father, hear us.

3 Thine arm will give the strength to bear
  Whate'er thy wisdom send us:
From thy strong love and tender care
  Nor life nor death can rend us.
O bid us feel thy Presence now,
Though we forget, forget not thou:
  In power and love be near us.

Frank Fletcher (1870-1954)

286

OLD 124th 10 10.10 10.10.

Melody from *Genevan Psalter* (1551)
(rhythm as in slightly later English version)

Turn back, O man, forswear thy foolish ways.
Old now is earth, and none may count her days,
Yet thou, her child, whose head is crowned with flame,
Still wilt not hear thine inner God proclaim—
'Turn back, O man, forswear thy foolish ways.'

2 Earth might be fair and all men glad and wise.
Age after age their tragic empires rise,
Built while they dream, and in that dreaming weep:
Would man but wake from out his haunted sleep,
Earth might be fair and all men glad and wise.

3 Earth shall be fair, and all her people one:
Nor till that hour shall God's whole will be done.
Now, even now, once more from earth to sky,
Peals forth in joy man's old undaunted cry—
'Earth shall be fair, and all her folk be one!'

Clifford Bax (1886-1962)

Prayer and Repentance

SECOND VERSION

OLD 124th 10 10.10 10.10.
Andante maestoso

(See First Version)
Harmony adapted from the choral setting
by GUSTAV HOLST (1874-1934)

1 Turn back, O man, for - swear thy fool-ish ways. Old now is earth, and none may count her days, Yet thou, her child, whose head is crowned with flame, Still wilt not hear thine in - ner God pro - claim— 'Turn back, O man, for - swear thy fool - ish ways'._

2 Earth might be fair and all men glad and wise. Age af - ter age their tra - gic em - pires rise, Built while they dream, and in that dream - ing weep: Would man but wake from out his haunt - ed sleep, Earth might be fair and all men glad and wise. _

3 Earth shall be fair, and all her peo - ple one: Nor till that hour shall God's whole will be done. Now, e - ven now, once more from earth to sky, Peals forth in joy man's old un - daunt - ed cry— 'Earth shall be fair, and all her folk be one!'_

vv. 1 and 2   v. 3

Clifford Bax (1886-1962)

✱ *Expression marks in brackets apply to Verse 3.*

The Christian Life:

FIRST TUNE

UFFINGHAM L.M.

Melody and bass by
JEREMIAH CLARKE (c. 1673-1707)

1 Cre-a-tor of the earth and skies, To whom the

words of life be-long, Grant us thy truth to

make us wise; Grant us thy power to make us strong.

SECOND TUNE

ST SEPULCHRE L.M.

G. COOPER (1820-76)

Penitence

CREATOR of the earth and skies,
 To whom the words of life belong,
Grant us thy truth to make us wise;
 Grant us thy power to make us strong.

2 Like theirs of old, our life is death,
 Our light is darkness, till we see
Th' eternal Word made flesh and breath,
 The God who walked by Galilee.

3 We have not known thee: to the skies
 Our monuments of folly soar,
And all our self-wrought miseries
 Have made us trust ourselves the more.

4 We have not loved thee: far and wide
 The wreckage of our hatred spreads,
And evils wrought by human pride
 Recoil on unrepentant heads.

5 For this, our foolish confidence,
 Our pride of knowledge and our sin,
We come to thee in penitence;
 In us the work of grace begin.

6 Teach us to know and love thee, Lord,
 And humbly follow in thy way.
Speak to our souls the quickening word
 And turn our darkness into day.

Donald Hughes (1911-   )

288 SANDYS S.M.

Melody from W. SANDYS' *Christmas Carols* (1833)
(as harmonized in *The English Hymnal,* 1906)

The Elixir

TEACH me, my God and King,
In all things thee to see;
And what I do in any thing,
To do it as for thee.

2 A man that looks on glass,
On it may stay his eye;
Or if he pleaseth, through it pass,
And then the heav'n espy.

3 All may of thee partake:
Nothing can be so mean,
Which with his tincture, 'for thy sake',
Will not grow bright and clean.

4 A servant with this clause
Makes drudgery divine;
Who sweeps a room, as for thy laws,
Makes that and th' action fine.

5 This is the famous stone
That turneth all to gold;
For that which God doth touch and own
Cannot for less be told.

George Herbert (1593-1633)

In the language of Alchemy, an 'Elixir' was something that would turn base metals into gold,
the Philosopher's Stone (v. 5) was supposed to do. A 'tincture' (v. 3) was a spiritual principle
that could be infused into matter, and in this line the word 'his' means 'its'.

Discipleship and Service

289 SHEPHERD BOY'S SONG C.M.

J. H. ALDEN (1900-   )

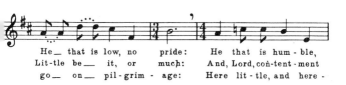

1 He that is down, needs fear no fall,
2 I am con - tent with what I have,
3 Full - ness to such a bur - den is That

He— that is low, no pride: He that is hum - ble,
Lit-tle be— it, or much: And, Lord, con-tent-ment
go— on— pil - grim - age: Here lit - tle, and here -

e - ver shall Have God to be his Guide.
still I crave, Be - cause thou sa - vest such.
af - ter bliss, Is— best from age to age.

John Bunyan (1628-88)

This poem, from Part 2 of 'The Pilgrim's Progress', is the Shepherd-Boy's song in the Valley of Humiliation.

The Christian Life:

290

WATERSMEET 87.87.

JOHN GARDNER (1917-   )

SECOND TUNE

OMNI DIE 87.87.

Melody from D. G. CORNER's *Gesangbuch* (1631)
Arranged by W. S. ROCKSTRO (1823-95)

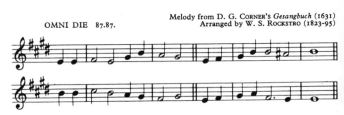

JESUS calls us: o'er the tumult
  Of our life's wild restless sea
Day by day his voice is sounding,
  Saying, 'Christian, follow me';

2 As of old Saint Andrew heard it
    By the Galilean lake,
  Turned from home and toil and kindred
    Leaving all for his dear sake.

3 Jesus calls us from the worship
    Of the vain world's golden store,
  From each idol that would keep us,
    Saying, 'Christian, love me more.'

4 In our joys and in our sorrows,
    Days of toil and hours of ease,
  Still he calls, in cares and pleasures,
    'Christian, love me more than these.'

5 Jesus calls us: by thy mercies,
    Saviour, may we hear thy call,
  Give our hearts to thy obedience,
    Serve and love thee best of all.

Mrs C. F. Alexander† (1818-95)

291 BRESLAU L.M.

German Traditional Melody, in
form used by MENDELSSOHN (1836)

'TAKE up thy cross,' the Saviour said,
  'If thou wouldst my disciple be;
Take up thy cross, with willing heart,
  And humbly follow after me.'

2 Take up thy cross; let not its weight
  Fill thy weak soul with vain alarm;
His strength shall bear thy spirit up,
  And brace thy heart, and nerve thine arm.

3 Take up thy cross, nor heed the shame,
  And let thy foolish pride be still:
Thy Lord refused not e'en to die
  Upon a Cross, on Calvary's hill.

4 Take up thy cross, then, in his strength,
  And calmly every danger brave;
'Twill guide thee to a better home,
  And lead to vict'ry o'er the grave.

5 Take up thy cross, and follow Christ,
  Nor think till death to lay it down;
For only he who bears the cross
  May hope to wear the glorious crown.

C. W. Everest‡ (1814-77)
Based on Mark 8.34

The Christian Life:

292 ALBERTA 10 4. 10 4. 10 10. WILLIAM H. HARRIS (1883-)

L<small>EAD</small>, kindly Light, amid the encircling gloom,
    Lead thou me on;
The night is dark, and I am far from home,
    Lead thou me on.
Keep thou my feet; I do not ask to see
The distant scene; one step enough for me.

2 I was not ever thus, nor prayed that thou
    Should'st lead me on;
I loved to choose and see my path; but now
    Lead thou me on.
I loved the garish day, and, spite of fears,
Pride ruled my will: remember not past years.

3 So long thy power hath blessed me, sure it still
    Will lead me on,
O'er moor and fen, o'er crag and torrent, till
    The night is gone;
And with the morn those angel faces smile,
Which I have loved long since, and lost awhile.

J. H. Newman (1801-90)

The author wrote these verses as a young man, never intending them as a hymn. In later li[fe]
when asked about the meaning of the imagery, he insisted that the art of a verse-writer lies in 't[he]
expression of imagination and sentiment', rather than of literal 'truth'.

293 LEXHAM II IO. II IO.   SYDNEY WATSON (1903-   )

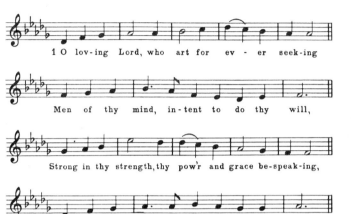

1 O lov-ing Lord, who art for ev - er seek-ing
Men of thy mind, in-tent to do thy will,
Strong in thy strength, thy pow'r and grace be-speak-ing,
Faith-ful to thee through good re-port and ill;

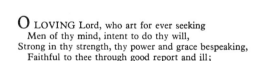

O LOVING Lord, who art for ever seeking
　　Men of thy mind, intent to do thy will,
Strong in thy strength, thy power and grace bespeaking,
　　Faithful to thee through good report and ill;

2 To thee we come, and humbly make confession,
　　Faithless so oft, in thought and word and deed,
Asking that we may have, in true possession,
　　Thy free forgiveness in the hour of need.

3 In duties small be thou our inspiration,
　　In large affairs endue us with thy might;
Through faithful service cometh full salvation;
　　So may we serve, thy will our chief delight.

4 Not disobedient to the heavenly vision,
　　Faithful in all things, seeking not reward;
Then, following thee, may we fulfil our mission,
　　True to ourselves, our brethren, and our Lord.

W. Vaughan Jenkins (1868-1920)

294 CAITHNESS C.M.

Melody from the *Scottish Psalter* (1635)
(as harmonized in *The English Hymnal*, 1906)

Walking with God

O FOR a closer walk with God,
A calm and heavenly frame;
A light to shine upon the road
That leads me to the Lamb!

2 The dearest idol I have known,
Whate'er that idol be,
Help me to tear it from thy throne,
And worship only thee.

3 So shall my walk be close with God,
Calm and serene my frame;
So purer light shall mark the road
That leads me to the Lamb.

William Cowper (1731-1800)

295 ST HUGH C.M.   E. J. HOPKINS (1818-1901)

DEFEND me, Lord, from hour to hour,
    And bless thy servant's way;
Increase thy Holy Spirit's power
    Within me day by day.

2 Help me to be what I should be,
    And do what I should do,
And ever with thy Spirit free
    My daily life renew.

3 Grant me the courage from above
    Which thou dost give to all
Who hear thy word and know thy love
    And answer to thy call.

4 So may I daily grow in grace,
    Continuing thine alone,
Until I come to sing thy praise
    With saints around thy throne.

George Snow (1903-   )
(Based on the prayer used at Confirmation)

The Christian Life:

296

FIRST TUNE

VIENNA 77.77. Melody and bass by J. H. KNECHT (1752-1817)

SECOND TUNE

INNOCENTS 77.77. Melody of uncertain origin
Arranged by W. H. MONK (1823-89)
in *The Parish Choir* (1850)

Discipleship and Service

TAKE my life, and let it be
Consecrated, Lord, to thee;
Take my moments and my days,
Let them flow in ceaseless praise.

2 Take my hands, and let them move
At the impulse of thy love.
Take my feet, and let them be
Swift and purposeful for thee.

3 Take my voice, and let me sing
Always, only, for my King.
Take my intellect, and use
Every power as thou shalt choose.

4 Take my will, and make it thine:
It shall be no longer mine.
Take my heart; it is thine own:
It shall be thy royal throne.

5 Take my love; my Lord, I pour
At thy feet its treasure-store.
Take myself, and I will be
Ever, only, all for thee.

Frances R. Havergal† (1836-79)

The Christian Life:

297

FIRST TUNE

ST JAMES   C.M.

Melody, and most of the bass,
from *Select Psalms and Hymns* (1697)
Probably by R. COURTEVILLE

SECOND TUNE

ST PETER   C.M.

A. R. REINAGLE (1799-1877)

Discipleship and Service

My God, accept my heart this day,
　　And make it always thine,
That I from thee no more may stray,
　　No more from thee decline.

2 Before the Cross of him who died,
　　Behold, I prostrate fall;
Let every sin be crucified,
　　Let Christ be all in all.

3 Anoint me with thy heavenly grace,
　　And seal me for thine own;
That I may see thy glorious face,
　　And worship at thy throne.

4 Let every thought, and work, and word
　　To thee be ever given:
Then life shall be thy service, Lord,
　　And death the gate of heaven.

5 All glory to the Father be,
　　All glory to the Son,
All glory, Holy Ghost, to thee,
　　While endless ages run.

Verses 1-4 by Matthew Bridges† (1800-94)

The Christian Life:

298 WOLVERCOTE 76.76. D.   W. H. FERGUSON (1874-1950)

O JESUS, I have promised
  To serve thee to the end;
Be thou for ever near me,
  My Master and my Friend;
I shall not fear the battle
  If thou art by my side,
Nor wander from the pathway
  If thou wilt be my Guide.

2*O let me feel thee near me:
  The world is ever near;
I see the sights that dazzle,
  The tempting sounds I hear;
My foes are ever near me,
  Around me and within;
But, Jesus, draw thou nearer,
  And shield my soul from sin.

3 O let me hear thee speaking
  In accents clear and still,
Above the storms of passion,
  The murmurs of self-will;
O speak to reassure me,
  To hasten or control;
O speak, and make me listen,
  Thou Guardian of my soul.

4 O Jesus, thou hast promised
  To all who follow thee,
That where thou art in glory
  There shall thy servant be;
And, Jesus, I have promised
  To serve thee to the end;
O give me grace to follow,
  My Master and my Friend.

5 O let me see thy footmarks,
  And in them plant mine own;
My hope to follow duly
  Is in thy strength alone;
O guide me, call me, draw me,
  Uphold me to the end;
And then in heaven receive me,
  My Saviour and my Friend.

J. E. Bode (1816-74)

299 LEXHAM 11 10.11 10.   SYDNEY WATSON (1903-   )

(At Confirmation)

O HEAV'NLY grace in holy rite descending
To those who kneel for laying on of hands;
Thine be the strength, O Lord, for their defending;
Theirs be the vows renewed at thy demands.

2 Here as they pledge to follow thee as Saviour—
Jesus their Lord, who for the Church hath died—
So may they live within that blest behaviour
Thou hast enjoined, and they have ratified.

3 May they continue thine, O God, for ever,
Daily increasing in the Spirit's gift,
Until they bring the gift unto the Giver,
Where time is ended, and earth's shadows lift.

Robert N. Spencer (1877-   )

300 SONG 34 L.M.

Melody and bass by
ORLANDO GIBBONS (1583-1625)

Before Work

FORTH in thy name, O Lord, I go,
  My daily labour to pursue;
Thee, only thee, resolved to know,
  In all I think or speak or do.

2 The task thy wisdom hath assigned
  O let me cheerfully fulfil,
In all my works thy presence find,
  And prove thy good and perfect will.

3 Thee may I set at my right hand,
  Whose eyes my inmost substance see,
And labour on at thy command,
  And offer all my works to thee.

4 Give me to bear thy easy yoke,
  And every moment watch and pray,
And still to things eternal look,
  And hasten to thy glorious day;

5 For thee delightfully employ
  What'er thy bounteous grace hath given,
And run my course with even joy,
  And closely walk with thee to heaven.

Charles Wesley† (1707-88)

The Christian Life:

Irish Traditional Melody
Harmonized by ERIK ROUTLEY (1917-   )

LORD of creation, to thee be all praise!
Most mighty thy working, most wondrous thy ways!
Who reignest in glory no tongue can e'er tell,
Yet deign'st in the heart of the humble to dwell.

2 Lord of all power, I give thee my will,
In joyful obedience thy tasks to fulfil.
Thy bondage is freedom; thy service is song;
And, held in thy keeping, my weakness is strong.

3 Lord of all wisdom, I give thee my mind,
Rich truth that surpasseth man's knowledge to find.
What eye hath not seen and what ear hath not heard
Is taught by thy Spirit and shines from thy Word.

4 Lord of all bounty, I give thee my heart;
I praise and adore thee for all that thou art;
Thy love to inflame me, thy counsel to guide,
Thy presence to shield me, whate'er may betide.

5 Lord of all being, I give thee my all;
If e'er I disown thee, I stumble and fall;
But, sworn in glad service thy word to obey,
I walk in thy freedom to the end of the way.

Jack C. Winslow (1882-   )

The Christian Life:

302 MONKS GATE 65.65.66.65.

Adapted from an English Traditional Melody
by R. VAUGHAN WILLIAMS (1872-1958)

Discipleship and Service

WHO would true valour see,
  Let him come hither;
One here will constant be,
  Come wind, come weather;
There's no discouragement
Shall make him once relent
His first avowed intent
    To be a pilgrim.

2 Who so beset him round
    With dismal stories
  Do but themselves confound;
    His strength the more is.
  No lion can him fright;
  He'll with a giant fight;
  But he will have a right
      To be a pilgrim.

3 Hobgoblin nor foul fiend
    Can daunt his spirit;
  He knows he at the end
    Shall life inherit.
  Then fancies fly away,
  He'll fear not what men say;
  He'll labour night and day
      To be a pilgrim.

John Bunyan (1628-88)
From 'The Pilgrim's Progress'

In this poem Bunyan is praising the constancy of Mr Valiant-for-Truth, whose account of the discouragement that a pilgrim must expect has just ended with the words: 'I believed and therefore came out [of Dark-land], got into the Way, fought all that set themselves against me, and by believing am come to this Place'.

The Christian Life:

UNIVERSITY COLLEGE 77.77.   H. J. GAUNTLETT (1805-76)

OFT in danger, oft in woe,
Onward, Christians, onward go;
Bear the toil, maintain the strife,
Strengthened with the Bread of Life.

2 Onward, Christians, onward go,
Join the war, and face the foe;
Will ye flee in danger's hour?
Know ye not your Captain's power?

3 Let your drooping hearts be glad;
March in heavenly armour clad;
Fight, nor think the battle long,
Victory soon shall tune your song.

4 Let not sorrow dim your eye,
Soon shall every tear be dry;
Let not fears your course impede,
Great your strength, if great your need.

5 Onward then in battle move;
More than conquerors ye shall prove;
Though opposed by many a foe,
Christian soldiers, onward go!

H. Kirke White (1785-1806),
F. S. Fuller-Maitland and others (1827)

304 KNECHT 76.76.

J. H. KNECHT (1752-1817)
(harmony of last line altered)

O HAPPY band of pilgrims,
    If onward ye will tread
With Jesus as your fellow
    To Jesus as your head!

2 O happy, if ye labour
    As Jesus did for men;
O happy, if ye hunger
    As Jesus hungered then!

3 The Cross that Jesus carried
    He carried as your due;
The Crown that Jesus weareth
    He weareth it for you.

4 The faith by which ye see him,
    The hope in which ye yearn,
The love that through all troubles
    To him alone will turn;

5 The trials that beset you,
    The sorrows ye endure,
The manifold temptations
    That death alone can cure;

6 What are they but his jewels
    Of right celestial worth?
What are they but the ladder
    Set up to heaven on earth?

7 O happy band of pilgrims,
    Look upward to the skies,
Where such a light affliction
    Shall win you such a prize!

            J. M. Neale (1818-66)

The Christian Life:

305

SUSSEX 87.87.

Adapted from an English Traditional Melody
by R. VAUGHAN WILLIAMS (1872-1958)

SECOND TUNE

MARCHING 87.87.

MARTIN SHAW (1875-1958)

Discipleship and Service

FATHER, hear the prayer we offer:
　Not for ease that prayer shall be,
But for strength that we may ever
　Live our lives courageously.

2 Not for ever in green pastures
　Do we ask our way to be,
But the steep and rugged pathway
　May we tread rejoicingly.

3 Not for ever by still waters
　Would we idly rest and stay,
But would smite the living fountains
　From the rocks along our way.

4 Be our strength in hours of weakness,
　In our wanderings be our guide;
Through endeavour, failure, danger,
　Father, be thou at our side.

Mrs L. M. Willis (1824-1908) *and others*

The Christian Life:

First Tune

ST ETHELWALD S.M.   W. H. Monk (1823-89)

Second Tune

FROM STRENGTH TO STRENGTH D.S.M.   E. W. Naylor (1867-1934)
Alla marcia

1 Sol-diers of Christ, a - rise, And put your ar-mour on,

Strong in the strength which God sup-plies Through his E - ter-nal Son.

2 Strong in the Lord of Hosts And in his migh - ty power;

Who in the strength of Je-sus trusts Is more than con - que - ror.

Discipleship and Service

The Whole Armour of God

SOLDIERS of Christ, arise,
And put your armour on,
Strong in the strength which God supplies
Through his Eternal Son.

2   Strong in the Lord of Hosts
    And in his mighty power;
Who in the strength of Jesus trusts
    Is more than conqueror.

3   Stand then in his great might,
    With all his strength endued;
And take, to arm you for the fight,
    The panoply of God.

4 · Leave no unguarded place,
    No weakness of the soul,
Take every virtue, every grace,
    And fortify the whole.

5   From strength to strength go on,
    Wrestle, and fight, and pray,
Tread all the powers of darkness down,
    And win the well-fought day;

6   That, having all things done,
    And all your conflicts past,
Ye may o'ercome through Christ alone,
    And stand entire at last.

Charles Wesley (1707-88)
Based on Ephesians 6. 10-18

The Christian Life:

H. P. ALLEN (1869-1946)

1 Chris - tian, dost thou see them On the ho - ly ground,

How the troops of Mi-dian Prowl and prowl a-round?

Chris-tian, up— and smite— them, Count-ing gain but loss;

Smite them by— the me - rit Of the ho - ly Cross.

Discipleship and Service

CHRISTIAN, dost thou see them
On the holy ground,
How the troops of Midian
Prowl and prowl around?
Christian, up and smite them,
Counting gain but loss;
Smite them by the merit
Of the holy Cross.

2 Christian, dost thou feel them,
How they work within,
Striving, tempting, luring,
Goading into sin?
Christian, never tremble;
Never be down-cast;
Smite them by the virtue
Of the Lenten fast.

3 Christian, dost thou hear them,
How they speak thee fair?
'Always fast and vigil?
Always watch and prayer?'
Christian, answer boldly,
'While I breathe, I pray':
Peace shall follow battle,
Night shall end in day.

4 'Well I know thy trouble,
O my servant true;
Thou art very weary—
I was weary too;
But that toil shall make thee,
Some day, all mine own;
And the end of sorrow
Shall be near my throne.'

J. M. Neale† (1818-66)

The Christian Life:

308

RUSHFORD L.M.

HENRY G. LEY (1887-1962)

FIGHT the good fight with all thy might,
Christ is thy strength and Christ thy right;
Lay hold on life, and it shall be
Thy joy and crown eternally.

2 Run the straight race through God's good grace,
Lift up thine eyes and seek his face;
Life with its way before thee lies,
Christ is the path and Christ the prize.

3 Cast care aside; upon thy Guide
Lean, and his mercy will provide;
Lean, and the trusting soul shall prove
Christ is its life, and Christ its love.

4 Faint not nor fear, his arms are near;
He changeth not and thou art dear;
Only believe, and thou shalt see
That Christ is all in all to thee.

J. S. B. Monsell (1811-75)

A small figure indicates the number of notes to a syllable.

Discipleship and Service

DUKE STREET L.M.

Melody, and most of the bass, from
H. BOYD's *Psalm and Hymn Tunes* (1793)
Later attributed to J. HATTON (*d.*1793)

FIGHT the good fight with all thy might,
Christ is thy strength and Christ thy right;
Lay hold on life, and it shall be
Thy joy and crown eternally.

2 Run the straight race through God's good grace,
Lift up thine eyes and seek his face;
Life with its way before thee lies,
Christ is the path and Christ the prize.

3 Cast care aside; upon thy Guide
Lean, and his mercy will provide;
Lean, and the trusting soul shall prove
Christ is its life, and Christ its love.

4 Faint not nor fear, his arms are near;
He changeth not and thou art dear;
Only believe, and thou shalt see
That Christ is all in all to thee.

J. S. B. Monsell (1811-75)

The Christian Life:

309 TRURO L.M.   Melody from T WILLIAMS's *Psalmodia Evangelica* (1789)

Discipleship and Service

*Land of our birth, we pledge to thee
Our love and toil in the years to be;
When we are grown and take our place,
As men and women with our race.*

FATHER in heaven who lovest all,
O help thy children when they call;
That they may build from age to age
An undefilèd heritage.

2 Teach us to bear the yoke in youth,
With steadfastness and careful truth;
That, in our time, thy grace may give
The truth whereby the nations live.

3 Teach us to rule ourselves alway,
Controlled and cleanly night and day;
That we may bring, if need arise,
No maimed or worthless sacrifice.

4 Teach us to look, in all our ends,
On thee for judge, and not our friends;
That we, with thee, may walk uncowed
By fear or favour of the crowd.

5 Teach us the strength that cannot seek,
By deed or thought, to hurt the weak;
That, under thee, we may possess
Man's strength to comfort man's distress.

6 Teach us delight in simple things,
And mirth that has no bitter springs;
Forgiveness free of evil done,
And love to all men 'neath the sun.

*Land of our birth, our faith, our pride,
For whose dear sake our fathers died;
O Motherland, we pledge to thee,
Head, heart, and hand through the years to be!*

Rudyard Kipling (1865-1936)

The Christian Life:

310

FIRST TUNE

WINTON 10 10.10 10.

GEORGE DYSON (1883-1964)

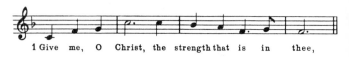

1 Give me, O Christ, the strength that is in thee,

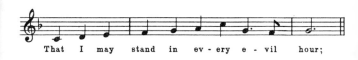

That I may stand in ev - ery e - vil hour;

Faints my poor heart ex - cept to thee I flee,

Rest - ing my weak - ness in thy per - fect power.

Discipleship and Service

SONG 24   10 10.10 10.

Melody and bass by
ORLANDO GIBBONS (1583-1625)

GIVE me, O Christ, the strength that is in thee,
  That I may stand in every evil hour;
Faints my poor heart except to thee I flee,
  Resting my weakness in thy perfect power.

2 Give me to see the foes that I must fight,
  Powers of the darkness, throned where thou shouldst reign,
Read the directings of thy wrath aright,
  Lest, striking flesh and blood, I strike in vain.

3 Give me to wear the armour that can guard:
  Over my breast thy blood-bought righteousness,
Faith for my shield, when fiery darts rain hard,
  Girded with truth, and shod with zeal to bless.

4 Give me to wield the weapon that is sure,
  Taking, through prayer, thy sword into my hand,
Word of thy wisdom, peaceable and pure,
  So, Christ my Conqu'ror, I shall conqu'ror stand.

H. C. Carter (1875-1954)
Based on Ephesians 6. 10-20

The Christian Life:

311

WOODLANDS 10 10.10 10. W. GREATOREX (1877-1949)

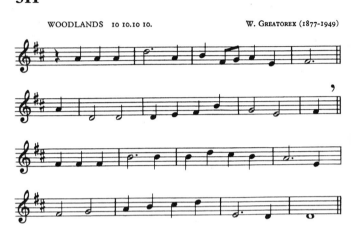

SECOND TUNE

MORESTEAD 10 10.10 10. SYDNEY WATSON (1903-)

Discipleship and Service

'LIFT up your hearts!' We lift them, Lord, to thee;
Here at thy feet none other may we see.
'Lift up your hearts!' E'en so, with one accord,
We lift them up, we lift them to the Lord.

2 Above the level of the former years,
  The mire of sin, the slough of guilty fears,
  The mist of doubt, the blight of love's decay,
  O Lord of Light, lift all our hearts to-day!

3*Above the swamps of subterfuge and shame,
  The deeds, the thoughts, that honour may not name,
  The halting tongue that dares not tell the whole,
  O Lord of Truth, lift every Christian soul!

4*Above the storms that vex this lower state,
  Pride, jealousy, and envy, rage, and hate,
  And cold mistrust that holds e'en friends apart,
  O Lord of Love, lift every brother's heart!

5 Lift every gift that thou thyself hast given;
  Low lies the best till lifted up to heaven;
  Low lie the bounding heart, the teeming brain,
  Till, sent from God, they mount to God again.

6 Then, as the trumpet-call in after years,
  'Lift up your hearts!', rings pealing in our ears,
  Still shall those hearts respond with full accord,
  'We lift them up, we lift them to the Lord!'

                    H. Montagu Butler (1833-1918)

312 WILDERNESS L.M.   R. S. THATCHER (1888-1957)

Verses 1-3

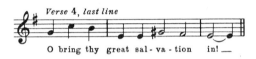

Verse 4, last line

O bring thy great sal - va - tion in! ____

ALMIGHTY Father, who dost give
The gift of life to all who live,
Look down on all earth's sin and strife,
And lift us to a nobler life.

2 Lift up our hearts, O King of Kings,
To brighter hopes and kindlier things,
To visions of a larger good,
And holier dreams of brotherhood.

3 The world is weary of its pain,
Of selfish greed and fruitless gain,
Of tarnished honour, falsely strong,
And all its ancient deeds of wrong.

4 Hear thou the prayer thy servants pray,
Uprising from all lands to-day,
And, o'er the vanquished powers of sin,
O bring thy great salvation in!

J. H. B. Masterman (1867-1933)

Discipleship and Service

313 BANGOR C.M.   Melody from W. Tans'ur's *Compleat Melody* (1735)

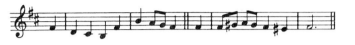

Science

G<small>OD</small>, who hast given us power to sound
   Depths hitherto unknown:
To probe earth's hidden mysteries,
   And make their might our own:

2 Great are thy gifts: yet greater far
   This gift, O God, bestow,
That as to knowledge we attain
   We may in wisdom grow.

3 Let wisdom's godly fear dispel
   All fears that hate impart;
Give understanding to the mind,
   And with new mind new heart.

4 So for thy glory and man's good
   May we thy gifts employ,
Lest, maddened by the lust of power,
   Man shall himself destroy.

G. W. Briggs (1875-1959)

National

314 CROFT'S 136th   66.66.88.

Melody and bass by
Dr William Croft (1678-1727)

O   Lord,   stretch   forth   thy   might - y   hand,

And   guard and   bless   our   fa - ther - land.

National

To thee our God we fly
For mercy and for grace;
O hear our lowly cry,
And hide not thou thy face.

> *O Lord, stretch forth thy mighty hand,*
> *And guard and bless our fatherland.*

2 Arise, O Lord of hosts!
Be jealous for thy name,
And drive from out our coasts
The sins that put to shame:

3 The powers ordained by thee
With heav'nly wisdom bless;
May they thy servants be,
And rule in righteousness:

4 The Church of thy dear Son
Inflame with love's pure fire,
Bind her once more in one,
And life and truth inspire:

5*Give peace, Lord, in our time;
O let no foe draw nigh,
Nor lawless deed of crime
Insult thy majesty:

6 Though all unworthy, still
Thy people, Lord, are we;
And for our God we will
None other have but thee:

W. Walsham How† (1823-97)

315

KING'S LYNN 76.76.D.

English Traditional Melody
Arranged by R. VAUGHAN WILLIAMS (1872-1958)

O GOD of earth and altar,
  Bow down and hear our cry,
Our earthly rulers falter,
  Our people drift and die;
The walls of gold entomb us,
  The swords of scorn divide,
Take not thy thunder from us,
  But take away our pride.

2 From all that terror teaches,
    From lies of tongue and pen,
  From all the easy speeches
    That comfort cruel men,
  From sale and profanation
    Of honour and the sword,
  From sleep and from damnation,
    Deliver us, good Lord!

3 Tie in a living tether
    The prince and priest and thrall,
  Bind all our lives together,
    Smite us and save us all;
  In ire and exultation
    Aflame with faith, and free,
  Lift up a living nation,
    A single sword to thee.

G. K. Chesterton (1874-1936)

National

LITTLE BADDOW 76.76.D. C. ARMSTRONG GIBBS (1889-1960)

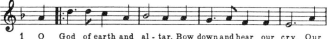

1 O God of earth and al - tar, Bow down and hear our cry, Our
2 (From) all that ter - ror teach-es, From lies of tongue and pen, From

earth - ly ru - lers fal - ter, Our peo - ple drift and die; The
all the ea - sy speech - es That com-fort cru - el men, From

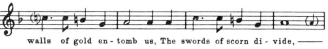

walls of gold en - tomb us, The swords of scorn di - vide, ——
sale and pro - fa - na - tion Of hon - our and the sword, From

Take not thy thun - der from us, But take a - way our pride.
sleep and from dam - na - tion, De - liv - er us, good Lord!

Before v. 2 *Before v.3*

2 From 3 Tie in a liv - ing teth - er The

315 (continued)

prince and priest and thrall, Bind all our lives to - geth-er,

Smite us and save us all; In __ ire and ex - ul -

ta - tion A - flame with faith, and free,

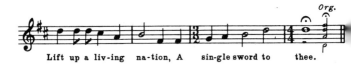

Lift up a liv-ing na-tion, A sin-gle sword to thee.

G. K. Chesterton (1874-1936)

316 WAREHAM L.M.

Melody by W. KNAPP (1698-1768)

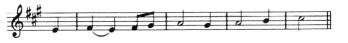

REJOICE, O land, in God thy might;
His will obey, him serve aright;
For thee the saints uplift their voice:
Fear not, O land, in God rejoice.

2 Glad shalt thou be, with blessing crowned,
With joy and peace thou shalt abound;
Yea, love with thee shall make his home
Until thou see God's kingdom come.

3 He shall forgive thy sins untold:
Remember thou his love of old;
Walk in his way, his word adore,
And keep his truth for evermore.

Robert Bridges (1844-1930)
Based on Joel 2. 21

National

First Tune

LINGWOOD 87.87.87.

C. Armstrong Gibbs (1889-1960)

1 Lord of Lords and King E - ter - nal, Who in ev - er

boun-teous ways This fair land hast blessed and gui - ded,

Shield-ing through tem-pest-uous days, Un - to thee in

rit. (v.5 only)

grate-ful hom-age Raise we ju - bi - lee and praise.

Second Tune

RHUDDLAN 87.87.87.

Welsh Traditional Melody
(as harmonized in *The English Hymnal*, 1906)

National

A Hymn for Church and Country

LORD of Lords and King Eternal,
  Who in ever bounteous ways
This fair land hast blessed and guided,
  Shielding through tempestuous days,
Unto thee in grateful homage
  Raise we jubilee and praise.

2 On thy Church in rich abundance
    Be thy quick'ning grace outpoured;
  Shame our pride and quell our factions,
    Smite them with the Spirit's sword,
  Till the world, our love beholding,
    Owns thy might and knows thee Lord.

3 Look in mercy on the nations;
    Bid their warring discords cease;
  To the homeless and the captives
    Send thy succour and release;
  And on all this earth's sore travail
    Breathe the healing of thy peace.

4 Speed the feet of thine apostles
    Who to every land and race
  Tell the tidings of salvation,
    Bear the treasures of thy grace,
  Till the flood-tide of thy Spirit
    Wakes new life in every place.

5 Lord, who by thy saving Passion
    Turnest all man's sin to gain,
  Wresting in thy risen glory
    Vict'ry from the cross of pain,
  Dawn, O dawn, upon our darkness
    With the splendours of thy reign.

Jack C. Winslow† (1882-   )

318 JERUSALEM D.L.M.
Slow, but with animation

C. HUBERT H. PARRY (1848-1918)

Org.

1 And did those

feet in an - cient time Walk up - on Eng-land's moun-tains

green? And was the ho - ly Lamb of — God On Eng-land's

pleas-ant pas-tures seen? And did the `coun-ten-ance di -

vine Shine forth up - on our cloud-ed hills? And was Je -

ru - sa - lem build - ed here A-mong those dark sa - tan - ic

National

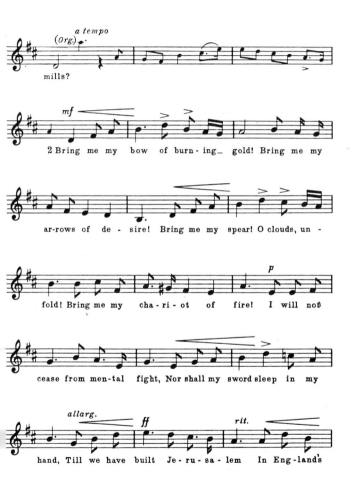

mills?

2 Bring me my bow of burn-ing_ gold! Bring me my ar-rows of de - sire! Bring me my spear! O clouds, un - fold! Bring me my cha - ri - ot of fire! I will not cease from men-tal fight, Nor shall my sword sleep in my hand, Till we have built Je - ru - sa - lem In Eng-land's

318 (continued)

green and pleas - ant land._____

AND did those feet in ancient time
    Walk upon England's mountains green?
And was the holy Lamb of God
    On England's pleasant pastures seen?
And did the countenance divine
    Shine forth upon our clouded hills?
And was Jerusalem builded here
    Among those dark satanic mills?

2 Bring me my bow of burning gold!
    Bring me my arrows of desire!
Bring me my spear! O clouds, unfold!
    Bring me my chariot of fire!
I will not cease from mental fight,
    Nor shall my sword sleep in my hand,
Till we have built Jerusalem
    In England's green and pleasant land.

William Blake† (1757-1827)

satanic mills] *The 'Mills of Satan' were part of the elaborate imagery of William Blake's late*
poems. Christianity, he said, was above all 'the liberty. . . to exercise the Divine Arts of Imagi
nation', and by contrast the Mills were his symbol for the workings of mere logic and reason—
whether in philosophy, religion, or the arts—when divorced from creative imagination.

National

Origin uncertain
First popularized in 1745

GOD save our gracious Queen,
Long live our noble Queen,
   God save the Queen!
Send her victorious,
Happy and glorious,
Long to reign over us;
   God save the Queen!

2*Thy choicest gifts in store
On her be pleased to pour,
   Long may she reign;
May she defend our laws,
And ever give us cause
To sing with heart and voice
   God save the Queen!

From the version of 1745†

320 CREDITON C.M.
Melody from THOMAS CLARK'S
2nd Set of Psalm Tunes [for] Country Choirs (c.1807)

Sunday

THIS is the day the Lord hath made,
He calls the hours his own;
Let heav'n rejoice, let earth be glad,
And praise surround the throne.

2 To-day he rose and left the dead,
And Satan's empire fell;
To-day the saints his triumph spread,
And all his wonders tell.

3 Hosanna to the anointed King,
To David's holy Son!
O help us, Lord, descend and bring
Salvation from thy throne.

4 Blest be the Lord, who comes to men
With messages of grace;
Who comes, in God his Father's name,
To save our sinful race.

5 Hosanna in the highest strains
The Church on earth can raise;
The highest heav'ns in which he reigns
Shall give him nobler praise.

Isaac Watts† (1674-1748)
Based on Psalm 118. 24-26

Sunday

321 LANSDOWNE L.M.   E. NORMAN GREENWOOD (1902-62)

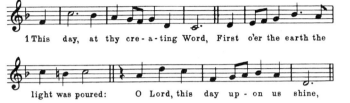

1 This day, at thy cre-a-ting Word, First o'er the earth the

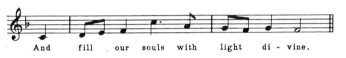

light was poured: O Lord, this day up-on us shine,

And fill our souls with light di - vine.

Sunday

THIS day, at thy creating Word,
First o'er the earth the light was poured:
O Lord, this day upon us shine,
And fill our souls with light divine.

2 This day the Lord, for sinners slain,
In might victorious rose again:
O Jesu, may we raisèd be
From death of sin to life in thee.

3 This day the Holy Spirit came
With fiery tongues of cloven flame:
O Spirit, fill our hearts this day
With grace to hear and grace to pray.

4 O day of light, and life, and grace,
From earthly toil a resting-place!
Thy hallowed hours, best gift of love,
Give we again to God above!

5 All praise to God the Father be,
All praise, Eternal Son, to thee,
Whom with the Spirit we adore
For ever and for evermore.

Vv. 1-4 by W. Walsham How† (1823-97)

322 SOLEMNIS HAEC FESTIVITAS L.M.   Melody from *Paris Gradual* (1685)

Iam lucis orto sidere
Deum precemur supplices,
Ut in diurnis actibus
Nos servet a nocentibus.

2 Linguam refrenans temperet,
Ne litis horror insonet;
Visum fovendo contegat,
Ne vanitates hauriat.

3 Sint pura cordis intima,
Absistat et vecordia;
Carnis terat superbiam
Potus cibique parcitas:

4 Ut, cum dies abscesserit,
Noctemque sors reduxerit,
Mundi per abstinentiam
Ipsi canamus gloriam.

5 Deo Patri sit gloria,
Eiusque soli Filio,
Sancto simul cum Spiritu,
Et nunc et in perpetuum.

Before 8th century

For translations, see Nos. 323 and 324.

Morning

323 SOLEMNIS HAEC FESTIVITAS L.M.   Melody from *Paris Gradual* (1685)

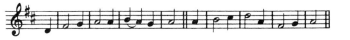

Iam lucis orto sidere

Now that the daylight fills the sky,
We lift our hearts to God on high,
That he, in all we do or say,
Would keep us free from harm today.

2 May he restrain our tongues from strife,
And shield from anger's din our life,
And guard with watchful care our eyes
From earth's absorbing vanities.

3 O may our inmost hearts be pure,
From thoughts of folly kept secure;
Be all our mortal pride of sense
Worn down by patient abstinence.

4 So we, when this new day is gone,
And night in turn is drawing on,
With conscience by the world unstained
Shall praise his name for victory gained.

5 All praise to God the Father be,
All praise, Eternal Son, to thee,
Whom with the Spirit we adore
For ever and for evermore.

Tr. J. M. Neale‡ (1818-66)

For another translation, see No. 324.

324 AMEN COURT 66.84.　　　　　　　　　J. DYKES BOWER (1905-　　)

Iam lucis orto sidere

THE star of morn has risen:
O Lord, to thee we pray;
O uncreated Light of Light,
Guide thou our way.

2　Sinless be tongue and hand,
　And innocent the mind;
Let simple truth be on our lips,
　Our hearts be kind.

3　As day rolls swiftly on,
　Still, Lord, our guardian be;
And keep the entry of our hearts
　From evil free.

4　Grant that our daily toil
　May to thy glory tend;
And as our hours begin with thee,
　So may they end.

Before 8th century
Tr. G. Phillimore (1821-84) and others

This is a free translation of No. 322. See also No. 323.

Morning

325 CHRISTE SANCTORUM 11 11 11.5.

Melody from *Paris Antiphoner* (1681)
Harmonized by R. VAUGHAN WILLIAMS.
(as arranged in *The BBC Hymn Book*, 1951)

Nocte surgentes vigilemus omnes

FATHER, we praise thee, now the night is over,
Active and watchful, stand we all before thee;
Singing we offer prayer and meditation:
    Thus we adore thee.

2 Monarch of all things, fit us for thy mansions;
  Banish our weakness, health and wholeness sending;
  Bring us to heavèn, where thy saints united
    Joy without ending.

3 All-holy Father, Son and equal Spirit,
  Trinity blessèd, send us thy salvation;
  Thine is the glory, gleaming and resounding
    Through all creation.

10th century or earlier
Tr. Percy Dearmer (1867-1936)

Times and Occasions:

Melody and figured bass
by F. H. Barthélemon (1741-1808)
(bass of 2nd bar altered)

PART I

Awake, my soul, and with the sun
Thy daily stage of duty run;
Shake off dull sloth, and joyful rise
To pay thy morning sacrifice.

2 Redeem thy mis-spent time that's past,
And live this day as if thy last;
Improve thy talent with due care;
For the great day thyself prepare.

3 Let all thy converse be sincere,
Thy conscience as the noon-day clear;
Think how all-seeing God thy ways
And all thy secret thoughts surveys.

4 Wake, and lift up thyself, my heart,
And with the angels bear thy part,
Who all night long unwearied sing
High praise to the eternal King.

5 Praise God, from whom all blessings flow,
Praise him, all creatures here below,
Praise him above, ye heavenly host,
Praise Father, Son, and Holy Ghost.

Morning

PART 2

ALL praise to thee, who safe hast kept
And hast refreshed me whilst I slept;
Grant, Lord, when I from death shall wake,
I may of endless light partake.

2 Lord, I my vows to thee renew,
Disperse my sins as morning dew;
Guard my first springs of thought and will,
And with thy self my spirit fill.

3 Direct, control, suggest, this day,
All I design or do or say;
That all my powers, with all their might,
In thy sole glory may unite.

4 Praise God, from whom all blessings flow,
Praise him, all creatures here below,
Praise him above, ye heavenly host,
Praise Father, Son, and Holy Ghost.

Thomas Ken† (1637-1711)

327 MEINE ARMUTH 847.D.

Melody and figured bass by
J. A. FREYLINGHAUSEN (1670-1739)

Morning

Seele! du musst munter werden

COME, my soul, thou must be waking,
    Now is breaking
  O'er the earth another day:
Come to him who made this splendour,
    See thou render
  All thy feeble strength can pay.

2 Gladly hail the light returning;
    Ready burning
  Be the incense of thy powers:
For the night is safely ended,
    God hath tended
  With his care thy helpless hours.

3 Pray that he may prosper ever
    Each endeavour,
  When thine aim is good and true;
But that he may ever thwart thee,
    And convert thee,
  When thou evil wouldst pursue.

4 May'st thou then on life's last morrow,
    Free from sorrow,
  Pass away in slumber sweet;
And, released from death's dark sadness,
    Rise in gladness,
  That far brighter Sun to greet.

5 God's own light meanwhile be heeding,
    Onward leading,
  Still his Spirit's voice obey:
Soon shall joy thy brow be wreathing,
    Splendour breathing,
  Fairer than the fairest day.

F. R. L. von Canitz (1654-99)
Tr. H. J. Buckoll† (1803-71)

Times and Occasions:

328 MELCOMBE L.M.   Melody by S. WEBBE the elder (1740-1816)

Morning

NEW every morning is the love
Our wakening and uprising prove;
Through sleep and darkness safely brought,
Restored to life, and power, and thought.

2 New mercies, each returning day,
  Hover around us while we pray;
  New perils past, new sins forgiven,
  New thoughts of God, new hopes of heaven.

3 If on our daily course our mind
  Be set to hallow all we find,
  New treasures still, of countless price,
  God will provide for sacrifice.

4 The trivial round, the common task,
  Will furnish all we ought to ask;
  Room to deny ourselves—a road
  To bring us, daily, nearer God.

5 Only, O Lord, in thy dear love
  Fit us for perfect rest above;
  And help us, this and every day,
  To live more nearly as we pray.

John Keble† (1792-1866)

329 HOMINUM AMATOR 76.76.88.   W. H. FERGUSON (1874-1950)

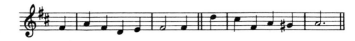

A Morning Hymn

THY love, O Lord, has kept us,
    And brought us through the night;
We seek thy power to guide us
    Who art the source of light.
Be near us, Father, when we pray,
And lead us through the coming day.

2 The perils that await us
    Are known, O Lord, to thee;
The sins that most beset us,
    Our insufficiency.
Uphold us with thy mighty hand,
And by thy grace we firm shall stand.

3 From error and self-seeking
    And all the snares that bind;
From pride that slays the spirit,
    And greed that warps the mind;
From hate and fear our souls defend,
And may we serve thee to the end.

                    Donald Hughes (1911-   )

Evening

330 LESSINGTON Irregular.

R. S. THATCHER (1888-1957)

1 Hail, glad-dening Light, of his pure glo-ry poured—

Who is th'im-mor-tal Fa-ther, heav'n-ly, blest,

Ho-li-est of Ho-lies, Je-sus Christ our Lord!

2 Now we are come to the sun's— hour of rest,——

The lights of eve - ning round us shine,

We hymn the Fa-ther, Son, and Ho-ly Spi-rit di - vine.

[*continued overleaf*

330 *(continued)*

3 Wor-thiest art thou at all times to be sung ___

With un - de - fil - èd tongue, Son of our

God, ___ Gi - ver of Life, a - lone;

There-fore in all the world thy glo-ries, Lord, they own.

Φῶς ἱλαρόν

HAIL, gladdening Light, of his pure glory poured
Who is the immortal Father, heavenly, blest,
Holiest of Holies, Jesus Christ our Lord!

2   Now we are come to the sun's hour of rest,
    The lights of evening round us shine,
We hymn the Father, Son, and Holy Spirit divine.

3   Worthiest art thou at all times to be sung
    With undefilèd tongue,
Son of our God, Giver of Life, alone:
Therefore in all the world thy glories, Lord, they own.

Before 4th century
Tr. J. Keble (1792-1866)

The Greek original of this (and of No. 331) is one of the very earliest Christian hymns. It was sung at evening service at the lighting of the lamps, and St Basil in the 4th century already refers to it as 'ancient'.

Evening

331 NUNC DIMITTIS 667.D.

Melody of metrical Nunc Dimittis in *Genevan Psalter* (1551). Probably composed by L. Bourgeois, *c*.1547

1 O glad-some Light, O grace Of God the Fa-ther's face,

Th'e - ter-nal splen-dour wear-ing; Ce - les-tial, ho-ly, blest,

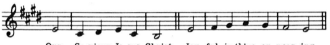

Our Sa-viour Je-sus Christ, Joy-ful in thine ap-pear-ing.

Φῶς ἱλαρόν

O GLADSOME Light, O grace
Of God the Father's face,
Th' eternal splendour wearing;
Celestial, holy, blest,
Our Saviour Jesus Christ,
Joyful in thine appearing.

2   Now, ere day fadeth quite,
We see the evening light,
Our wonted hymn outpouring;
Father of might unknown,
Thee, his incarnate Son,
And Holy Spirit adoring.

3   To thee of right belongs
All praise of holy songs,
O Son of God, Lifegiver;
Thee therefore, O Most High,
The world doth glorify,
And shall exalt for ever.

Before 4th century
Tr. Robert Bridges (1844-1930)

See also the translation opposite.

332 TE LUCIS L.M.   Plainsong Melody, Mode viii

1 Te lu-cis an-te ter-mi-num, Re-rum cre-a-tor, pos-ci-mus,

Ut sol-i-ta cle-men-ti-a Sis prae-sul ad cus-to-di-am.

A - men.

TE lucis ante terminum,
Rerum creator, poscimus,
Ut solita clementia
Sis praesul ad custodiam.

2 Procul recedant somnia
Et noctium phantasmata,
Ut expulsis insaniis
Quies in te sit integra.

3 Praesta, Pater omnipotens,
Per Iesum Christum Dominum,
Qui tecum in perpetuum
Regnat cum sancto Spiritu.

Before 8th century‡

For translation see No. 333.

Evening

333 ILLSLEY L.M.

Melody, and most of the harmony,
by J. Bishop (1665-1737)

Te lucis ante terminum

BEFORE the ending of the day,
Creator of the world, we pray
That with thy wonted favour thou
Wouldst be our guard and keeper now.

2 From all ill dreams defend our eyes,
From nightly fears and fantasies;
That we from cares and follies free
May find unbroken rest in thee.

3 O Father, that we ask be done,
Through Jesus Christ, thine only Son;
Who, with the Holy Ghost and thee,
Doth live and reign eternally.

Tr. J. M. Neale‡ (1818-66)

334 TALLIS' CANON L.M.

Melody, and most of the harmony,
by THOMAS TALLIS (c.1505-1585)
As shortened by T. RAVENSCROFT (*Psalmes*, 1621)

GLORY to thee, my God, this night
For all the blessings of the light;
Keep me, O keep me, King of Kings,
Beneath thy own almighty wings.

2 Forgive me, Lord, for thy dear Son,
The ill that I this day have done,
That with the world, myself, and thee,
I, ere I sleep, at peace may be.

3 Teach me to live, that I may dread
The grave as little as my bed;
Teach me to die, that so I may
Rise glorious at the aweful day.

4 O may my soul on thee repose,
And with sweet sleep mine eyelids close,
Sleep that may me more vigorous make
To serve my God when I awake.

5*When in the night I sleepless lie,
My soul with heavenly thoughts supply;
Let no ill dreams disturb my rest,
No powers of darkness me molest.

6 Praise God, from whom all blessings flow,
Praise him, all creatures here below,
Praise him above, ye heavenly host,
Praise Father, Son, and Holy Ghost.

Thomas Ken (1637-1711)

335 AR HYD Y NOS 84.84.88.84. Welsh Traditional Melody

GOD, that madest earth and heaven,
    Darkness and light;
Who the day for toil hast given,
    For rest the night;
May thine angel-guards defend us,
Slumber sweet thy mercy send us,
Holy dreams and hopes attend us,
    This livelong night.

2 Guard us waking, guard us sleeping;
    And, when we die,
May we in thy mighty keeping
    All peaceful lie:
When the last dread call shall wake us,
Do not thou our God forsake us,
But to reign in glory take us
    With thee on high.

Verse 1 by R. Heber (1783-1826)
Verse 2 by R. Whateley (1787-1863)

336 SEELENBRÄUTIGAM 55.88.55. Melody from *Geistreiches Gesang-Buch* (Darmstadt, 1698)
Attributed to A. DRESE (1620–1701)

ROUND me falls the night;
  Saviour, be my light;
Through the hours in darkness shrouded
Let me see thy face unclouded;
  Let thy glory shine
  In this heart of mine.

2   Earthly work is done,
      Earthly sounds are none;
   Rest in sleep and silence seeking,
   Let me hear thee softly speaking;
      In my spirit's ear
      Whisper, 'I am near'.

3   Blessèd, heav'nly Light,
      Shining through earth's night;
   Voice, that oft of love hast told me;
   Arms, so strong to clasp and hold me;
      Thou thy watch wilt keep,
      Saviour, o'er my sleep.

W. Romanis (1824–99)

Evening

337 ST CLEMENT 98.98.

C. C. SCHOLEFIELD (1839-1904)

THE day thou gavest, Lord, is ended,
    The darkness falls at thy behest;
To thee our morning hymns ascended,
    Thy praise shall sanctify our rest.

2 We thank thee that thy Church unsleeping,
    While earth rolls onward into light,
Through all the world her watch is keeping,
    And rests not now by day or night.

3 As o'er each continent and island
    The dawn leads on another day,
The voice of prayer is never silent,
    Nor dies the strain of praise away.

4 The sun that bids us rest is waking
    Our brethren 'neath the western sky,
And hour by hour fresh lips are making
    Thy wondrous doings heard on high.

5 So be it, Lord; thy throne shall never,
    Like earth's proud empires, pass away;
Thy kingdom stands, and grows for ever,
    Till all thy creatures own thy sway.

J. Ellerton (1826-93)

338

FIRST TUNE

Evening

SAVIOUR, again to thy dear name we raise
With one accord our parting hymn of praise.
Guard thou the lips from sin, the hearts from shame,
That in this house have called upon thy name.

2 Grant us thy peace, Lord, through the coming night;
   Turn thou for us its darkness into light;
   From harm and danger keep thy servants free;
   For dark and light are both alike to thee.

3 Grant us thy peace throughout our earthly life;
   Peace to thy Church from error and from strife;
   Peace to our land, the fruit of truth and love;
   Peace in each heart, thy Spirit from above:

4 Thy peace in sorrow, balm of every pain;
   Thy peace in death, the hope to rise again;
   Then, when thy voice shall bid our conflict cease,
   Call us, O Lord, to thine eternal peace.

J. Ellerton (1826-93)

Times and Occasions:

339

INNSBRUCK   776.778.

German Traditional Melody, as set by
J. S. BACH in the *St Matthew Passion* (1729)

Second Version

INNSBRUCK   776.778.

Variant form of the melody,
with harmony chiefly based on J. S. BACH

Evening

Nun ruhen alle Wälder

THE duteous day now closeth,
Each flower and tree reposeth,
  Shade creeps o'er wild and wood:
Let us, as night is falling,
On God our Maker calling,
  Give thanks to him, the Giver good.

2 Now all the heav'nly splendour
Breaks forth in starlight tender
  From myriad worlds unknown;
And man, the marvel seeing,
Forgets his selfish being,
  For joy of beauty not his own.

3 His care he drowneth yonder,
Lost in the abyss of wonder;
  To heav'n his soul doth steal:
This life he disesteemeth,
The day it is that dreameth,
  That doth from truth his vision seal.

4 Awhile his mortal blindness
May miss God's loving-kindness,
  And grope in faithless strife:
But when life's day is over
Shall death's fair night discover
  The fields of everlasting life.

Robert Bridges (1844-1930)
  Based on the German of P. Gerhardt (1607-76)

340 RENDEZ À DIEU 98.98.D.

Melody from *La Forme des Prieres et Chantz Ecclesiastiques* (Strasbourg, 1545) (2nd line as in *Genevan Psalter* of 1551)

1 As now the day draws near its end-ing, While eve-ning

steals o'er earth and sky, Once more to thee our hymns as-cend-ing

Sound forth thy prais-es, Lord Most High. Thine is the splen-dour of the

morn-ing, Thine is the eve-ning's tran-quil light; Thine too the

veil which till the dawn-ing Shrouds all the earth in peace-ful night.

Evening

As now the day draws near its ending,
  While evening steals o'er earth and sky,
Once more to thee our hymns ascending
  Sound forth thy praises, Lord Most High.
Thine is the splendour of the morning,
  Thine is the evening's tranquil light;
Thine too the veil which till the dawning
  Shrouds all the earth in peaceful night.

2 Maker of worlds beyond our knowing,
    Realms which no human eye can scan,
  Yet in thy wondrous love bestowing
    Through Christ thy saving aid to man;
  Lord, while the hymns of all creation
    Rise ever to thy throne above,
  We too would join in adoration,
    Owning thee God of changeless love.

> *Jack C. Winslow* (1882-   )
>   *Partly based on a hymn by J. Ellerton* (1826-93)

Times and Occasions:

341 WIR PFLÜGEN 76.76.D.66.84.

Melody by J. A. P. SCHULZ (1747-1800), as
arranged by J. B. DYKES in *Hymns A & M* (1868)
(harmony slightly revised)

All good gifts a - round us   Are sent from heav'n a - bove;

Then thank the Lord, O thank the Lord, For all ___ his love.

Harvest Thanksgiving

Wir pflügen und wir streuen

WE plough the fields, and scatter
  The good seed on the land,
But it is fed and watered
  By God's almighty hand;
He sends the snow in winter,
  The warmth to swell the grain,
The breezes and the sunshine,
  And soft refreshing rain.

  All good gifts around us
    Are sent from heav'n above;
  Then thank the Lord, O thank the Lord,
    For all his love.

2 He only is the Maker
  Of all things near and far,
He paints the wayside flower,
  He lights the evening star.
The winds and waves obey him,
  By him the birds are fed;
Much more to us, his children,
  He gives our daily bread:

3 We thank thee then, O Father,
  For all things bright and good;
The seed-time and the harvest,
  Our life, our health, our food.
No gifts have we to offer
  For all thy love imparts,
But that which thou desirest,
  Our humble, thankful hearts:

M. Claudius (1740-1815)
Tr. J. M. Campbell (1817-78)

342 ES FLOG EIN KLEINS WALDVÖGELEIN 76.76.D.

German Traditional Melody
(17th century or earlier)

SING to the Lord of harvest,
   Sing songs of love and praise;
With joyful hearts and voices
   Your alleluias raise.
By him the rolling seasons
   In fruitful order move;
Sing to the Lord of harvest
   A joyous song of love.

2 By him the clouds drop fatness,
   The deserts bloom and spring,
The hills leap up in gladness,
   The valleys laugh and sing.
He filleth with his fullness
   All things with large increase,
He crowns the year with goodness,
   With plenty and with peace.

3 Bring to his sacred altar
   The gifts his goodness gave,
The golden sheaves of harvest,
   The souls he died to save.
Your hearts lay down before him
   When at his feet ye fall,
And with your lives adore him,
   Who gave his life for all.

J. S. B. Monsell† (1811-75)
Based on Psalm 65

For Those at Sea

343 MELITA 88.88.88. J. B. DYKES (1823-76)

For Those at Sea

ETERNAL Father, strong to save,
Whose arm doth bind the restless wave,
Who bidd'st the mighty ocean deep
Its own appointed limits keep:
    O hear us when we cry to thee
    For those in peril on the sea.

2 O Saviour, whose almighty word
The winds and waves submissive heard,
Who walkedst on the foaming deep,
And calm amid its rage didst sleep:
    O hear us when we cry to thee
    For those in peril on the sea.

3 O sacred Spirit, who didst brood
Upon the waters dark and rude,
And bid their angry tumult cease,
And give, for wild confusion, peace:
    O hear us when we cry to thee
    For those in peril on the sea.

4 O Trinity of love and power,
Our brethren shield in danger's hour;
From rock and tempest, fire and foe,
Protect them wheresoe'er they go;
    And ever let there rise to thee
    Glad hymns of praise from land and sea.

W. Whiting† (1825-78)

344 FAMOUS MEN   R. VAUGHAN WILLIAMS (1872-1958)
Andante con moto

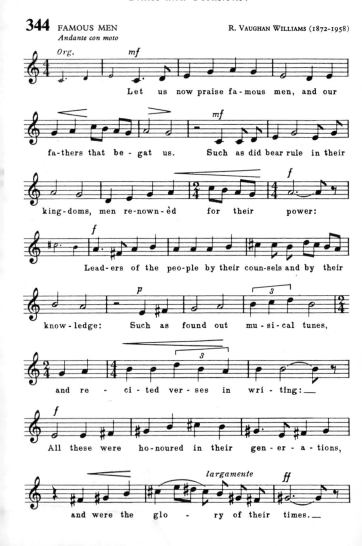

Let us now praise fa-mous men, and our fa-thers that be-gat us. Such as did bear rule in their king-doms, men re-nown-èd for their power: Lead-ers of the peo-ple by their coun-sels and by their know-ledge: Such as found out mu-si-cal tunes, and re-ci-ted ver-ses in wri-ting:__ All these were ho-noured in their gen-er-a-tions, and were the glo - ry of their times.__

Commemoration

And some there be, which have no me-mo-ri-al; who are pe-rished, as though they had ne-ver been.— Their bo-dies are bu-ried in peace;— but their name liv-eth for ev-er-more.—

Words selected from Ecclesiasticus 44.

345

FIRST TUNE

LONGWOOD 10 10.10 10.   J. BARNBY (1838-96)

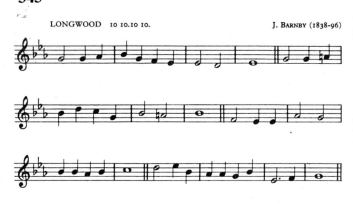

SECOND TUNE

MAGDA 10 10.10 10.   R. VAUGHAN WILLIAMS (1872-1958)

End of Term

For the End of Term (Evening)

LORD, thou hast brought us to our journey's end:
Once more to thee our evening prayers ascend;
Once more we stand to praise thee for the past;
Grant prayer and praise be honest at the last!

2 For all the joys which thou hast deigned to share,
For all the pains which thou hast helped to bear,
For all our friends, in life and death the same,
We thank thee, Lord, and praise thy glorious name.

3 If from thy paths, by chastening undismayed,
If for thy gifts ungrateful, we have strayed,
If in thy house our prayers were faint and few,
Forgive, O Lord, and build our hearts anew.

4 If we have learnt to feel our neighbour's need,
To fight for truth in thought and word and deed,
If these be lessons which the years have taught,
Then stablish, Lord, what thou in us hast wrought.

5 So be our rest thy palaces most fair,
Not built with hands, whose stones thy praise declare:
Where war is not, and all thy sons are free,
Where thou art known, and all is known in thee!

C. A. Alington (1872-1955)

At a Farewell

346 RANDOLPH 98.89.   R. Vaughan Williams (1872-1958)

At a Farewell

GOD be with you till we meet again,
  May he through the days direct you;
  May he in life's storms protect you;
God be with you till we meet again.

2 God be with you till we meet again;
  And when doubts and fears oppress you,
  May his holy peace possess you.
God be with you till we meet again.

3 God be with you till we meet again;
  In distress his grace sustain you;
  In success from pride restrain you;
God be with you till we meet again.

4 God be with you till we meet again.
  May he go through life beside you,
  And through death in safety guide you;
God be with you till we meet again.

Donald Hughes (1911-   )
  Partly based on a hymn by J. E. Rankin (1828-1904)

INDEXES

INDEX OF AUTHORS, TRANSLATORS, AND SOURCES OF WORDS

The use of italics for a hymn-number indicates a Translation.

Authors, Translators, and Sources of Words

Authors, Translators, and Sources of Words

GENERAL INDEX

General Index

General Index

General Index

General Index

General Index

General Index

General Index

General Index

General Index

CANTICLES

AND

PSALMS

Te Deum Laudamus
A Hymn of the Western Church, *circa* A.D. 400

Praise to the Holy Trinity

1 We praise | thee O | God:
  we acknowledge | thee to | be the | Lord.

2 All the earth doth | worship | thee:
  the | Father | ever- | lasting.

3 To thee all Angels | cry a- | loud:
  the Heav'ns and | all the | Powers there- | in.

*4 To thee | Cherubin · and | Seraphin ‖ con- | tin-ual- | ly do
  | cry,

5 Holy | Holy | Holy:
  Lord | God of | Saba- | oth;

*6 Heav'n and | earth are | full ‖ of the | Majes-ty | of thy
  | Glory.

7 The glorious company of the Apostles | praise — | thee:
  the goodly fellowship of the | Prophets | praise — | thee;

*8 The noble | army · of | Martyrs ‖ praise | — | — | thee.

9 The holy Church throughout all the world doth ac-
  | knowledge | thee:
  the Father | of an | infin-ite | Majesty;

This verse should be sung without a break.

Canticles and Psalms

10 Thine honourable true and | only | Son:
  also the | Holy | Ghost the | Comforter.

Invocation of Christ the Son

11 Thou art the King of | Glory · O | Christ:
  thou art the ever- | lasting | Son · of the | Father.

12 When thou tookest upon thee to de- | liver | man:
  thou didst not ab- | hor the | Virgin's | womb.

2nd part 13 When thou hadst overcome the | sharpness · of | death:
  thou didst open the kingdom of | heav'n to | all be-
  | lievers.

14 Thou sittest at the right | hand of | God:
  in the | glory | of the | Father.

*15 We be- | lieve that | thou ⫴ shalt | come to | be our | Judge.

16 We therefore pray thee | help thy | servants:
  whom thou hast redeem'd | with thy | precious | blood.

17 Make them to be number'd | with thy | Saints:
  in | glory | ever- | lasting.

†Prayers for the Divine Mercy

18 O Lord save thy people and | bless thine | heritage:
  govern them and | lift them | up for | ever.

19 Day by day we | magni-fy | thee:
  and we worship thy Name | ever | world with-out | end.

20 Vouchsafe O Lord to keep us this | day with-out | sin:
  O Lord have mercy upon us * have | mer — | cy up-
  | on us.

21 O Lord let thy mercy | lighten · up- | on us:
  as our | trust — | is in | thee.

22 O Lord in | thee · have I | trusted:
  let me | never | be con- | founded.

* *This verse should be sung without a break.*

† *Verses 18-22 may be treated as a series of Versicles and Responses, the first half of each being sung by a Cantor or by the Choir, and the second by All.*

Benedictus

The Song of Zacharias at the birth of John the Baptist—last Prophet of the Old Testament and first of the New (Luke 1. 68)

1 Blessed be the Lord | God of | Israel:
   for he hath visited | and re- | deem'd his | people;

2 And hath rais'd up a mighty sal- | vation | for us:
   in the | house of · his | servant | David;

3 As he spake by the mouth of his | holy | Prophets:
   which have | been · since the | world be- | gan;

4 That we should be | sav'd · from our | enemies:
   and from the | hands of | all that | hate us;

5 To perform the mercy promis'd | to our | forefathers:
   and to re- | member · his | holy | Covenant;

*6 To per- | form the | oath ‖ which he | sware · to our
   | fore-father | Abraham,

7 That he would give us * that we being deliver'd out of the
   | hand of · our | enemies:
   might | serve · him with- | out — | fear;

8 In holiness and | righteousness · be- | fore him:
   all the | days — | of our | life.

9 And thou Child shalt be call'd the | Prophet · of the
   | Highest:
   for thou shalt go before the face of the | Lord · to pre-
   | pare his | ways;

10 To give knowledge of salvation | unto · his | people:
   for the re- | mission | of their | sins,

11 Through the tender mercy | of our | God:
   whereby the dayspring | from on | high hath | visited us;

12 To give light to them that sit in darkness * and in the
   | shadow · of | death:
   and to guide our feet | into · the | way of | peace.

   Glory be to the Father * and | to the | Son:
   and | to the | Holy | Ghost;
   As it was in the beginning * is now and | ever | shall be:
   world without | end. — | A — | men.

   * *This verse should be sung without a break.*

Canticles and Psalms

Alternative pointing for GLORIA

Glory | be · to the | Father:
 and to the Son | and · to the | Holy | Ghost;

As it | was in · the be- | ginning:
 is now and ever shall be * | world with-out | end.
 A- | men.

Magnificat

The thanksgiving of Mary at the promise of Christ's birth
(Luke 1. 46*)*

1 My soul doth | magni-fy the | Lord:
 and my spirit hath re- | joic'd in | God my | Saviour.

2 For he | hath re- | garded:
 the | lowli-ness | of his | handmaiden.

3 For be- | hold from | henceforth:
 all gene- | rations · shall | call me | bless-ed.

4 For he that is mighty hath | magni-fied | me:
 and | holy | is his | Name.

2nd part 5 And his mercy is on | them that | fear him:
 throughout | all — | gene-rations.

6 He hath shew-ed | strength · with his | arm:
 he hath scatter'd the proud * in the imagi- | nation
 | of their | hearts.

7 He hath put down the mighty | from their | seat:
 and hath ex- | alted · the | humble · and | meek.

8 He hath fill'd the hungry with | good — | things:
 and the rich he hath | sent — | empty · a- | way.

9 He remembering his mercy hath holpen his | servant
 | Israel:
 as he promis'd to our forefathers * Abraham | and his
 | seed for | ever.

GLORIA

Canticles and Psalms

Nunc Dimittis

The aged Simeon rejoices at the fulfilment of his hopes
(Luke 2. 29)

1 Lord now lettest thou thy servant de- | part in | peace:
ac- | cording | to thy | word.

2 For mine eyes have | seen thy · sal- | vation:
which thou hast prepar'd before the | face of | all —
| people;

3 To be a light to | lighten · the | Gentiles:
and to be the | glory · of thy | people | Israel.

GLORIA

Psalm 8

The majesty of God, and man's place of honour in God's
creation

1 O Lord our Governor * how excellent is thy Name in
| all the | world:
thou that hast set thy | glory · a- | bove the | heav'ns!

2 Out of the mouth of very babes and sucklings hast thou
ordain'd strength * be- | cause of · thine | enemies:
that thou mightest still the | enem-y | and · the a- | venger.

3 For I will consider thy heav'ns * even the | works of · thy
| fingers:
the moon and the stars | which thou | hast or- | dain'd.

4 What is man * that thou art | mindful · of | him:
and the son of man | that thou | visit-est | him?

5 Thou madest him | lower · than the | angels:
to | crown · him with | glory · and | worship.

6 Thou makest him to have dominion of the | works of · thy
| hands:
and thou hast put all things in sub- | jection | under · his
| feet;

7 All | sheep and | oxen:
yea | and the | beasts · of the | field;

8 The fowls of the air and the | fishes · of the | sea:
and whatsoever walketh | through the | paths · of the
| seas.

2nd part 9 O | Lord our | Governor:
how excellent is thy | Name in | all the | world!

GLORIA

Psalm 15

"Blessed are the pure in heart, for they shall see God"

(*Single chant*)

1 Lord who shall | dwell in · thy | tabernacle:
or who shall rest up- | on thy | holy | hill?

2 Even he that leadeth an | uncor-rupt | life:
and doeth the thing which is right * and | speaketh · the
| truth · from his | heart.

3 He that hath us'd no deceit in his tongue * nor done evil
| to his | neighbour:
and | hath not | slander'd · his | neighbour.

4 He that setteth not by himself * but is lowly in his | own —
| eyes:
and maketh much of | them that | fear the | Lord.

5 He that sweareth unto his neighbour * and disap-
| pointeth · him | not:
though it | were · to his | own — | hindrance.

6 He that hath not given his | money up-on | usury:
nor taken re- | ward a- | gainst the | innocent.

§7 Whoso doeth these | things shall | never | fall.

GLORIA

§ *This verse to be sung to the last phrase of the chant.*

Psalm 19

*God revealed in the natural law of the universe, and in the
moral law for mankind*

1 The heav'ns declare the | glory · of | God:
and the | firma-ment | sheweth · his | handywork.

Canticles and Psalms

2 One day | telleth · a- | nother:
    and one night | certi- | fieth · a- | nother.

3 There is neither | speech nor | language:
    but their | voices · are | heard a- | mong them.

4 Their sound is gone out into | all — | lands:
    and their words | into · the | ends · of the | world.

5 In them hath he set a tabernacle | for the | sun:
    which cometh forth as a bridegroom out of his chamber
    * and rejoiceth as a | giant · to | run his | course.

6 It goeth forth from the uttermost part of the heav'n * and
    runneth about unto the | end of · it a- | gain:
    and there is nothing | hid · from the | heat there- | of.

7 The law of the Lord is an undefil'd law con- | verting · the
    | soul:
    the testimony of the Lord is sure * and giveth | wisdom
    | unto · the | simple.

8 The statutes of the Lord are right and re- | joice the | heart:
    the commandment of the Lord is pure * and giveth
    | light — | unto · the | eyes.

9 The fear of the Lord is clean and en- | dureth · for | ever:
    the judgments of the Lord are true and | righteous | alto-
    | gether.

10 More to be desir'd are they than gold * yea than | much
    fine | gold:
    sweeter also than | honey | and the | honeycomb.

2nd part 11 Moreover by them is thy | servant | taught:
    and in keeping of them | there is | great re- | ward.

12 Who can tell how | oft · he of- | fendeth:
    O cleanse thou me | from my | secret | faults.

13 Keep thy servant also from presumptuous sins * lest they
    get the do- | minion | over me:
    so shall I be undefil'd * and innocent | from the | great of-
    | fence.

2nd part 14 Let the words of my mouth and the meditation of my heart
    * be alway acceptable | in thy | sight:
    O Lord my | strength and | my Re- | deemer.

                                            GLORIA

Psalm 23

God's loving care and providence

1 The Lord | is my | shepherd:
    therefore | can I | lack — | nothing.

2 He shall feed me in a | green — | pasture:
    and lead me forth be- | side the | waters · of | comfort.

3 He shall con- | vert my | soul:
    and bring me forth in the paths of righteousness | for
    his | Name's — | sake.

4 Yea though I walk through the valley of the shadow of
    death * I will | fear no | evil:
    for thou art with me * thy | rod · and thy | staff —
    | comfort me.

5 Thou shalt prepare a table before me * against | them that
    | trouble me:
    thou hast anointed my head with oil | and my | cup ·
    shall be | full.

6 But thy lovingkindness and mercy shall follow me * all the
    | days of · my | life:
    and I will dwell in the | house · of the | Lord for | ever.

                                      GLORIA

Psalm 24

*An anthem to be sung in procession to God's sanctuary by
those who are worthy to enter*

1 The earth is the Lord's * and all that | therein | is:
    the compass of the world and | they that | dwell there- | in.

2 For he hath founded it up- | on the | seas:
    and pre- | par'd · it up- | on the | floods.

3 Who shall ascend into the | hill of · the | Lord:
    or who shall rise | up · in his | holy | place?

4 Even he that hath clean hands and a | pure — | heart:
    and that hath not lift up his mind unto vanity * nor
    | sworn · to de- | ceive his | neighbour.

5 He shall receive the | blessing · from the | Lord:
    and righteousness from the | God of | his sal- | vation.

6 This is the generation of | them that | seek him:
    even of them that | seek thy | face O | Jacob.

7 Lift up your heads O ye gates * and be ye lift up ye ever-
    | lasting | doors:
    and the King of | Glory | shall come | in.

8 'Who is the | King of | Glory?';
    'It is the Lord strong and mighty * even the | Lord —
    | mighty · in | battle'.

9 Lift up your heads O ye gates * and be ye lift up ye ever-
    | lasting | doors:
    and the King of | Glory | shall come | in.

10 'Who is the | King of | Glory?':
    'Even the Lord of hosts * | he · is the | King of | Glory'.

GLORIA

Psalm 46

A nation's confidence in God

1 God is our | hope and | strength:
    a very | present | help in | trouble.

2 Therefore will we not fear though the | earth be | mov'd:
    and though the hills be carried | into · the | midst · of the
    | sea.

3 Though the waters thereof | rage and | swell:
    and though the mountains shake at the | tempest | of the
    | same.

4 The rivers of the flood thereof shall make glad the | city · of
    | God:
    the holy place of the tabernacle | of the | Most —
    | Highest.

5 God is in the midst of her * therefore shall she | not · be re-
    | mov'd:
    God shall | help her · and | that right | early.

6 The heathen make much ado and the | kingdoms · are
| mov'd:
but God hath shewed his voice and the | earth shall
| melt a- | way.

2nd part 7 The Lord of | hosts is | with us:
the God of | Jacob | is our | refuge.

8 O come hither and behold the | works · of the | Lord:
what destruction he hath | brought up- | on the | earth.

9 He maketh wars to cease in | all the | world:
he breaketh the bow and knappeth the spear in sunder *
and burneth the | cha-riots | in the | fire.

10 Be still then and know that | I am | God:
I will be exalted among the heathen * and I will be ex-
| alted | in the | earth.

11 The Lord of | hosts is | with us:
the God of | Jacob | is our | refuge.

GLORIA

Psalm 67

*As the nations invoke God's blessings, so they must render him
their praise.*

1 God be merciful unto | us and | bless us:
and shew us the light of his countenance * | and be
| merci-ful | unto us.

2 That thy way may be | known up-on | earth:
thy saving | health a- | mong all | nations.

3 Let the people | praise thee · O | God:
yea let | all the | people | praise thee.

4 O let the nations re- | joice and · be | glad:
for thou shalt judge the folk righteously * and govern the
| nations · up- | on — | earth.

5 Let the people | praise thee · O | God:
let | all the | people | praise thee.

6 Then shall the earth bring | forth her | increase:
and God even our own | God shall | give us · his
| blessing.

2nd part 7 God | shall — | bless us:
     and all the | ends · of the | world shall | fear him.

GLORIA

Psalm 84

The joy of being in God's house

1 O how amiable | are thy | dwellings:
    thou | Lord — | of — | hosts.

2 My soul hath a desire and longing * to enter into the
    | courts · of the | Lord:
    my heart and my flesh re- | joice · in the | living | God.

3 Yea the sparrow hath found her an house * and the swallow
    a nest where she may | lay her | young:
    even thy altars O Lord of hosts * my | King — | and my
    | God.

4 Blessed are they that | dwell in · thy | house:
    they will be | alway | praising | thee:

5 Blessed is the man whose | strength is · in | thee:
    in whose | heart are | thy — | ways.

6 Who going through the vale of misery | use it · for a | well:
    and the | pools are | fill'd with | water.

2nd part 7 They will go from | strength to | strength:
    and unto the God of gods appeareth every | one of | them
    in | Sion.

8 O Lord God of hosts | hear my | prayer:
    hearken | O — | God of | Jacob.

9 Behold O God | our de- | fender:
    and look upon the | face of | thine An- | ointed.

*10 For one day | in thy | courts ‖ is | better | than a | thousand.

11 I had rather be a doorkeeper in the | house of · my | God:
    than to | dwell · in the | tents of · un- | godliness.

12 For the Lord God is a | light · and de- | fence:
    the Lord will give grace and worship * and no good thing
    shall he withhold from them that | live a | godly | life.

13 O Lord | God of | hosts:
    blessed is the man that | putteth · his | trust in | thee.

GLORIA

* *This verse should be sung without a break.*

Canticles and Psalms

Psalm 91

Trust in God's protection, and his response to it.

1 Whoso dwelleth under the defence of the | Most — | High:
   shall abide under the | shadow | of the · Al- | mighty.

2 I will say unto the Lord * Thou art my | hope and · my
   | stronghold:
   my | God in | him · will I | trust.

3 For he shall deliver thee from the | snare · of the | hunter:
   and | from the | noisome | pestilence.

4 He shall defend thee under his wings * and thou shalt be
   safe | under · his | feathers:
   his faithfulness and truth shall | be thy | shield and
   | buckler.

5 Thou shalt not be afraid for any | terror · by | night:
   nor for the | arrow · that | flieth · by | day;

6 For the pestilence that | walketh · in | darkness:
   nor for the sickness that de- | stroyeth | in the | noonday.

7 A thousand shall fall beside thee * and ten thousand at | thy
   right | hand:
   but it shall | not come | nigh — | thee.

8 Yea with thine eyes shalt | thou be- | hold:
   and see the re- | ward of | the un- | godly.

9 For thou Lord | art my | hope:
   thou hast set thine house of de- | fence — | very | high.

10 There shall no evil happen | unto | thee:
   neither shall any | plague come | nigh thy | dwelling.

11 For he shall give his angels charge | over | thee:
   to | keep · thee in | all thy | ways.

12 They shall bear thee | in their | hands:
   that thou hurt not thy | foot a- | gainst a | stone.

2nd part 13 Thou shalt go upon the | lion · and | adder:
   the young lion and the dragon shalt thou | tread — | under
   · thy | feet.

14 Because he hath set his love upon me * therefore will | I de-
| liver him:
I will set him up be- | cause · he hath | known my | Name.

15 He shall call upon me and | I will | hear him:
yea I am with him in trouble * I will deliver him and
| bring — | him to | honour.

2nd part 16 With long | life · will I | satisfy him:
and | shew him | my sal- | vation.

GLORIA

Psalm 96

The whole earth is called to worship God as King and Judge

1 O sing unto the Lord a | new — | song:
sing unto the Lord | all the | whole — | earth.

2 Sing unto the Lord and | praise his | Name:
be telling of his sal- | vation · from | day to | day.

3 Declare his honour | unto · the | heathen:
and his wonders | unto | all — | people.

4 For the Lord is great * and cannot | worthily · be | prais'd:
he is more to be | fear'd than | all — | gods.

5 As for all the gods of the heathen | they are · but | idols:
but it is the | Lord that | made the | heav'ns.

6 Glory and worship | are be- | fore him:
power and | honour · are | in his | sanctuary.

7 Ascribe unto the Lord O ye | kindreds · of the | people:
ascribe unto the | Lord — | worship · and | power.

8 Ascribe unto the Lord the honour due | unto · his | Name:
bring presents and | come in- | to his | courts.

9 O worship the Lord in the | beauty · of | holiness:
let the | whole earth | stand in | awe of him.

10 Tell it out among the heathen that the | Lord is | King:
and that it is he who hath made the round world so fast
that it cannot be mov'd * and how that he shall | judge the
| people | righteously.

11 Let the heav'ns rejoice and let the | earth be | glad:
   let the sea make a noise and | all that | therein | is.

12 Let the field be joyful and | all · that is | in it:
   then shall all the trees of the wood re- | joice be- | fore
   the | Lord.

2nd part 13 For he cometh * for he cometh to | judge the | earth:
   and with righteousness to judge the world * and the
   | people | with his | truth.

                                                    GLORIA

Psalm 98

A call to the universal praise of God, the righteous Judge.

1 O sing unto the Lord a | new — | song:
   for he hath | done — | marvel-lous | things.

2 With his own right hand and with his | holy | arm:
   hath he | gotten · him- | self the | victory.

3 The Lord declared | his sal- | vation:
   his righteousness hath he openly | shew'd · in the
   | sight of · the | heathen.

4 He hath remember'd his mercy and truth toward the | house
   of | Israel:
   and all the ends of the world have seen the sal- | vation
   | of our | God.

5 Shew yourselves joyful unto the Lord | all ye | lands:
   sing re- | joice and | give — | thanks.

6 Praise the Lord up- | on the | harp:
   sing to the | harp · with a | psalm of | thanksgiving.

7 With trumpets | also · and | shawms:
   O shew yourselves joyful be- | fore the | Lord the | King.

8 Let the sea make a noise * and all that | therein | is:
   the round world and | they that | dwell there- | in.

9 Let the floods clap their hands * and let the hills be joyful
   together be- | fore the | Lord:
   for he is | come to | judge the | earth.

10 With righteousness shall he | judge the | world:
and the | people | with — | equity.

GLORIA

Psalm 100

Joy in God's service

1 O be joyful in the Lord | all ye | lands:
serve the Lord with gladness * and come before his
| presence | with a | song.

2 Be ye sure that the Lord | he is | God:
it is he that hath made us and not we ourselves * we are
his | people · and the | sheep of · his | pasture.

3 O go your way into his gates with thanksgiving * and into
his | courts with | praise:
be thankful unto | him and · speak | good of · his | Name.

4 For the Lord is gracious * his mercy is | ever- | lasting:
and his truth endureth from gene- | ration · to | gene-
| ration.

GLORIA

Psalm 121

The pilgrim's confidence that God is his help at all times

1 I will lift up mine eyes | unto · the | hills:
from | whence — | cometh · my | help?

2 My help cometh even | from the | Lord:
who hath | made — | heav'n and | earth.

3 He shall not suffer thy | foot · to be | mov'd:
and he that | keepeth · thee | will not | sleep.

*4 Behold he that | keepeth | Israel ‖ shall | neither | slumber ·
nor | sleep.

5 The Lord him- | self is · thy | keeper:
the Lord is thy defence up- | on thy | right — | hand;

* *This verse should be sung without a break.*

6 So that the sun shall not | burn · thee by | day:
   neither the | moon — | by — | night.

7 The Lord shall preserve thee from | all — | evil:
   yea it is even | he that · shall | keep thy | soul.

8 The Lord shall preserve thy going out and thy | coming | in:
   from this time | forth for | ever- | more.

GLORIA

Psalm 122

A happy vision of the community whose centre is God.

1 I was glad when they | said un-to | me:
   'We will | go in-to the | house of · the | Lord'.

*2 Our | feet shall | stand ‖ in thy | gates — | O Je- | rusalem.

3 Jerusalem is | built · as a | city:
   that is at | uni-ty | in it- | self.

4 For thither the tribes go up * even the | tribes · of the | Lord:
   to testify unto Israel * to give thanks | unto · the | Name of · the | Lord.

2nd part 5 For there is the | seat of | judgment:
   even the | seat · of the | house of | David.

6 O pray for the | peace · of Je- | rusalem:
   they shall | prosper · that | love — | thee.

7 Peace be with- | in thy | walls:
   and | plenteous-ness with- | in thy | palaces.

8 For my brethren and com- | panions' | sakes:
   I will | wish — | thee pros- | perity,

9 Yea because of the house of the | Lord our | God:
   I will | seek to | do thee | good.

GLORIA

* *This verse should be sung without a break.*